Hudson Bay Bound

HUDSON BAY BOUND

Two Women, One Dog,
Two Thousand Miles to the Arctic

NATALIE WARREN

Foreword by Ann Bancroft

University of Minnesota Press
Minneapolis
London

For photographs, videos, and more information about the Hudson Bay Bound expedition, visit http://www.natalie-warren.com.

Map on page xvii drawn by Lee Vue. Photographs by Ann Raiho and Natalie Warren; courtesy of the author.

Published by the University of Minnesota Press
111 Third Avenue South, Suite 290
Minneapolis, MN 55401-2520
http://www.upress.umn.edu

ISBN 978-1-5179-0784-6 (hc/j)

A Cataloging-in-Publication record for this book is available from the Library of Congress.

Printed in Canada on acid-free paper

The University of Minnesota is an equal-opportunity educator and employer.

25 24 23 22 21 20   10 9 8 7 6 5 4 3 2 1

For my best friend and lifelong paddling partner, Ann Raiho

CONTENTS

FOREWORD

Ann Bancroft

WHEN I FIRST MET Ann Raiho and Natalie Warren along the shores of the Mississippi River in Minneapolis, I knew our brief introduction would not be the last time we would find ourselves together on the shores of a river. That afternoon before they shoved off on their trip, they were in a foggy swirl of the excitement and chaos of friends and strangers celebrating them, their journey, and the river. As I stood back and watched the commotion of the gathering, I had more than a twinge of envy, because I recognized the scene and could almost taste the familiar feelings that a big excursion kicks up. There's almost nothing like it. With all the preparation behind you, for a brief time you are swept up in the current and froth of anticipation, nervousness, wonder, and the warmth of the love and friendship of those who have come to wish you well on your journey. Soon you will hear just the sound of your breath, the movement of the water, and perhaps the steady beat of your heart. Before long you will settle into a new pace of life on the water for the months ahead with your best friend.

In reading *Hudson Bay Bound,* I couldn't help but see the similarities to my first major expedition and how that odyssey charted a course for my work decades into the future. Years ago as a young teacher, I would depart with a team of men and dogs on a childhood dream expedition across frozen water to the North Pole. There was no larger purpose than just the deep desire to discover our personal limits inspired by those who went before us more than seven decades earlier. Like Natalie, I would come to understand that my journey would continue in ways I could never have known at the time. Taking my place in history, I now became committed to giving each expedition going forward the distinct purpose of inspiring young people through my experiences.

Likewise, this grand adventure of theirs would be the start of something much more far-reaching than Hudson Bay.

Natalie and Ann embarked on their enterprise by mirroring one of my favorite books, *Canoeing with the Cree,* written by Eric Sevareid. My father gave me my first copy while I was in high school, to feed my growing passion for paddling and adventure. Soon after I consumed the pages of Sevareid's adventure in 1930 with his paddling companion, Walter Port, my little brother, my dad, and I shoved our metal Grumman canoe off the mud and gravel shore of the Mississippi River near our home in St. Paul. Our adventure that April was less than a week long, but for our family the short excursion provided plenty of excitement as we found ourselves windbound and tardy for our scheduled return. Unbeknownst to us, barges had been sent out, panning the fading gray light of islands and shorelines with spotlights in search of us, to no avail. When the conditions shifted a day later, we found our way to a pay phone downriver to call a worried mom for a pickup.

There are endless parallels between the two accounts by Sevareid and Warren of their expeditions to Hudson Bay. Both shared their modest depictions through youthful eyes embarking on their first major expedition. They acknowledged that their companions were catalysts for stewarding the excursions into reality. They traveled with best friends, all anxious about their futures after the trips, and something inside them stirred to suggest a knowing that they *must* take the challenge—if they did not try, regret would follow them later in life. Ann and Natalie would be heralded for showing that adventure can still be had in a changing environment and that women have not only a place in the landscape of adventure but an important voice that needs to be heard.

Hudson Bay Bound offers an important and unique perspective on how much had indeed changed with the lakes, rivers, communities, and people who live along these shores in the eighty-one years since Sevareid and Port encountered them. Pollution, agriculture, erosion, flooding, and, of course, the injection of human-made structures have altered the river's personality and course. Eric Sevareid gives us a portrait of the life of the Cree and fur traders, and the narrative continues as Natalie bears witness to both the dying and the thriving communities along these waterways. She illuminates for us that urban waterways are complex because of the human element.

After reading Natalie's honest account, I am inspired by what I glimpsed on the shores of the Mississippi when we first met: her twinkle, zest, and determination in all she goes after. Her journey with Ann reveals the physical landscapes, hardships, and human encounters; it also uncovers the heart of any good journey, the human spirit. A spirit that pushes through long hours of a day, wrong turns, dams, tough weather, fears, and the stresses such a journey puts on even your closest friendship. Rain, wind, night skies, and endless days are the elements that lead to self-inspection and the ability to listen to yourself. Natalie's fearless internal exploration is the miracle of every good journey. It is there where the real discovery of your courage, determination, and love will take you next.

While on their journey, Natalie and Ann inspired curiosity among people living along the rivers and lakes, many of whom had never engaged in or thought about the waters before. I hope this story, with all its humor and humility that burbles to the surface, enlivens your spirit and curiosity as it did mine.

PROLOGUE

SOMETIMES A GREAT ADVENTURE lands in your lap. That's exactly what happened on a chilly February day in my dorm room at St. Olaf College in Northfield, Minnesota. Ann flung open the door of my room with fire in her eyes and a book in her hand. I had been cooped up all day writing a paper. The interruption, although abrupt, was a welcome break to a gloomy and uneventful day. She lingered in the doorway with a familiar smirk on her face.

"Yes, Ann? How can I help you this fine evening?" I asked facetiously. We'd been scheming trips together for four years, and it seemed every adventure started with Ann standing in the doorway with that same expression. She threw the book at me from the across the room. "Read this," she said. "We should do it." I looked down at the book, *Canoeing with the Cree,* now lying on the bed in front of me. There was a silhouette of two people paddling a canoe on the cover. I looked back up to respond, but Ann was gone.

The monotony of the day was getting to me; I needed a break. Reading a chapter or two would provide a welcome respite from schoolwork. But after the first few chapters I just kept going, flying through the story of two men, Eric Sevareid and Walter C. Port, who in 1930 paddled from Minneapolis to Hudson Bay. They were fresh out of high school and didn't have sleeping bags or maps for the long journey. Their story was documented by the *Minneapolis Star,* and their adventurous spirit brought them to the shores of Hudson Bay, inspiring supporters and skeptics across the country. Sevareid and Port traveled through agricultural rivers and wild waters of the north. I began wondering what those rivers looked like today. If we decided to make the trip, would we too get lost on Mud Lake near the headwaters of the Minnesota River and be hopelessly windbound on Lake Winnipeg? Hours passed as I continued reading, furiously flipping pages about the Native community at Norway House and how Eric and Walter went to church at York Factory on the shores of Hudson Bay. Meanwhile, the gray sky outside my window had turned to black.

The cafeteria was long closed by now, so I shoved a granola bar into my mouth and finished the last few pages of the book by headlamp. I closed the book and shut my eyes. "Yes, I want to do this trip," I thought. Why not? Everyone around me was frantically applying for jobs, and very few people were hearing back from prospective employers. What else was I going to do after graduation? I wanted something more than the seemingly predictable life path in front of me. I felt an itch to do something crazy. An energy inside me was overflowing, yearning to get out and get going, and no internship or entry-level job could fulfill my desire to live and breathe and feel the earth around me. The next day I threw the book back at Ann and said, "I'm in."

What I didn't know was just what I was signing up for or how it would profoundly change my perceptions of everything around me. My city upbringing and higher education did not prepare me to unbiasedly interact with people who were different from myself. Yet on this expedition, I would be forced into uncomfortable situations with people from a variety of backgrounds, especially political, and would slowly begin to witness the complex web of humanity. Preparing for our expedition to Hudson Bay taught us several life skills. In many ways, it was like starting our own business. I learned more about communication, public relations, fundraising, event planning, and marketing than I ever had at school. I initially saw this trip as a hole in my resume. In reality, it was the key component to unfolding my career.

There is a big difference between going on an expedition and just going camping. On an expedition you feel a sense of urgency to continue on a trail and will relax only long enough to rejuvenate. When camping you're there to relax and enjoy the surroundings. You don't feel the need to push yourself beyond your comfort zone just to cover more ground. I'm not sure what made us so focused and driven to reach Hudson Bay. I often thought about the psychology behind what makes anyone hell-bent on one thing while knowing that, in the big scheme of things, their greatest passions seem minuscule and unimportant. Before and during the trip, Ann and I knew that nothing would stop us from making it to the Bay. Sometimes we would turn it into a game:

"What if a bear bites my leg off?" Ann would ask.

"We'd temporarily evacuate, go to a hospital for bandages, and then I would portage you for the rest of the trip."

"What if our boat capsizes and sinks to the bottom of Lake Winnipeg?" I'd ask.

"We'd swim to shore, find help, and use all our money to get another boat."

This game of "what if?" gave us the confidence and determination to continue on through the most challenging parts of our journey. For eighty-five days we faced fierce weather, wild animals, and changing communities. The biggest unforeseen challenge, however, was to our own relationship. How could two best friends reach a point where they had to resort to communicating through handwritten letters, even though, day in and day out, they were always within feet of each other?

This is the story of how Ann Raiho and I became the first two women to re-create Eric Sevareid and Walter Port's route to Hudson Bay—a route that has been attempted, and sometimes completed, many times since it was popularized in 1930. It is also an account of the present-day condition of the lakes and rivers between the Twin Cities and Hudson Bay, the people who live on these waters, and the communities that shape them. It explores the intrinsic connection that human beings have to moving water and reflects on the raw challenges we faced as two women making history.

~~~~

JUST LIKE PADDLING A CANOE, writing a book is not a solo effort. Thank you to all who supported our dream to paddle to Hudson Bay. Our lives were changed by the people we met and the landscapes we traversed. Thanks to my family and friends who believed and invested in me during this process. Specifically, to my best friend, Ann Raiho, for trusting me with our story; John Synhavsky, my loving partner, for making extra coffee on long writing days and listening to me read drafts out loud before bed; Steve Kinsella, my book-writing mentor and friend; Richard Warren, my lifelong first-draft editor; Ann Bancroft, for writing the Foreword and being a constant source of inspiration; Lee Vue, for designing the map and making everything I do look beautiful; YMCA Camp Menogyn, for sparking my love of nature and adventure; and my supportive parents, for shipping me off to camp in Minnesota every summer, giving me the opportunity to be wild and free. I thank Kristian Tvedten, my editor at the University of Minnesota Press, for providing support, knowledge, and constructive feedback while expertly keeping my voice and vision alive. This expedition was made possible by the many donations and sponsorships we received. From gear to food to money—we could not have done this without the support of our community, friends and strangers far and wide. Thank you!

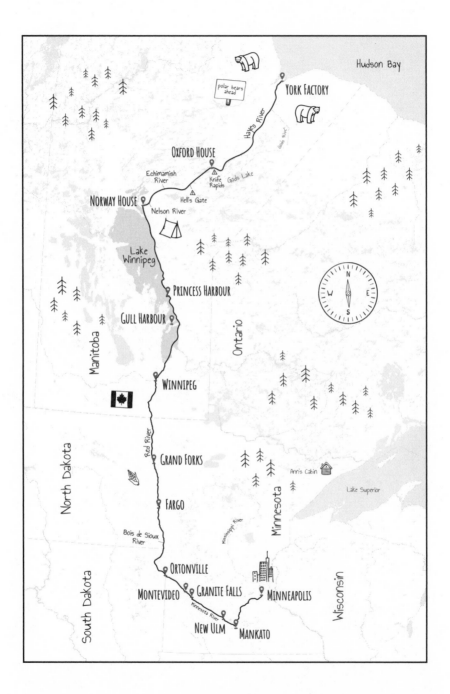

FROM PALMS TO PINES

WITH ALL GREAT JOURNEYS, the seed of adventure is planted long before the first step on a trail or the first stroke of a paddle. Looking back, I think a part of my soul was always searching the river. When I was young, I remember peering out the car window every time my mom drove over a bridge just to catch a glimpse of water. Rivers always drew me in. But unlike many of the adventurers I have known, I did not grow up surrounded by trees, lakes, or streams. My itch for wild places grew out of my desire for something different from the urban metropolis of Miami, Florida, and started many years before my paddle strokes carried me to Hudson Bay.

"Mom! I'm going canoeing in Minnesota this summer!" I brassily announced as I stomped through the door of my family's house. As the youngest child of three, I loved to stir the pot. I kicked my untied shoes off my inside-out socks and threw my backpack and saxophone down on the floor. I knew this, too, would cause trouble later. But I didn't care. I had spent the entire ride home from high school waiting for this moment, imagining what I would say and how my mom would respond. More than anything, I felt like I finally had something to really look forward to in life, something that would get me through the school year. After almost two years of struggling through an arts school for saxophone performance, I wondered if my previous dream of becoming the modern-day Cannonball Adderley or John Coltrane was realistic.

"Oh, really?" my mom replied from the other room. She had a tone I could work with. Everything is back-alley trading when

1

you're in high school. What can I get away with? Where is the line? I knew strategy was key. I had to come on slowly—enthusiastic but not *too* excited, a sprinkle of "I haven't been very happy" with a glimmer of hope for the future in my eyes. Perhaps I'd throw in a smile she hadn't seen in a while. Teenagers can be the best con artists, and I thought I was pretty damn good at sixteen. Little did I know that, from my mom's perspective, she was just thinking, "Cool. My kid is proactive about going to camp. That's great!"

One of my friends always missed the first few days of class because he was "off canoeing." While the rest of us had to drudge through picking outfits, organizing pens and pencils, and pretending we were going to use our itineraries for real this year, he would appear a few days into the school year looking tan and happy, glowing like someone who knew there was a bigger world to explore beyond our classroom walls. There is nothing like someone glowing to make you realize that you are *not* glowing. I asked my friend where he went during the summer and why he looked so obnoxiously happy when he returned. He told me about a camp in the Boundary Waters Canoe Area (BWCA) in Minnesota, where rivers run free and lakes are connected by treacherous paths that you traverse from one lake to the next while carrying all of your gear. With fondness, he described the pain he still had in his shoulders from carrying canoes, as if it were the last thing connecting him to a fleeting memory of summer days spent paddling with friends.

Sign. Me. Up. I knew immediately it was something I wanted to do. It was less the *act* of canoeing, since I didn't even know how to canoe, and more the *idea* of escaping into the woods that excited me. And not so much the woods themselves but more the thought of adventure in a magical distant land. Minnesota, as I understood, was located in the gray blob in the top middle of the country (geography was not a priority in arts school) and definitely qualified as distant. I looked out the window of our environmental science classroom at the sprawling Miami cityscape.

It was almost too much to take in, but I wanted more. I wanted a different view altogether. My eyes glazed over as the skyscrapers shape-shifted into large trees. The people scurrying on the streets below became fish navigating rivers of cars and concrete. I had never traveled into the wilderness before, so bits and pieces of images from movies and books combined to create my imagined scenery in the city. School field trips to the Florida Everglades and a few visits to North Carolina in the summer were not enough to stitch together the true beauty of the North Woods. The bell rang. The trees turned back into buildings; the river, back into dirty streets. I trudged through my concrete jungle to catch the train back home, desperate to move from daydreaming about the natural world to actually seeing it.

That night my mom listened carefully as I explained how my day had changed between my usual depressing departure on the 6:00 a.m. Metrorail and my return as the most excited I'd been in months, maybe years, at the prospect of going canoeing in Minnesota. Her smile alone was a preliminary stamp of approval—my pitch had been accepted.

~~~~~

THE MONTHS FOLLOWING were a whirlwind of preparations for a two-week canoe trip in the Boundary Waters through a camp called Menogyn, located on the outskirts of the BWCA on the Gunflint Trail. When I received the trip packing list in the mail, my entire family sat around the dining room table trying to figure out what the heck a "fleece" was (this was Miami, remember). We struggled to collect everything I needed for the trip. There weren't many outdoor retail stores in Miami except for the boating and fishing shops by the beach. At one of the smaller ones, my eyes landed on a cheap Swiss Army knife by the register that set my heart aflutter. Growing up, I played with Barbie dolls only to tear their heads off to play "Barbie basketball." I hated pink and "girly things," sometimes solely on principle. Now, in the world of knives and hiking boots, I was finding my stride. I belonged before I had even arrived.

After school, I would walk around the neighborhood in my hiking boots with my trusty pocketknife to "practice" for the trip. In spite of this exercise, I still had no real idea where I was going or what I was getting into. This is how I would feel again years later before starting out on a paddling expedition from the Twin Cities to Hudson Bay with my best friend, not fully understanding what it would feel like to travel through polar bear country or to paddle as a team of two for eighty-five days. When in doubt, don't think too much, and walk around the block in your hiking boots.

The day finally came. My mom flew with me to Minneapolis. We drove to the outdoor gear store REI and waited for the bus with other people my age wearing hiking boots and sporting pocketknives. Fighting back tears, I got on the bus and waved a final farewell to my mom through the window. The new scenery quickly made me forget I was on a bus with total strangers far from my friends and family in Florida. I was experiencing a world so different from my own that it felt like another planet. Goodbye, palm trees; hello, pine forests! I stared in awe at the lush woods zipping past us on the highway. If the view from the bus blew my mind, then the view from a canoe was surely going to rock my world. And thus began the monumental unfolding of the rest of my life.

~~~~~~

MY SEQUENCE OF SUMMERS in the North Woods started with a two-week canoe trip through the BWCA with six other young women and one guide. I zigzagged my way through lakes on my first few days, trying to maneuver the foreign boat through unfamiliar territory. Some days the sky shook as thunder and lightning clamored down from the clouds above us while we waited out the weather in the woods. Other days the lakes were so calm that ripples from our paddle strokes would dance for several feet before sinking back into the glassy surface.

After dinner one night, our guide took all of her clothes off and went swimming in the lake at sunset. She had eyes that could pierce the patriarchy. She looked comfortable in her tan tattooed skin. We all followed suit for a simple but life-changing twilight swim. I had never been comfortable with my body until that night in the dimming light. From then on I felt more at home in my own body. This came in handy when, days later, I fell asleep naked on a rock and woke up to a group of Boy Scouts staring at me as they canoed by. My paddle mates had heard the oncoming canoes and ran behind the tent to hide, not realizing that I was fast asleep. That evening our laughter traveled far and wide, echoing through the woods and across the crystal water.

Another night, I heard wolves howling outside our tent. Horrified, I thought to myself, "I took a risk leaving the comfort of my home and now I am going to be eaten by wolves." I was so afraid that I woke everyone up to inform them of our impending doom. They listened and then laughed. It was not a wolf. It was a loon. I got them back the next day by informing them that "bagel" is actually pronounced *bay*-gull and not *bag*-ul. Needless to say, we learned a lot from each other that summer. My mom had written me a letter and told me to open it while I was "on trail." She had written the usual heartfelt note about how proud she was of my ability to try new things. Visible dried-up teardrops smudged the ink in some spots. At the end of her letter she expressed, "I hope you have a wonderful time exploring the beautiful mountains of Minnesota." It was official—no one really knew where I was.

The disconnect between South Florida and northern Minnesota would continue to grow over the years as my family and friends struggled to understand where I disappeared to for those magical summer months spent in a canoe. On my future expedition to Hudson Bay, I would call my mother from the Minnesota River in Mankato, a city of almost forty thousand people, to have her ask, "How are you calling me? Aren't you supposed to be in the wilderness?" The physical distance between Minnesota and

Florida was great, but the cultural difference, especially when it came to my canoe adventures (and saying "pop" for "soda"), was more challenging for my friends and family to wrap their heads around.

My personal journey continued the next summer with a thirty-day canoe expedition through Wabakimi Provincial Park in Ontario, where I first learned how to paddle whitewater on the Allanwater, Brightsand, and Kopka Rivers. My time at Camp Menogyn culminated with a fifty-day expedition through Nunavut, Canada's northernmost province, paddling the Kazan and Kunwak Inuit Heritage Rivers through the Arctic tundra. This trip was a dream that I wished would last forever. But more impactful than the migrating caribou stampeding by the river, the musk oxen lazily acknowledging our presence while grazing, or the crystal-blue rushing rivers that we drank and fished from was the woman who was assigned to be my paddling partner: Ann Raiho.

<hr />

ANN HAD BEEN GOING ON CANOE TRIPS through Camp Menogyn since she was twelve years old and, at the age of seventeen, was already a skilled outdoorswoman ready to conquer the world by canoe. I was intimidated by her knowledge of knives and knots and her ability to make her mark in social settings. The first day I met Ann, she asked one of the other women going on our trip if they liked meat. They responded, "Yes," and Ann concluded, "It's gonna be a great trip!" We then proceeded to make T-shirts that said "Do you like meat?" on the front and "It's gonna be a great trip!" on the back. Everything Ann said or did greatly impacted those around her. I knew immediately I wanted to be her friend. I saw something in Ann that I admired, that I wanted to be, too. She embodied a spirit of the outdoors that I strived for. I felt like I was pretending to be an outdoorswoman. Ann was the real deal.

Ann grew up in a suburb of St. Paul where she spent much of her childhood playing in the woods with her dog. An only child,

Ann had a unique ability to love those around her like family, always keeping in touch with faraway friends. Her wandering spirit has taken her across the globe and keeps her constantly on the move, but her strong network provides her a home wherever she goes. One thing that especially intrigued me about Ann is that she truly believes anything is possible, even when the forces of nature, society, science, and technology are against her. She once tried to convince me that we could run an errand in half an hour even though the GPS said it would take an hour to drive there and back. Even time and space are no limitations for Ann. This same spirit makes her a creative scientist and a bold feminist; she always sees what is possible instead of focusing on the barriers.

Our ability to have fun no matter where we are became apparent early on while traveling by van to reach a float plane that would carry us north across the tundra. An hour into our two-day drive, I had run out of small talk and wondered if the bored glaze of infinite road trips would soon coat us all. After some silence I asked Ann, "Wouldn't it be cool if we made a way to deliver notes to each other in the van?"

"Let's do it!" she responded immediately.

We got to work stringing twine from the back of the van to the front and creating an apparatus that would slide, like a zipline, from one end to the other. On it was an envelope with everyone's names and an arrow that you could move to point to the intended receiver of the note. Ann used her skills in math and science to focus on the technical creation and operation of the "note sender" while I was all about usability and hyping our audience. Together, we worked seamlessly to create something quite impressive out of very limited resources. It was something we would do over and over again as the years went by.

Our synergy in a canoe reflected our partnership in the van. Paddling a canoe with someone can easily spark miscommunication and challenges in a relationship, especially when navigating whitewater. A delicate dance of ego and control, stepping in and letting go, came naturally to us as we maneuvered those fast, rock-filled rivers. Because of my immediate connection with Ann on and off the water, our trail guide designated us official paddling partners for the expedition. I remember one of our first conversations in the boat:

"Where are you going to school in the fall?" I asked Ann.

"St. Olaf College. You?"

"Me too!" I replied.

Lo and behold, we ended up in the same freshman dorm. There are few happenstances in my life that I can attribute to fate. Unknown to me at the time, meeting Ann Raiho was one of those moments. Our meeting realigned the stars. Other possibilities for our future—different careers, friends, adventures—faded into shadow, allowing for a new shiny story line to take center stage.

PACKING OUT

BY THE TIME WE GRADUATED from St. Olaf College, Ann and I had been on many canoe trips together, building our skills and confidence as canoeists and outdoor adventurers. That confidence led us to believe that we could survive, or even thrive, paddling together for three months through unknown territory with only each other, a canoe, and our gear. Ann was excited that I was interested in doing the expedition, but both of us were skeptical. We didn't have any money (the float plane alone would cost two thousand dollars), the necessary gear, or much of anything beyond our thirst for adventure. We rarely had time to relax between schoolwork, jobs, and extracurricular activities. Planning a canoe trip on top of all of that seemed impossible. Beyond the logistics, insecurities flooded my mind. I was worried that my life would be greatly impacted if I "got off the train": school, work, marriage, house, kids, and so on. I felt that if I went on this expedition my life would crumble in front of me. Would this three-month gap in my resume keep me from getting a job? Would anyone want to date someone who didn't shave or shower often? I assured myself I could get a dog and live in a canoe if things didn't work out. There was always that to fall back on.

We needed advice. One especially cold night in early February, Ann and I drove up to Minneapolis to visit Scott Miller, one of the men who paddled the route in 2005. We parked Ann's old car along a snowbank and hesitantly walked up to his house. "Well, here goes nothing!" We knocked loudly, eager to get out of the cold. Scott was also a graduate of St. Olaf, and he opened the door with a reassuring smile. He bustled around making us tea and pulling out old photo albums. In between his trips to the kitchen, he inquired about when we were thinking of launching and what gear we needed. He was excited to talk to us about the expedition and show us the pictures from his trip. The images were gorgeous: the bright colors of the Minnesota River during the summer, the various people they met along the Red River, the vast expanse of Lake Winnipeg, and the unyielding flow of the Hayes River. It was enough to convince anyone to paddle the route. After a bit of jovial conversation, Scott looked at us very seriously and said, "If you decide, I mean *really* decide, to do the trip, then it will happen."

That was hard for us to believe. A desire to do something does not mean it will happen. How was *deciding* to do it any different? We didn't even have a boat, let alone the money to get home. Would those things magically appear if we decided to do the trip? We were skeptical. But that night, inspired by Scott's advice and despite our lack of preparation, we officially decided to do the trip. Our excited energy bounced around Ann's car on the drive back to campus. "Let's do it!" we agreed. That night as I lay in bed, I closed my eyes and imagined I was in my sleeping bag, in a tent somewhere along the Hayes River near Hudson Bay. The sounds of the night magnified in my mind. I imagined that the soft foot-steps of students scurrying back to their dorms was a polar bear circling the tent or maybe a pack of wolves. Fear overcame me. I quickly turned on my headlamp to scare away the darkness. But it wasn't fear of the wilderness that kept me up. It was the risk of doing the trip at all. Would it derail my career? How would it change me? I thought to myself, "I will tell Ann tomorrow that I'm not sure, that I am still waiting to hear back from a few jobs." I fell asleep with my headlamp still shining bright.

~~~~~~

I NEVER EXPRESSED THOSE FEARS or doubts to Ann, and if she had any I never heard about them. Instead of focusing on what could go wrong, we dedicated our energy to all of the things that could go right. Our positive attitude spiraled upward until we were spending our days planning and daydreaming about the trip as spring quickly turned into summer. June 2, 2011, our departure date, was quickly approaching.

A few weeks after our visit with Scott, my phone rang in the library, and I quickly ran outside to answer it. Ann was in Grand Marais, Minnesota, calling to inform me that we had been given a canoe for our trip.

"What?!" I exclaimed, perplexed by the news.

"Yep. I just walked into an outfitter and told them what we want to do. They said they'd give us a boat! It's a 17′4″ Langford Prospector. Kevlar."

Eric Sevareid and Walter Port had named their canoe *Sans Souci*—"no worries" in French. Similarly, we decided to call ours *Kawena Kinomaeta*, a Cree phrase that translates to "no worries" (but most times we just called it "Canoey"). It was truly happening! We were elated. Community members came out of the woodwork to assist us. By April, all of our gear and food had been sponsored and we had raised five thousand dollars. Once the float plane was paid for, we agreed to give the excess money to a scholarship fund at Menogyn, the camp where we met, to help fund wilderness trips for young women.

Not all sponsorships were easy, though. Most companies saw two life jackets and two paddles as a no-brainer opportunity to get their logo on our website and a mention in our blog, which, by the end of the trip, would have more than forty thousand views. But we quickly learned that when you do things out of the ordinary there are always a few people who just will *not* believe in you. Earlier in the spring, we attended an outdoor trade show called Canoecopia in Madison, Wisconsin. The show was a great forum for us to talk about our expedition and pitch our gear needs to potential sponsors. Ann and I created a packet of information about our trip, what we needed, and what we could provide in return.

We approached the booth of a Canadian company in the hope that they would sponsor our expedition with a spray skirt, an essential piece of gear that would keep water out of our canoe while paddling the large waves on Lake Winnipeg or the whitewater rapids on the Hayes River.

The sales rep at the booth talked to us a bit and seemed friendly and interested. "Send me more information. Here is my email." He kindly handed us his business card. So we did just that. We sent him more information about our goal to be the first two women to paddle from Minneapolis to Hudson Bay along with a sponsorship agreement detailing "gives and gets." I was working late at a pizza place on campus when we received his long-awaited response.

> Natalie and Ann,
>
> . . . Typically, I may have sent you a note saying thanks, but no thanks; however, I think you would benefit from a little more detailed explanation, and I'm not willing to close the door just yet . . .

I already didn't like where this was going and wished he had stopped at "thanks but no thanks." We were accustomed to either not hearing back or getting outright rejections, but this response was far different. He continued:

> I will be blunt. I need to know what you are doing that is going to garner me good publicity for the features and benefits of our products. . . . I wouldn't be impressed with two men paddling to Hudson Bay from Minnesota, this is not 1915 before women had the vote, so why am I to be impressed by two women doing it today? Is it harder for you to do it than two males your age? I am not trying to be rude or disrespectful, but that is what you are trying to sell me—or have I read your messaging incorrectly? I would like to do this trip also. It sounds to me like

you are going on your summer vacation and want to defray the costs. . . . I suggest that between ultimate tournaments and exams you proofread and not just spell check your correspondence. . . . I'm looking for partners who are champions. . . . I want people to promote our brand because they believe in who we are, what we do and why we do it. I want to see your writing samples. Some concepts of the pieces you are pitching to the various magazines. I want to know how you are going to work the "product placement" into your photos and your editorial and your radio interviews, then I'll see what we might work out.

Tears filled my eyes and overflowed down my cheeks. I hid them as best as I could for the last half hour of my shift and hurried back to my dorm, anxious to find Ann. I flung her door open, and there she was, crying in the corner by her computer. She had read the email, too. We hugged and cried together, understanding exactly how the other felt—intimidated for the first time, thinking we might be totally out of our league.

There were plenty of things wrong with that email, but the main blow was to us as women in the outdoors (and, frankly, women anywhere doing anything). Was it physically harder for two women to do this trip? Of course not. Ann and I were setting out to paddle every day for eighty-five days, which is something that (believe it or not) most able-bodied people can do. But was it socially and politically harder? Yes, absolutely. That email is proof in itself of the barriers women face while attempting to stake ground in the outdoors. At the time it was difficult for me to understand how Ann and I could break into a world that had historically been built for white men.

The outdoor industry is still wildly homogenous in terms of gender and racial equality. This is a problem. But it is not an accident. According to a study done by REI during its "Force of Nature" campaign, nearly 75 percent of women feel they are under more pressure to conform to social norms than men, and

72 percent say they feel liberated and free when they are outdoors. Women in the study noted the pressure they feel from social and mainstream media, men, and even other women to be sexy, lose weight, smile more, be less emotional, and be less dramatic. We are told we should feel less social restraint in the outdoors, yet more than half of the women surveyed could not think of a female role model in the outdoor industry. How can we rise up if we do not see ourselves in the roles we aspire to? Women are especially underrepresented and oversexualized in outdoor advertising. Even fewer women go on outdoor expeditions like ours, and, consequentially, there are fewer of us featured in outdoor articles. When you dig into it, the inequalities are stark.

Ann and I were not professional marketers out to gain the public's support of certain outdoor brands. But we embodied the true spirit of adventure, the raw emotion of "screw it, let's do it" despite all barriers and a lack of female role models. The fact that we were the first two women to complete a three-month canoe expedition recreating a historic route was marketing gold for those who could see through the glass ceiling. Contrary to what the writer of that email may believe, sponsorships should be first and foremost an investment in people and only second a tool for companies to market their products and brands. I truly believed we were a worthy investment that represented the spirit of adventure and grit on which many outdoor companies were founded.

If lots of people wanted to do this trip, then why didn't they? Outdoor adventures are always highly romanticized, often as carefree and relaxing summer vacations to escape the busyness of life or as strenuous physical endeavors that involve conquering mountains and slaying whitewater rapids—a dance with death that requires physical strength and yields a magnificent reward. But separate from the miserable weather and the dangers of the wild, it's easy to forget the compromises that people make when they venture out into canoe country. It's scary, and sometimes it's easier to just stay home.

In my case, I was afraid that I would lose the momentum to build my career after college. For others, that fear may involve leaving family and a job behind. It is a scary decision because we cannot predict how it will end and how it will change us. And it *will* change us. The most challenging part of an expedition is committing to do it—accepting the unknown changes that will inevitably occur in you and around you. That bravery alone is worth celebrating (and sponsoring). We would often think back to the email from the sales rep during the most challenging parts of our journey. The skepticism we received was motivation. It fueled us to prove that we could do it and make it our own, with our homemade spray skirt and all.

That spring, Ann and I were far too busy with trip details to think about graduation or our separation from our friends and community. Ann was so focused on planning our trip that she almost failed her math class, which would have cost her a diploma and would not have looked good on her college transcript, especially since she was majoring in the subject. One day we skipped class to practice paddling upstream on the Cannon River to prepare for our journey up the Minnesota River, the first leg of our trip. On our way back, we ran into the professor whose seminar I had just skipped. I apologized for not attending his class. With a smile and wink, he said that we must have had more important things to do. It seemed as if everyone around us was starting to share in our excitement and support our adventure.

We planned to bring a gun with us for extra protection in polar bear country but never hoped to use it. Before we left on the trip I drove to Ann's parents' house to learn how to load and shoot the 12-gauge shotgun from her neighbor Bob. We both took turns putting together and taking apart the gun multiple times before we practiced shooting it in the backyard. I thought it was strange to shoot a gun in the woods at someone's house near the city but didn't think too much about it. Only later did we hear that someone had called the police after hearing the gunshots in the suburban neighborhood. When the police knocked on the Raihos' door, Ann's dad said he didn't know what they were talking about and wished them farewell with a wink and a wave.

We held a launch party in St. Paul the night after graduation where we roasted a pig and toasted our supporters. At the party, our family and friends wrote us letters to open throughout the trip, some serious, some inspiring, and some goofy. After months of planning, it was finally time to pack and depart. The days that followed were a blur of gear, maps, and granola bars (a lot of them) littering the Raihos' basement. We repackaged all of our food into thick plastic bags to eliminate any excess trash on trail and carefully tied each bag to keep water out. There were three scheduled resupply stops on our route: Fargo, Winnipeg, and Norway House in Manitoba. We organized supplies by their drop-off point and carefully labeled each pile. Ann would drive back with her parents to pick up the Fargo resupply while I made a quick detour to Philadelphia for my sister's wedding in July. After that, the Raihos offered to resupply us in Winnipeg. We shipped the last box of maps and food to Norway House. Each resupply was unique based on our location. We packed lightly for the upstream section, bringing only sleeping bags, tent, personal gear, and food. In Winnipeg we would switch out our lighter sleeping bags for warmer ones for the journey north. Handwritten checklists carpeted the basement floor between mountains of gear and food. With only a few days to get everything ready, we barely had time to reflect on the life of comfort and convenience—of showers, home-cooked meals, and good company—that we were about to leave behind. It was packing purgatory, and in packing purgatory, everything starts to look (and smell) like a granola bar.

FLOODED UPSTREAM

WE WERE DETERMINED to meet our launch date of June 2. We had given ourselves ninety days to get to Hudson Bay. If we waited any longer to launch from the muddy banks of the Minnesota River, the cold winds might beat us north. Ann and I had planned to start our journey from Pike Island at Fort Snelling State Park in St. Paul, the location where Eric Sevareid and Walter Port had launched their famed canoeing expedition eighty-one years earlier, but there was a problem: it was underwater. We had to quickly revise our plans, something that, unbeknownst to me at the time, we would have to do again and again on our journey. So instead of Pike Island, we found a flooded inlet in the park that provided safe access to the river for the first leg of our expedition to Hudson Bay—330 miles against the unpredictable current of the Minnesota River.

On the day of departure, I looked out at the rushing current and then down at my paddle, hoping somehow it held a strength that my arms did not. I kept repeating in my head the phone call I had received the day before:

"Hi, is this Natalie of Hudson Bay Bound? I work for the Minnesota Department of Natural Resources. I'm calling to let you know that the Minnesota River is in a severe flood stage and that we recommend you and Ann postpone your trip until the water level goes down. I'm not sure you'll be able to paddle upstream against the current now anyway."

Rivers during flood stage have a strong and unpredictable flow. They rapidly twist and turn over underwater obstacles, often creating challenging conditions for paddlers beyond just a strong current, as if the hydrology of the river was specifically at war with canoeists. There was only one way to find out if the current was too strong for us to attain. We had to try.

I couldn't sleep the night before our launch. My mind was stuck somewhere between the excitement I felt as a child before Christmas and the nervousness I felt in college before a big test. Part of me wanted to shake Ann awake and say, "Let's just go now!" I already had my trail clothes on, ready for a quick escape. What if the current *was* too strong to paddle? How many people would arrive on the banks of the Minnesota River in the morning just to watch us fail? I wished we could go get the canoe and test the current before the production of our departure. I tried counting sheep to distract myself, but those sheep kept ending up in canoes and getting swept downstream. The first light shone through the window, justifying my jostling Ann awake for our big debut.

About thirty friends, family, and members of the media, cameras in tow, stood in the mud with us at 8:00 a.m. to say farewell. We wouldn't see them for another three months at least. The flooded forest made for a less than glamorous location for a photo shoot. Everyone maneuvered through the swamp to get to our canoe, struggling to keep their shoes dry. I wondered if we were supposed to give a speech. It felt unnatural to say goodbye, as if nothing we said could express our gratitude. But after months of planning there was nothing left to do but paddle. With an awkward smile and a final wave, Ann and I got into our new floating home and pushed off from the mud onto the standing water. Our hips instinctively danced with the unsteady rocking of the boat, like a secret password to let the canoe know we could handle her. It felt strange to launch in front of a crowd of people cheering us on. In that moment, it felt like our journey, and eventual success, was more for them than for us. We navigated through the flooded woods until we had a clear path to the river. The event of the launch had briefly distracted me from my concerns of paddling upstream. But now our boat was headed straight toward the unforgiving current. I glanced to the opposite shore and saw an entire cottonwood tree floating downstream. The warning of the Minnesota DNR official began playing in my mind again.

In the seconds before the canoe's bow hit the river, I imagined getting sideswept downstream. We even briefly debated paddling the Mississippi River to New Orleans instead. I literally felt Ann's anxiety in the water. Her strokes were the strongest I'd experienced in our many years of canoeing together. I responded in kind. The cheers from our friends onshore became faint and distant; all of my energy focused on strong, consistent paddle strokes as our canoe finally hit the current. I closed my eyes, expecting a sudden blow. Instead, there was nothing but slow, steady stillness. We were set free at last, crawling up the Minnesota River at a steady 1.5 miles per hour. Our friends and family disappeared behind the lush foliage of Fort Snelling State Park as we pushed through our first of 330 miles paddling upstream. I monitored our slow pace in relation to the passing land and wondered if we could walk the river faster than we could paddle it.

The muscles in my arms roused with each paddle stroke, tearing apart in preparation to grow stronger. The river resisted like molasses. If we stopped paddling for even a second the current would send us back to where we began, like a film on rewind. I felt euphoric in the first few hours despite the physical challenge and the mental strain of traveling upstream. But soon the sun was out and the wind was at our backs. In the afternoon, we wasted the hours away developing a new language that only we could speak. We made new words for *bird* ("flit-to-weet") and *paddle* ("woo-spish"). Creative conversation had been waiting in the wings of my busy life for too long, and now we had hours, days, weeks, and months to talk about whatever our minds could imagine. We made up a game where one person says something and the other person says something grosser, and so on and so forth, until someone gets too disgusted to carry on. I excelled at this game. I couldn't tell whether Ann didn't like losing or really didn't like the bizarre revolting things that I came up with, but this was definitely not one of her favorite games. She was much better at, well, almost everything else.

"Big stick floating our way!" Ann called from the bow.

"Think you can hit it with your paddle?"

Ann wound up her paddle above her head while I struggled to keep us moving forward against the current. SMACK! The sound pierced through the thick blanket of humidity around us. She turned back and smiled.

"Well done, chap! I'd say 7 out of 10!" I said in a British accent that would come out fairly often on our expedition.

Games like this came and went throughout our journey. It is nearly impossible to set accurate expectations for an adventure. Over long trips, rapport and routines unfold over time. We were raw material for the conditions to mold. That meant not always forcing conversation, which was challenging for both of us, and simply enjoying each other's company in whatever way felt natural in the moment. There was no TV or any other activity beyond paddling, eating, and sleeping day after day. For us, the expedition became an open space to inject our own fun into what could be, without imagination and creativity, an otherwise monotonous routine.

When we were planning our trip, there were a few things people warned us about for the different legs of the trip: the dirty, polluted Minnesota River (aka "the river of chocolate milk"), the dangerous dams on the Red River, the weather and waves on Lake Winnipeg, and, once we got closer to Hudson Bay, the polar bears ("They will hunt you for days and then eat you"). Each of these sections had its unique challenges. But hearing about them from others and thinking about them in advance did little to truly prepare us for what lay ahead. Paddling upstream on the Minnesota in the heavy heat of summer was the first challenge.

~~~~~

LOOKING AROUND THE VAST Minnesota River Valley, I thought about my family name, Warren. I contemplated whether it was fate or coincidence that my name was the same as the river that created this river basin almost twelve thousand years prior. Glacial Lake Agassiz, formed from the meltwaters of the Laurentide Ice Sheet during the last ice age, was once the largest lake in the world, even larger than all of the Great Lakes combined. It covered parts of what is now Minnesota, the Dakotas, and Canada. A natural dam made of rocks and ice that held Agassiz's waters broke open, unleashing the great River Warren. She was a force to be reckoned with—a wall of water hundreds of feet deep and several miles wide that rushed through the landscape, carving out the wide river valley that we now traversed. She cut rock, created waterfalls (some of which are still here today and many of which have fallen into shadow), and eventually joined the Mississippi River in search of the sea. The Minnesota River, even during flood stage, was a mere remnant of the River Warren, an ancient and powerful force of nature. I felt honored to share her name, even though in truth she was nameless. "Warren" was ascribed to her more than ten thousand years after her tremendous travels through what is now the Minnesota River Valley, Mni Sóta Makoce in the language of the Dakota: the land where the water reflects the skies.

Few people recreate on the Minnesota River due to its reputation as a polluted, agricultural waterway. We paddled nearly every day for three weeks and never saw another paddler. I would often close my eyes and imagine what this land was like three or four hundred years ago. Endless prairies once extended as far as the eye could see, reaching into the distance to touch the wide blue sky above. Bison and elk made their home here before they were replaced by domestic livestock. Wetlands and wild rice were abundant. Today, the river is so polluted that swimming is not recommended and anglers are warned to limit their consumption of fish taken from the water. For decades we made our mark on the fertile soil; a full 92 percent of land in the Minnesota River

Basin is used for agriculture. Its farming legacy is proof that what happens on land is inextricably tied to the health of our lakes and rivers.

The Minnesota was once considered the most polluted river in America. Like many others across the nation, it has seen improvements in water quality over the last few decades because of regulations that aim to protect our water resources, such as the Clean Water Act of 1972. Improvements have occurred through better wastewater treatment, land use practices, and restrictions on dumping. But long-standing agricultural practices, exempt from the Clean Water Act, have had a huge negative impact on water flow and quality in the Minnesota River Basin. Just outside of the Twin Cities, Ann and I began to see farmland along the riverbank, but we would soon see only miles of corn planted all the way to the water's edge. Much of the nitrogen and other chemicals used to produce row crops like corn and soybeans eventually flows into the river, which joins the Mississippi at Fort Snelling. These chemicals travel with the current down to the Gulf of Mexico, where they settle and stimulate algae growth. That algae depletes the oxygen levels in the water, creating a dead zone—a toxic environment where aquatic life can no longer live.

Chemical pesticides are frequently used in Minnesota corn production, often at the expense of water quality and public health. Yet we continue to grow more and more corn to fuel growing industries. I always mused at the idea that "farmers feed the world." While certainly true, the majority of the corn in the Minnesota River Valley is not edible. You could stand in the middle of a cornfield and be miles away from any real food. Instead, the crops go toward ethanol production or to feedlots for cattle. Ann and I would soon have the opportunity to explore this complex issue with the farmers who took us in on nights when we couldn't find enough solid ground to pitch a tent.

Even with its messy environmental history, from the very first day onward Ann and I found the river to be a secret gem, a hidden wilderness. The sun illuminated the leaves on the trees as they danced in the wind, creating wildly different shades of green across the shoreline. The water was murky but rushing. It played a soothing sound that many people would pay to hear all day. As we continued on that first day, we saw a family of otters, orioles, finches, and turkeys along the riverbank. The wind was strong at our backs, so we built a sail out of extra paddles and rain jackets to help us attain the current.

Later we found out that, before our departure, an article had appeared in the paper titled "Ann and Natalie Delay Hudson Bay Expedition Due to Flooding on the Minnesota." This came as a surprise to us since we never even considered delaying our trip. People warned us that we couldn't paddle upstream during a flood because "trees would fall from the sky and float toward us" and we wouldn't be able to find dry land for camping. Both of these warnings had elements of truth, but they by no means made the river unpaddleable. When trees floated our way we simply paddled around them. When the riverbanks were too flooded to camp we simply searched for drier land. Ann and I were very conscious of the ever-changing water level on the Minnesota, but we worked with it and learned little tricks every day that allowed us to safely traverse the river in its flooded state.

That first night we camped in tall grass between an interstate and a state highway bridge. We fell asleep to the constant rush of passing cars, safely hidden in our patch of urban wilderness. After playing a few lullabies on the travel guitar to help Ann fall asleep and to soothe my musical itch, the weight of my sore, growing muscles forced me retire to my sleeping bag. It was too hot to crawl in, so I sprawled out on top, sweating and sticking to its fabric. It had taken us eleven hours to paddle 14 miles upstream. "Only 316 more to go," I thought as my mind easily drifted off to sleep.

AGAINST THE WIND

$$\times$$

THE NEXT MORNING we downed a delicious breakfast of eight-grain cereal and continued crawling up the Minnesota's strong currents. The odds were against us: upstream with a headwind. Every day we set concrete goals of where to stop for lunch and how far to travel (averaging twelve to fifteen miles daily), but ultimately our mileage was dependent on the wind and sun. Today, we aimed to stop for lunch at Murphy's Landing, a historic site where reenactors tell the story of the local history, mostly for tourists and schoolchildren. Our stomachs churned as we rounded the bend before our destination. As the current quickened, the wind whipped our boat around, and it took us nearly an hour to paddle the half mile to our destination. Exhausted, we finally pulled ashore at "The Landing," a well-maintained abandoned town managed by the Three Rivers Park District. We sat on an old stone wall to eat our salami and cheese in the shade of a large cottonwood tree.

"Wanna walk around a bit?" Ann asked.

I was all in favor of delaying the challenging paddle ahead. We had planned to make it another seven miles to Chaska that night, but ultimately the wind and current would decide our fate. The strong breeze found us even in the thick woods where we ate our lunch.

"Yep. It's probably free, right?" I thought about the few hundred dollars saved in my bank account, the remnants from working several campus jobs. With no income, I did not plan on spending part of my savings on admission to a reenactment village.

We hopped the stone fence to explore the site. The quiet empty grounds quickly came to life in our minds. We imagined the loud banging of a blacksmith working on tools, the joyful giggles of girls with braids, and the click-clack of horses echoing throughout the village. Aromatic apple pie pulled men in suits away from their meetings at the town hall. The scene was rife with the romance of nineteenth-century pioneer life, even though no one was there to reenact its history for us. I thought about how truly difficult life must have been back then. But the dolled-up structures we walked through portrayed a seemingly happier and simpler time. I wondered how they settled here and whom they may have displaced. The merry fiddlers slowly faded in my imagination as we turned to walk back to the canoe. My muscles pleaded for a break that my mind knew would not come.

We were tempted to stop for the day. Ann and I are very competitive, and on this occasion neither of us wanted to be the "weak one" and suggest that we set up camp and call it quits. That same attitude was what brought us here in the first place; it was why we agreed to do this trip when there were so many reasons not to. We always pushed each other to go further or to be better, which led to great things in our friendship and encouraged our proactive lives. That competitive spirit impelled us to push back out into the strong headwind and continue upstream.

Luckily, the river was easier to paddle for the remainder of the day. We arrived in Chaska around 7:00 p.m. after a twelve-hour paddle. It was difficult to find dry land to set up the tent, so we went into town to ask residents if we could camp on their property. We were excited to talk to people in the community. Heck, maybe we could even get a meal out of the deal! To our dismay and surprise, the people we met were wary of us and would not let us camp in their yards. Returning to the river, we joked that "nonwelcoming Minnesotans" was an oxymoron since they have such a nice reputation. Tired and hungry, we got back into trusty *Kawena Kinomaeta* and paddled downstream to a sandbar.

We stuffed ourselves with deliciously bland mac 'n' cheese and set up camp for the night.

The alarm went off at 6:30 a.m. I peeked blearily over my sleeping bag at Ann. She looked back with similar eyes. It was only the third day of our trip, but our bodies were sore and still adjusting to our new lifestyle. Without words, we agreed to sleep in. The morning sun slowly turned our tent into a sauna until the miserable heat pulled us from our slumber. Sweaty and desperate for a breeze, we crawled out of our tent into the hot and humid air of Minnesota summer.

We had been prepared for inclement weather, animal encounters, and large waves, but we never thought that heat would be an issue. Sweltering heat. It was unbearable to wear long sleeves to protect our skin, and when we discarded our layers, the UV rays blistered our arms and lower backs. My skin was covered in pus bubbles, which I enjoyed popping throughout the day during breaks. The hottest day we experienced on the Minnesota River was 101 degrees with no wind. On the plus side, the heat was evaporating the water quickly and the river level was going down. As the water lines descended on the tree trunks every hour, each day paddling upstream became easier.

Currents tend to run faster in the middle of a river and on the outside bends. Ann and I strategically navigated the waters throughout the day, crossing from bank to bank to find the weakest current. I have never taken a class in fluid dynamics, but I know from experience how water responds to barriers, both visible and below the surface. Paddling rivers has taught me how to find rest in natural eddies, to predict and respond to "water spirals," which can form after large whitewater rapids, and to read the ripples of the water for clues to hidden obstacles.

On June 4, near Jordan, Minnesota, Ann and I encountered our first real fight with the current. We turned the corner to find a railroad bridge cutting diagonally across the river. The river under it was completely jammed by logs and trees, old and new.

High waters had loosened the roots of trees on the riverbank, causing them to fall and drift downstream, until they got stuck. The railroad bridge in front of us looked like an impenetrable tree graveyard.

Farming practices are partially to blame for our upstream battle. It is common for farmers to "tile" agricultural fields, draining water into underground systems that quickly transport it from land to river. This keeps valuable crops from flooding. The ability to move water has turned once marshy lands into prime real estate for agriculture. Water used to precipitate and seep into the ground to recharge the groundwater system, feed the plants, and maybe meander its way to a nearby stream. It now gets escorted directly to the river like a high-speed train with no time to absorb into the soil. The result? When it rains, when it pours, it floods. The Minnesota River now holds more water than it has in recent history, especially during heavy-rain events. Water rushing through the channel tears away the land on the riverbank, uprooting trees and ravaging the landscape. These days, it happens so frequently that the land often does not have time to recover before the next flood event.

To deal with the situation in front of us, Ann and I used a whitewater paddling technique called "forward ferrying" to get from one side of the river to the other without moving backward or forward in the channel. To do this, the person in the stern keeps the boat at about a 45-degree angle with the bow pointing toward the direction we want to go. This angle, combined with enough forward paddling to compensate for the current, gracefully carries the boat laterally across the river. Once we got to the other side of the river, we found a small opening between two logs under the bridge, but the current was too quick for us to attain it. We pulled over on some rocks on river right (which was our left— putting "river" in front of a direction always assumes the downstream direction). I had a plan: I wanted to jump over to one of the bridge supports, have Ann throw the painter lines (the long ropes tied to either end of the canoe) to me from the shore, weave in and out of the wooden pillars holding up the rickety railroad tracks, and pull the boat against the rushing water to the sandbar on the upstream side of the bridge.

Now, I know Ann Raiho. She likes to get her way (as do I), and I knew that if we were going to execute my idea I would have to finesse it by leading her to a similar conclusion on her own. After much discussion she agreed that this was the best (albeit not the safest) option. This was the first time I had advocated for the more dangerous option; it would not be the last.

I jumped onto the nearest bridge support and received the painter lines from Ann. Weaving in and out of the large wooden pillars was exhilarating; I was climbing trees with a mission. If I made one wrong move or if the old wooden crossbeams beneath me gave way, I would end up in the flooded river with the fallen trees. Whenever we were in dangerous situations I always thought of the newspaper headline that would appear if something went wrong: "Hudson Bay Women Float Back to Minneapolis on Tree Logs, Looking for Boat Downstream."

My abs clenched as I hugged the first pillar. I slowly lifted and carefully placed one foot after the other, shuffling across the crossbeams. I paused, took a deep breath, quickly released the first pillar, and swiftly embraced the next under the bridge. The painter lines were wrapped around my wrist, digging into my skin as I pulled the canoe through the narrow opening. The current was strong, but the boat did not resist. I hugged the last pillar, gave the painter lines a big tug, and jumped onto a sandbar just upstream with the boat in tow. Ann scrambled around the bridge onshore and met me there to help lift the loaded boat over the sandbar and put ol' Canoey back in the water.

"I guess we could have just portaged around that, huh?" I said, feeling relieved.

"Hudson Bay Bound—we'll do anything to avoid a portage!" joked Ann. It was funny but true. Future obstacles were waiting

for us, and we would always try a creative approach before suc-
cumbing to the onerous chore of unloading, carrying, and reload-
ing our gear.

Navigating rivers is fairly straightforward: stick to the current. But due to the high water in 2011, the Minnesota River had
sprawled out across the watershed like a wily, wayward hose. Ann
and I avoided the side channels, which often ended up to be trib-
utaries or small farm channels. But sometimes we would gamble
on a shortcut to save time. One day we approached a mile-long
oxbow that had a fairly strong current. River bends are like rubber bands. The current pushes them out, causing them to stretch
further and further over time until the bend looks like a big U
shape from above. Then one day, usually during a flood event, the
water rushes through, connecting the top ends of the U shape,
and the bend snaps back to its most direct channel. The oxbow
we were approaching was in flux—a rubber band about to snap
back. The river flowed every which way across the U-shaped
bend, through the woods and across the mud and sand. We calculated that it would take about half an hour to paddle around the
entire thing. Due to our shared passion for covering miles, Ann
and I saw the flooded woods as an opportunity. "Time for a shortcut!" we agreed.

The dark woods felt like a gateway into another reality. The
bright sounds of summer—the wind, the birds, and the constant
rush of the river—disappeared behind us as we entered the quiet
flooded forest. Ann and I eased the canoe forward with caution;
moving through the lagoon was like paddling through a maze. We
diverted our path many times to avoid floating logs. Tent worms
fell from the sky like soldiers parachuting from planes above. Our
shortcut quickly became a nightmare of low-lying branches, spiders, cobwebs, and frustrating dead ends. We spent half an hour
navigating the flooded woods until we finally emerged back into
the rushing current and summer light. After examining our location, however, we realized we were right back to where we had

started. Within that half hour we could have paddled around the entire oxbow! We appreciated the bizarre side adventure nonetheless. Small excursions and unexpected decisions often enriched our days with great memories.

Paddling upstream is the slowest form of transportation I had ever taken. On our way to Le Sueur, Minnesota, we paddled fifteen miles in ten hours. I appreciated that I could feel my arms and shoulders growing in strength every day. I enjoyed the pains of physical achievement. I flexed my muscles almost every night before falling asleep to celebrate my newly developed strength. I wanted to be a woman with strong arms, shoulders, and thighs. I wanted to feel powerful and capable wherever I went.

We reached Le Sueur after six days on the water. At Camp Menogyn, Ann and I had been trained to pack out enough food for each meal based on pounds per person per day. For this expedition, we each packed out one and a half pounds of food per day, increasing in half-pound increments each month. We carefully planned out all of our meals and rations without taking into account that, since we were paddling through communities for the first month, we could just stop in town to grab a burger at the end of the day. Due to this oversight, we had a stockpile of extra dinners that sat sadly at the bottom of our food bag, waiting to be eaten. After our long push toward Le Sueur, it was time for a beer and some pizza at the local bar. We got used to strange, skeptical looks from locals. After nearly a week on the water, we were both in need of a shower, and we often felt out of place. Ann and I split a large pizza at the bar. As usual, we shared our story with those who were interested. In return for our tales, we'd usually get good conversation, sometimes a free beer, and occasionally prayed over. This time we scored a free pizza from a nice woman bartending that night.

The next morning, we left Le Sueur with our eyes set on St. Peter, Minnesota. Before our trip, we heard a lot about the wind and waves on Lake Winnipeg, which were "so strong that we could spend a day paddling only to find ourselves right back where we started!" We knew that challenge awaited us farther north, but we never expected wind to be an issue in the sheltered Minnesota River Valley. We were wrong.

The wind was against us on our paddle to St. Peter, with gusts over thirty-five miles per hour. I did not speak to Ann for the last half of the day because the wind was so strong that we couldn't hear each other. Each stroke barely nudged us forward. After hours of battling the wind and current, the bridge at St. Peter finally came into view. I almost wished it hadn't. On the last stretch of river leading to town we hit a wind tunnel. Instead of the occasional strong gust, the wind here was unrelenting. My muscles tensed and shriveled up in protest. It felt like we were in some sort of slapstick comedy with a dangling carrot in front of a horse. I was convinced we could get there, but the more we tried the farther away the bridge seemed.

It took us over an hour to paddle the final mile into town. In retrospect, these were not the best conditions for a lightweight Kevlar canoe. Physically exhausted, we finally arrived at the boat landing and, in between heavy breathing, expressed our shared desire after the long day on the river: milkshakes. Glorious, creamy, cold milkshakes.

We hauled our relatively light load to the nearby campground: one large pack with personal gear, a tent, cooking supplies, a pack with a month's worth of food, and our ol' pal Canoey. Before we could charge into St. Peter demanding milkshakes, we met with a local news reporter. Like we did for many of our early interviews, we felt awkward about and confused by people's interest in our expedition. It didn't help that we had a milkshake mission to take care of and this reporter was delaying it.

We walked into town like two women emerging from weeks in the jungle, our tan skin darkened by a layer of dirt and our hair tangled like Medusa's. Our fierce gazes scanned the town for milkshakes. We went into a few establishments and coffee shops but always came out empty-handed. It turned into a fun night for us, walking around St. Peter in our mucky Muck Boots and ranting about how no one in the town serves milkshakes.

Eventually we gave up and settled for smoothies. The cold drinks woke up our stomachs as hunger took control and brought us to an Irish bar, where we scarfed down cheeseburgers, french fries, and a very delicious rhubarb crisp with ice cream. We were drunk from food when we finally cozied into our tent by the river and gave in to exhaustion. Luckily our bodies shut down easily after the long day. Otherwise, it would have been hard to fall asleep thinking about how we'd have to do it all again in the morning.

WE WOKE THE NEXT MORNING with renewed hunger. This was the first time we had expended so many calories in a single day, and hunger was beginning to feel like a constant companion. We spent lots of time thinking and talking about where to camp and what to eat each day because there was little else to worry about. It's amazing how so many things unrelated to basic survival had frustrated us back home while we were preparing for the expedition. Life was simple on the river. Anything that wasn't a basic need or a life-threatening issue wasn't worth a worried thought.

We left St. Peter in the early afternoon. The wind apologized for the previous day as it reversed direction and pushed us toward Mankato. One thing I appreciate about paddling a whole river is that you get to experience all of her moods and temperaments. Similar to living with another person, you get to witness the best and worst of another living entity. You begin to see and read the signs of distress and joy and to learn the difficult dance of living together harmoniously. In a way, the river cared for us, too. She had expressed her power—her strong current, whitecapped waves, and sisterhood with the wind—on our paddle to St. Peter. But we had a pact. She would not be like that forever. It would not rain every day. There would not be a headwind for our entire expedition. Over our long journey, there would be one day of pure bliss and easy paddling to compensate for every day the wind whipped over the water and the rain poured down. Our paddle from St. Peter to Mankato felt like a reward, or perhaps an apology, for our hard work the day before.

Despite the beautiful weather and easy paddling that day, Ann and I managed to really get on each other's nerves for the first time. Our moods shifted suddenly when I wanted to take out in Mankato on the muddy shores of Land of Memories Park to scope it out and Ann wanted to find the boat launch. I noticed that this small disagreement sparked a resentful voice in my head. Memories of all of the times Ann made the final call flooded my mind. Perhaps Ann was also spinning memories of the times I took the quickest route instead of the safest one. It was not just this disagreement that put me in a sour mood but the accumulation of similar small arguments throughout our friendship, many of which had gone unaddressed. I didn't know it at the time, but this thick history of shared experiences and closed perceptions of each other would eventually lead to a tipping point in the middle of one of the largest lakes in the world.

The next morning we met with the Mankato Canoeing Club to tour Minneopa State Park, whose name translates from the Dakota language as "water falling twice." The main attraction at the park is a two-tiered cascading waterfall that flows through a majestic limestone gorge. We learned how the Dakota people used the river for thousands of years before the first Europeans arrived in the 1700s and how tourism to the park increased in the mid-1800s due to the construction of a railroad. The park was created in 1905 to protect the land from being turned into agricultural fields and has since expanded from 145 acres to more than 800 acres that are still protected today. Our local guides hinted at the historic battles that took place nearby, saying, "You'll learn all about that during your visit to New Ulm."

Back on the river, we paddled only ten miles before our "gas tanks" hit empty around Judson, Minnesota. We were exhausted. Whenever we stopped somewhere, even just for the afternoon, we found it difficult to hop right back into our rigorous paddling schedule. So, we set up camp above the floodwaters on the river-bank. Soon rain began to pitter-patter on our tent, lulling us into a deep sleep. The next morning we paddled to New Ulm, Minnesota, in a record seventeen miles in 9.5 hours. After having camped along the beautiful sandbanks of the Minnesota River for five nights, we were offered our first homestay. It would be the first of many. A family had contacted us days earlier and offered a hot meal and a bed when we got to the area.

A woman, her husband, and their teenage son were all waiting for us at the boat launch. We mistakenly paddled past it and had to turn around for a glorious glimpse of what it was like to paddle downstream. Our boat glided through the water, and our strong, persistent paddle strokes were no longer necessary to propel us forward. It was a thirty-second journey of pure joy, and we relished in what would come once we entered the Red River.

The family greeted us when we landed. Before we knew it, the father and son were carrying all of our gear to their car. They refused to let us help because God forbid that we carry the heavy things we'd been lugging around for a week already. Ann and I obliged out of courtesy as we watched our gear slowly relocate to the trunk of their van, not quite sure what to do with ourselves. Then they put the canoe on top of their car. The father assured us that his son was a Boy Scout and that there was nothing to worry about because "he's got it covered." Ann and I smiled and nodded as we watched the young boy fumble over knots and eventually declare the boat was secure. We hopped in the back seat of the family van. While the mother casually chatted with us, I had my eyes on the bow of the canoe through the front windshield. It was bouncing up and down, swaying back and forth. I grabbed Ann's thigh and squeezed it every time I thought the boat was going to topple off the car onto the road. We shared terrified glances and half-hearted responses to a drill of questions from the woman until we, and miraculously the boat, arrived in their driveway.

The next morning we toured Flandrau State Park and began to understand what our guides at Minneopa had hinted at. The battles at New Ulm were a pivotal moment in the US-Dakota War. The Dakota people, rightfully angered by the government's failure to adhere to the terms of the treaty they had been forced to sign, rebelled, attacking settlers and settlements, such as New Ulm. The final chapter of the war occurred in December 1862 when thirty-eight Dakota men were hanged in Mankato—the largest mass execution in the nation's history. The lives of the Dakota were forever altered, and that tragic history remains fresh in the minds of Native and non-Native Americans in Minnesota to this day.

Once we resumed our trip, the usual sights—trees, water, mud—felt different. The quiet woods and rushing current we had been traveling for almost a week now became a historical looking glass. How many people had paddled this same stretch of river during times of war? How many bodies bled in the woods where we camped each night? The land here holds many secrets and stories hidden beneath the layers of lush vegetation. Time passes. The earth's soils shift and fold in a constant process of burying and unearthing. It becomes nearly impossible to see the scars of war on the landscape. Unjust deaths become stories in books that we tell to remember. Those stories, too, change with time, as we continuously reexamine what we think we know.

Time seemed to slow down as we struggled logistically to get back on the water. It felt like days since we were last on the river, even though we had only hopped off for the night. As comfortable as it was to sleep in a bed, I already missed the ease and simplicity of camping by the water. The river welcomed us home with the familiar sounds of water flowing alongside us, leaves dancing in the wind, and birds singing in the green trees and blue skies above us as we attained the strong current. After a good twelve-mile paddle, we decided to camp early and play music on our travel guitar and ukulele. We looked at the map—only one more week of paddling upstream! I played a lullaby for Ann and then fell into another peaceful sleep by the river.

MEET ME AT THE POPCORN STAND

The water trail from New Ulm to Montevideo is one of my favorite stretches of the Minnesota River. A water trail is a body of water that is managed for recreation. The Minnesota Department of Natural Resources manages more than thirty-five water trails across the state, maintaining campsites, signage, and access to the water. They also make detailed maps for every state water trail, which we used to navigate this section of our expedition. Thanks to this state-funded program, paddlers and boaters can safely venture down (or up, in our case) a waterway knowing there will be clear passage, amenities, and campsites along the way. Even though we were only a few hours away from the Twin Cities by car on this stretch of the river, it often felt like we were in the middle of a remote wilderness area. The only sounds we could hear were the leaves on the trees and the occasional flap of wings from nearby ducks or geese, startled by our presence. Floating on the water, it was easy to forget that the river below was so unhealthy. Above the murky waters, the forest played home to traveling birds, deer, and, on a very rare occasion, bobcats.

Sometimes we would go days without seeing other people on this secluded section of the river. To entertain ourselves, in the heat of the day, we would paddle standing up in the boat, singing and interpretive paddling to our favorite folk songs. Music always felt like a third member of our expedition. The weather took a turn for the worse two days after our departure from New Ulm. Ann had arranged for us to meet a news reporter from Redwood Falls, Minnesota, at a boat launch near a bridge on the west side of the river. We paddled beneath the darkening clouds, eyeing the sky as a mother might eye her child before an inopportune tantrum, as if to say, "Don't you dare, not now." The reporter was going to meet us at noon, but we were not about to paddle through a storm just to get there in time. We skipped our usual pre-lunch granola bar break to make headway on the river. We were a mile away when the sky released the heavy rain it had threatened all morning. Lightning exploded all around, terrifying both of us. Ann spotted the boat launch ahead, and we struggled toward it through the storm, staring at the bottom of the canoe to protect our faces from the oncoming rain and wind. Finally, we reached the concrete platform under the bridge and quickly stowed our gear under the canoe onshore.

The reporter was waiting in his car and offered to drive us to a pavilion so we wouldn't get wet during our interview. Looking down at my drenched rain gear, I didn't see how I could get any wetter. We got into his car and drove to a nearby park, where Ann and I shared tales from our adventure, shivering despite the warm weather. After the meet and greet, the reporter drove us through Redwood Falls for a quick tour. "Over there is Dari King," he gestured. "Some of the best food in town! Next time you come through Redwood you should definitely stop there to eat." My stomach growled uncontrollably. But alas, I had been living in Minnesota too long to suggest something that could possibly inconvenience someone else—to ask if we could stop in for a juicy cheeseburger and sizzling french fries. Ann and I were cold, hungry, wet, and not particularly eager to get back on the water in a thunderstorm as we slowly watched the Dari King disappear from sight.

We returned to our boat and dug up some granola bars, not wanting to whip out the lunch de jour during the downpour. The bars we had rationed for the day were lemon chamomile—our least favorite flavor. They tasted like lemon-scented cleaning solution. As we crouched in the rain, ravenously savoring our mediocre granola bars, I looked over at Ann and began to laugh. I had learned that sometimes in these situations, that's all you can do. We fell asleep that night dreaming of burgers and fries.

~~~~~

THANKS TO NONPROFIT and community groups in the basin, the Minnesota River has improved in the last few decades, but there is clearly much more work to be done. More people, and especially policy makers, need to realize that healthy waterways and healthy communities are directly connected. Every now and then we would meet someone who really cared about the Minnesota River. In recent decades, some towns have turned their backs on the river because of its polluted reputation. That made it so much more meaningful when we could talk with inspirational people who see the recreational and economic advantages of living close to a river. They were often excited to hear about our experiences on the water and share their own river stories with us in return.

As Ann and I traveled up the Minnesota River we spent lots of time talking and thinking about what we were seeing around us. The impacts of flooding and pollution were obvious. We saw fields of row crops planted right up to the edge of the riverbank and cows defecating in the water. After sixteen days, we had learned how to read the river and travel where the current was weakest. We loved seeing bridges because they helped us keep track of our progress on the map, but we never realized how much they change the hydrology of the river. Bridges funnel the river and create stronger currents and patches of what is technically known as "vortex shedding" but what we referred to as "confused water" around the support pillars. This water changes the ebb and flow of the river and is difficult to navigate in a canoe. Over thousands of years, rivers like the Minnesota have cut their own routes, using land elevation as a guide, which will continue to change for thousands more.

En route to Granite Falls, Minnesota, we stopped at Upper Sioux Agency State Park to meet with the park ranger there. Ann and I waited by the campground along the river and eventually spotted a pickup truck bouncing down the unpaved road in our direction. It stopped a few yards away from us, and a short, stout, middle-aged woman with blond curly hair descended from the truck. She introduced herself as Terri the park ranger and directed us into the truck to begin our tour of the park. She shared with us the Native history of the river and described how the 1851 Treaty of Traverse des Sioux relocated the Dakota from their land in Iowa to the banks of the Minnesota River, establishing the Yellow Medicine Agency. Nearly 150 years ago the land we now casually traversed with the park ranger was home to a bloody battle in the US-Dakota War that wiped out the Yellow Medicine Agency. The state park was established in 1963 to preserve the historic site.

In the middle of her well-rehearsed spiel, Terri looked at us and said, "Would you girls like to see my favorite tree?"

A favorite tree? I was perplexed. Terri had lived here her entire life and did little traveling. When I was growing up I took every opportunity to explore other places. At age nineteen, I blew all my money on a two-month solo trip through Europe, working on farms in exchange for room and board. I had spent summers living in different states and had collected endless travel stories. Sure, I had come across several trees I liked and maybe took a nap or ate lunch under their shade, but I did not have a *favorite* tree. The truck rolled to a stop at a truly magnificent tree. Its sturdy crooked fingers, perfect for climbing, reached high and wide as if trying to grasp the sun. Below, there was a welcoming patch of grass waiting for someone to waste the summer day away, staring up at the clouds or out over the prairie. Suddenly I realized I was envious of Terri, of her deep attachment to this place. The history and culture of Terri's home were deep within her. I was just a curious visitor longing for a true sense of place. I hoped that someday I, too, would have a favorite tree.

We said our farewells after lunch and continued upstream, quietly digesting the stories and faces from our visit to the park. We reached the Minnesota Falls Dam and pulled over on river left to portage our canoe over the massive concrete structure. We grew to love paddling a Kevlar canoe on the upstream section of this trip because, coming in at only forty-five pounds, one person could lift and carry it alone, which made for smooth, independent portages. A few yards into our trek over the dam (which was built in the early 1900s and has since been demolished to allow the river to run free), a local pulled up to tell us that we were trespassing on private land and that the portage was on the other side of the river. We carelessly repacked our boat and paddled to the river right side, where we found a sad excuse for a portage. I carried the canoe up a hill and into a cornfield, losing sight of the river and any hint of a path. Retracing my steps, I found the water once more and beached the boat above the dam.

〰〰

DAMS ARE A FREQUENT SIGHT on rivers like the Minnesota. Numbers from the Army Corps of Engineers indicate that the United States has more than ninety thousand dams, impacting more than six thousand miles of river. It's as if we've built a dam a day since Thomas Jefferson was president. Once considered symbolic of the grandeur of America's empire building, dams are now damaging the environment and destroying vital natural systems that have been in place for thousands of years. The World Wildlife Foundation published research in 2019 showing that around two-thirds of the world's longest rivers are no longer free-flowing. As a result, freshwater plants and animals are declining twice as fast as terrestrial and marine populations.

In the late nineteenth and early twentieth centuries, dams sprang up across the country in response to the government's call to turn the river "menace" into a resource for flood control, irrigation, and hydropower. But in some cases, dams prove to be more dangerous than the "menaces"—the free-flowing rivers—they were intended to tame. When structures like dams and levees are built, there is often no life-cycle plan in place, no consideration of what to do when those structures inevitably fail. Today, our nation's dams are beginning to crumble, creating a natural point of intervention: do we sink money into maintaining them or remove them completely? Removing dams can create drastic changes in the landscape, cost tens of millions of dollars, and, not surprisingly, spark heated debates among energy corporations (hydropower); politicians; federal, state, and local governments; and local community members vying for their economic and political interests. But that point of intervention also creates space for people to decide the future of a river, a space that requires us to come together as a community, to ask big questions about our future and advocate for policies that reflect a greater human connection with the natural landscape.

The current quickened, and paddling became tricky as we approached the Granite Falls Dam. I tried to clear my mind and focus on my breathing to overpower the voice in my head telling me I was in pain. Inhale, exhale, one paddle stroke at a time. Repeat. The current is typically faster downstream of a dam, but the full force of flood stage on the Minnesota River made it feel like we were paddling up a waterfall. Ann paddled harder and I responded in kind. In my periphery I could see a tree trunk onshore to our left that looked stationary. If the tree wasn't moving that meant we weren't moving—we were on a canoe treadmill. To distract myself from the aches and pains of fast, nonstop paddling, I pretended we were racing the tree to the dam. We were neck and neck. Finally, our canoe inched forward, and I started racing the next tree in competition.

Beyond the trees I saw a concrete path leading up to the dam. In between heavy breaths, I suggested to Ann that we just pull over and portage the rest of the way. She nodded in support of the plan. Anything was better than our current battle upstream. Just then, two reporters from the local newspaper jumped out of the bushes and began photographing our attempt to reach the dam. Ann and I silently agreed to put the brakes on our portage plan when one of them exclaimed, "You can do it! You can paddle all the way to the dam!" One by one, residents of Granite Falls came down to the riverbank to watch our traveling performance. The pressure was now on; we had to give them a good show.

We enviously watched dozens of large white pelicans swimming, fishing, and relaxing on rocks by the river, seemingly mocking our efforts. What felt like hours later (in reality it was just thirty minutes), we arrived at the takeout point just downstream of the Granite Falls Dam, gasping for breath. The crowd of spectators gathered around us and cheered loudly when we finally stepped out of our canoe. The reporters were there to greet us along with the mayor, who exclaimed, "Wow, great job! I've never even seen two *guys* do that before!"

"Why would *anyone* do that?" I thought.

Tom Cherveny, one of the reporters, graciously offered to host us for the night, and we accepted. He parked his old blue truck by the river, and we loaded our gear before heading out to meet his family.

Granite Falls has a population of around three thousand people and relies heavily, like other communities we were paddling through, on agriculture. I had never been exposed to small towns like these and hadn't even stepped foot on a farm until I was in college. I thought hunting was something from folklore, like unicorns or treasure maps, and was not even aware that flannel was a thing until I put effort into fitting in with other students in college. Needless to say, I was way out of my element. But I wasn't just clueless when it came to small-town life in the Midwest. I'd often thought that rural areas lacked culture and education. I was beginning to learn that I was way off the mark on that assumption, too.

Tom was a journalist for the *West Central Tribune* and had thick white hair and the smile of a man who would make a great mayor but knew better than to run for office. I figured he must be in his midsixties and, based on the more than three hundred thousand miles on his truck, assumed he had done a fair bit of traveling outside Granite Falls. Tom shared quite a bit about the community with us that evening while entertaining his grandkids by making jokes and running around the kitchen.

"You portaged around the Minnesota Falls Dam, I presume?" Tom asked during dinner. We both nodded. I hadn't realized how hungry I was until we started eating, and it was hard to stop, even to talk.

"They're talking about removing it, you know. Hopefully it'll be natural rapids in a few years, like it was a long time ago." Tom explained that the Minnesota Falls Dam just south of the Granite Falls Dam was owned by Northern States Power, now known as Xcel Energy. The Minnesota Falls Dam had created hydropower until the early 1960s and then was used to store cooling water for the Minnesota Valley Generating Plant nearby, which closed down in 2004. By the time Ann and I visited in 2011 the dam served no function at all. It was a barrier for us and many other paddlers on the Minnesota, and it kept native fish and mussel species from moving freely throughout the river system. Three years after our expedition, the Minnesota Falls Dam was removed.

While Tom shared the local arguments for and against the removal of the dam, I felt a new feeling growing inside of me. I knew this wasn't my river, but it was for the moment my home, and I wanted it to flow freely and to thrive, to expand outward onto its floodplain in the spring and early summer and flow lazily in the fall. Something I love most about rivers is that they are capable of change. Even when they are seemingly damaged beyond repair by development or pollution, they can still bounce back. We've seen this phenomenon on rivers like the Cuyahoga in Ohio, which was once so polluted that it caught on fire (several times, most notably in 1969) but today is a popular paddling trail with renewed wildlife and water quality. We need to give rivers room to breathe, to protect and improve not only the water but the land surrounding the river, too. Agricultural waterways like the Minnesota River are capable of change. For the first time I felt like it was my responsibility to take action for the greater good of our rivers. We told Tom to let us know if he ever needed us to represent the paddling community's viewpoint in the future.

"For now, let's take a walk down to the popcorn stand," he responded with a big smile. The grandkids cheered and ran out of the kitchen to find their shoes. Apparently this was a familiar and highly anticipated excursion.

We were not alone on our walk. Just as residents had trickled down to the river to watch us paddle, families began popping out of their houses after dinner to join the parade to the popcorn stand. A small candy-cane-striped red and white building came into view near the river. Behind it were hordes of people laughing, drinking, and shoveling popcorn into their mouths. A little sign displayed on the old carnival-like stand said it was open every night from May Day to Labor Day. This stand has been a focal point of nightlife in Granite Falls since its opening in 1919. It looked like everyone was drinking beer on the street, even some apparently underage people. I was getting a serious Key West vibe, rural Minnesota style.

"What's the drinking age here?" I asked Tom. He realized why I was asking and laughed.

"Look at the labels," he said.

When we got closer I could read the bottles: 1919 Root Beer. During Prohibition, breweries turned their production to low-alcohol beer, soft drinks, and candy to survive. The August Schell Brewing Company of New Ulm introduced 1919 Root Beer that same year. Coincidentally, Andrew Volstead, the author of the Eighteenth Amendment, was a resident and former mayor of Granite Falls. His old house, just a short walk from the popcorn stand, is now a museum and a National Historic Landmark. I assumed it wasn't a coincidence that the stand opened the same year alcohol was banned, replacing local bars with a salty sweet family event on the riverfront.

The streetlamps illuminated the smiling faces of residents and visitors enjoying the warm summer night along the Minnesota River. Typically around this time most people would be inside watching TV or getting ready for bed. Instead, families, lovers, and friends were out on the town in this unassuming river city, connecting and sharing stories into the late hours of the evening, until the last kernel was popped and the root beer ran dry. Something so simple as a little popcorn stand created a strong sense of community here, all centered around the river.

"Hey, ladies! I'll walk back with you," said Scott, the other journalist who had popped out of the bushes during our upstream tree race. "Whaddaya think if we tore down that dam through downtown and made a whitewater park for kayakers and canoers? Would you drive here from the city to paddle?" Scott went on and on about his vision for Granite Falls as the next best paddling town. He was young and lanky and had moved to Granite Falls to write for the local paper. His hope for a better future was inspiring, and his enthusiasm had me convinced that he could help turn Granite Falls from a community almost solely dependent on agriculture to a thriving river town, with paddling as its rising star. I couldn't wait to return someday to paddle the rapids through Granite Falls.

RIVER RACES AND ROLE MODELS

Ann's family met us in Montevideo, Minnesota, for the local Festival Days celebration, which coincided with Father's Day. There were people everywhere, and the town was buzzing with live music, food, and games in the park. We signed up for a canoe race on the Chippewa River, a tributary of the Minnesota River that flows through Montevideo, but decided to split up in different boats. Expectations were high for our performance, and Ann and I, both extremely competitive, wouldn't have taken failure easily. "Two Women Canoe 2,000 Miles to Hudson Bay, Get Second Place in Local Canoe Race" was not a newspaper headline that I wanted to see the next day. I paddled with Ann's cousin, and she paddled with her other cousin. Things got heated. We ignored all the other competitors and solely focused on the growing tension between our two canoes. Neck and neck for almost the whole stretch, my boat sprinted ahead on the final leg, much to Ann's dismay. Probably from overcelebrating or because of just plain karma, my glasses flew off my face and into the muddy river at the finish line. I had already accepted that they were gone forever when Ann pulled her boat up onshore next to ours, stepped in the water with her Muck Boots, plunged her hand in, and immediately pulled out my glasses. "That's the kind of friend Ann is," I thought. "The superhero kind."

After the canoe battle, we were asked to take pictures with and give autographs to a group of kids waiting nearby. I was taken aback by the unforeseen celebrity status. A mother who noticed our surprise at the attention explained, "We're so grateful to have such great role models for our kids other than Justin Bieber." She and her family had driven all the way to Montevideo from Minne-apolis to see us. It was the first time I felt like we were making a real difference in the world. I hoped there were many more kids like them following our expedition, perhaps inspired to plan their own adventures, big or small.

In between the live bands at the park, a local organization gave out badges to everyone who had paddled the length of the Min-nesota River, honoring us as guests at their event. We said a few words on stage and walked over to receive our badges from a man who whispered, "Now you *have* to finish padding the Minnesota River," in a half-skeptical, half-encouraging tone.

Ann's aunt and uncle brought bikes to the event, and, after an overstimulating afternoon of schmoozing, Ann and I borrowed them and bolted from the park out onto country roads. Paddling upstream for two weeks had changed my sense of speed—biking on the smooth concrete felt like flying compared to the slow pace we were accustomed to on the water. On our bikes we found new solitude and freedom from the social duty of repeating our stories to the press back in town. We left Montevideo renewed and re-freshed for the last stretch of upstream paddling.

Returning to the river felt like being welcomed by an old friend into their home. I understood the Minnesota River's movements and temperaments. On this beautiful day, the river welcomed us to her waters with the wind at our backs and the sun dancing off of small waves. Familiar with paddling through all types of weather, Ann and I knew it was a day to be cherished. After Montevideo, word of our adventure spread further throughout the river valley. A man named Dennis offered to host us in a retrofitted silo along the river just before Lac Qui Parle Lake. After paddling the twenty or so miles that day to get there, we pulled up along the bank be-fore the Lac Qui Parle Dam and waited for Dennis to show up. The bugs were horrendous, and Ann and I competed silently to see who could withstand them the longest.

Dennis showed us around his hunting grounds and led us to

the silo: a two-story "man cave" complete with a kitchen and bedroom loft. We thought it would be a great idea to have a network of these up and down the river for paddlers to use—a good way to repurpose old farm buildings and to encourage recreation. We settled in for the night like we always did. I made dinner, and Ann set up and organized our gear. That evening I climbed to the very top of the silo, where I enjoyed a beautiful sunset and wrote an entry in my journal:

> Today I think about my father. I'm sitting on top of an old silo looking over the Minnesota River as the sun sets over the golden prairie grass. . . . This land is a far cry from my upbringing and I can't help thinking of my home. It is Father's Day today. I do not get to see my parents often, due to my wandering nature, but I have learned to love and appreciate them through this separation. With all my flaws, I truly love who I am, and I thank my parents for raising me with such care. They let me go, and I grew; they kept me in and I grew louder; they spent hours looking out windows, so I learned to climb trees. As I sit here I am reminded of my mother's love of birds. Which ones are chirping now? She would love to listen to this choir. She would sit excitedly, nagging me about which bird was which, and I would let her talk to herself since I was not going to be much help. My father would love this place as well.

In the morning, Dennis brought us blueberry muffins and orange juice. Apparently he had already taken our canoe to the other side of the dam, so we quickly packed up in his truck and headed over. Small-town hospitality continued to baffle us. We put in at Lac Qui Parle, the first lake on our journey to the Red River.

The day started with a glorious tailwind. But as we progressed farther along the lake, the winds shifted and large waves crashed into our boat. I began to sing old jazz standards, which is my "tell" that I feel nervous. Singing calms me. When I saw monsters under my bed and witches in the dark, my mother told me to sing to make them go away. Unfortunately, my singing on this day was distressing to Ann, so I belted out the songs in my head instead.

We made it to a large bridge where the river split east and west. After much deliberation, we decided to veer right under the bridge. The river slowly turned from a clear channel to marshy grass to a flooded forest—we were desperately lost. With each paddle stroke I pushed off the forest ground as we propelled in circles, shoving off trees with our hands, around what was normally dry land. A bright green film covered the water. Large fish splashed in the shallow waters as we canoed by, startling us every time like a jack-in-the-box. After a two-hour detour, we realized we had gone the wrong way and returned to the bridge to explore the other route. When we saw the dam before Marsh Lake we knew we were heading in the right direction. But that feeling of certainty soon disappeared when we portaged over the dam into the lake's maze, joining the ranks of countless paddlers who had lost their way searching for the mouth of the Minnesota River. I half expected to encounter ghosts still trying to live out their life's work of finding the river through the reeds. Or perhaps that would be us someday.

The islands of Marsh Lake are a big attraction for pelicans. I listened to the loud flap of their wings as they took off and watched them effortlessly maneuver in the sky. When one bird moved, so did the next, and the next, as if they were all connected by a long string. I passed the time watching them dance in the wind while we paddled northwest. When we approached one of the islands our nostrils filled with a foul fishy stench. It turns out that pelicans vomit as a defense mechanism. Perhaps we got a little too close to them.

When we reached the other end of the lake there was no clear path back to the river. Instead, multiple small waterways branched out into tall grasses that we couldn't see over. It felt like a TV game show—what's behind door 1, 2, or 3? We took the first channel into the weeds, paddled until we hit a dead end, and then retraced our steps to the lake to try the next door. Another dead end. With each one our frustration grew. The waterways were narrow and swampy, with several twists and turns. On our third attempt we detected a small current gently pushing the tall grass below the surface of the water. We stuck to the route and, sure enough, discovered the channel out of Marsh Lake.

Wildlife seemed to emerge from the reeds to celebrate our success. We saw deer, pelicans, cormorants, beavers, raccoons, carp, yellow-headed blackbirds, red-winged blackbirds, mallards, and wood ducks. We were told the area is even home to lynx and the occasional cougar. The river continued to astonish us with its bounty and beauty, even as it dwindled away into the lake.

Because of our marshy surroundings, we couldn't find solid ground to set up camp. It was 9:30 p.m. when we resolved to pull up onto what seemed like private property on a small dirt road by the river. In the same way you might realize that someone has been staring at you for a long time, I realized how still and humid it was, and had been for some time. Not in the typical heat-of-the-summer way, either. Something at the core of me felt threatened and sensed oncoming danger. Ann turned on her phone, like she did most nights, to communicate with media and people along our route. I heard six buzzes, one for each new voicemail we had received that day.

Ann put the speaker on so we could listen to the messages as we set up camp. Tom, Terri, Dennis . . . each was from someone we had met along the river, urgently informing us of the tornado warning that was now upon us. The hot stillness taunted us with serious weather to come. Ann contacted Dennis, who knew a guy (everyone along the river seems to "know a guy") who lived in a nearby town. He instructed us to pack up and paddle another mile to a bridge where he would pick us up and let us stay in his fishing cabin for the night. We paddled hard in the dark without speaking, unsure of our decision to pack up and leave the river.

We saw the car lights before we could see the bridge. Mike, Dennis's friend, picked us up with all of our gear and let us stay in his fish house, which he used for winter ice fishing. We had just settled in when the rain and wind began. The fish house rocked us to sleep, and even though we probably wouldn't have perished out there we were thankful to be indoors during the severe weather. But I knew that opportunities like this would disappear once we reached the vast wilderness areas of Lake Winnipeg and the Hayes River.

~~~~~

MIKE TOOK US OUT TO BREAKFAST in the morning after giving us a quick tour around Odessa, Minnesota. "This place used to be really cool," he said over and over again, as Ann and I looked around at several closed and boarded buildings. Noticing the decreasing populations in these river towns was unavoidable. Massive metal machines replaced the families and communities that were once needed to farm. The local shops could not compete with the nearby Walmart. Many residents, especially younger generations, fled to the city, never to return. All eyes were on us at breakfast, as if we had been walking around town wearing clown costumes and big silly shoes. I looked at Ann and then down at myself. I supposed we did look out of place: dirty, tan, Muck Boot–wearing young ladies from a distant planet.

We got back on the river and portaged over a small dam into a reservoir, entering into Big Stone National Wildlife Refuge, an 11,500-acre sanctuary consisting of tallgrass prairie, wetlands, granite outcrops, and river woodlands. Eleven miles of the Minnesota River flow through the refuge. We paddled northeast, looking for the entrance to the river, but had to retrace our steps back to the dam. It was Marsh Lake all over again. After about two hours, we maneuvered around a grass peninsula to the right, and an entrance to the river quickly revealed itself, as if it had been intentionally hiding the whole time.

This part of the river was very narrow and twisted around tight corners like a long ribbon folded over on itself. It was a gray, rainy day, with little visibility. Ann and I paddled until we came across a fallen tree. Using the expert problem-solving skills we were honing on the river, we carefully pulled the boat onto the tree like a teeter-totter; then the person in the bow got in while the other person lifted and pushed the boat forward off of the tree trunk. We naively celebrated our success before turning the bend to see even more fallen trees. The high water had likely infiltrated their roots, loosening the soil beneath, until the trees toppled over, creating a barrier from bank to bank. It was as if someone had laid a giant ladder over the last stretch of the river from Odessa to Ortonville.

At first, we made a game of getting around the trees. If they were too low to go under, we got into the groove of efficiently, and often wordlessly, maneuvering over the top of them. My favorite fallen trees were the ones that had just enough space for our canoe to pass under. I would crouch below the gunnels in the bow and push off the tree until I passed under it. Then I paddled like crazy while Ann ducked below the gunnels in the stern until emerging on the other side of the fallen tree to paddle again. While the current was weaker in this narrow section on the river, we were still paddling upstream, daydreaming of our upcoming downstream days on the Red River.

After hours of slowly attaining the river, fallen tree by fallen tree, we pulled over under a bridge to call a few people in Ortonville who were expecting us to arrive that day (which was clearly not going to happen via paddling). They were going to throw us a potluck, and we figured it wouldn't be quite the same without the guests of honor. To arrive on time, we'd have to get a ride into town, and in the morning we would return to continue on the river. Duane, a St. Olaf alumnus we had met in Montevideo, picked us up. We loaded our gear into his car and left our boat hidden under the bridge.

We made it to the celebration on time and with rumbling stomachs—a great way to show up to any potluck! We were so ravenous that it was hard to focus on people's names and conversation topics. Our manners improved significantly once our stomachs were full and content. We were used to consuming an average of three thousand to four thousand calories a day, which only felt like a lot when we were around other people.

The next morning Rebecca, who worked with the Land Stewardship Project and helped organize the potluck, drove us to a farm to have breakfast with two community members we met the night before. Heidi and Elaine and their two massive, fluffy dogs were outside waiting for us when we pulled up to their house. We enjoyed a breakfast of Pannekoeken, yogurt, fresh berries, and juice. Ann and I laughed about the amount of food we had packed out for the Minnesota River section of our trip—we probably could have survived without packing any food, thanks to the kindness of river folk.

Heidi and Elaine are a couple who farm organic produce and conventional corn, selling to the local market and to the grain co-op. Their house was cozy with a warm, lived-in feel: two dogs, pots hanging from the ceiling, and muddy boots by the door. Fresh fruits and vegetables were scattered around their kitchen. I hoped that someday my home would feel as warm and comforting. The five of us entertained ourselves for hours, including a group skinny-dip in the outdoor hot tub. I admired their life, their spirit, and their stories. The women were inspired by our trip. We thanked them and said farewell, unaware of the activities they were scheming for the next day. Canoey was waiting for us under the bridge, and we felt, as we often did when good times lingered, that we must be on our way. Moments of elation off the river were often tainted by our anxiety to keep moving. It felt like we were on vacation when we should have been working, like any fun we had before making it to the Bay was undeserved.

Duane brought us back to the bridge where we had left our

canoe the day before. The rain and wind picked up as we hopped out of the car, anxious to see if our boat was still safe. It was. Ann and I looked out at the river of fallen trees before us and decided to portage the boat four miles to Ortonville. The wind was strong and persistently pushed against our forty-five-pound Kevlar boat. We switched off carrying the canoe on the bike path along the river: one person carried it on their shoulders while the other held on to the rope tied to the front of the canoe. This kept it from spinning around in the wind. When in the bow, I felt like I was leading an uncooperative horse by its reins. We must have been quite a sight portaging through town.

Near the dam in Ortonville we approached a large sign: "The Headwaters of the Minnesota River." Finally, the upstream section of our trip was over, and Ann and I were filled with anticipation for what was to come: "livin' the dream, downstream," we would say. Since it was already too late to start paddling Big Stone Lake, we stayed one more night in Ortonville. At dinner that evening, Ann and I celebrated the end of the first part of our journey by telling stories and laughing with our new friends in town.

Around 8:30 a.m. the next morning, Ann and I launched our canoe into Big Stone Lake. We pushed off into a headwind that was not immediately overpowering but was slowly building waves. We had paddled through much rougher water in windier conditions in the past, but for some reason we couldn't keep the boat straight. The wind kept pushing the bow from one side to the other, while the person in the stern fought an unnecessary battle to keep the boat steady in one direction. Confused and racking our brains about why we couldn't move forward (maybe we were out of shape from a few days off the water?), Ann and I pulled over on the rocky shore to problem solve.

We couldn't *not* paddle. We had to paddle. We silently sat on the rocks by the lake. "Rocks," I thought. "Rocks! Ann, what about rocks?" I exclaimed. We filled the boat with heavy rocks, hoping that our added weight would give us the upper hand against the wind. We pushed off hesitantly, paddling stroke after stroke, until we were convinced we had successfully fixed our problem. We were off once again, this time with a boat filled to the brim with large rocks. The headwind made for slow progress throughout the day. Right before lunch, I spotted a small plane circling around the lake. It got very near to us, so we waved our paddles to say hello but didn't think too much more about it. "A casual summer joyride," I thought.

We arrived at a beautiful campsite with a soft sand beach landing as the sun was sinking behind the trees. It was the Fourth of July, so I made a festive dinner of calzones and leftover cupcakes from the potluck. I got started in the "kitchen," as was our routine, when I heard Ann laughing by the tent site. I looked over, and she was on her phone listening to a voicemail. It was a message from Heidi saying that she had chartered a plane to fly over us to take aerial pictures of our expedition. It was especially entertaining because the pictures would show us paddling a canoe filled with rocks. After dinner we paddled out onto the now calm lake to eat cupcakes and watch fireworks. I felt peaceful floating in the middle of the lake at night, feeling Ann's company coupled with a strong sense of geographic isolation. All I had to think about was our trip: where to camp, what to eat, and how to make decisions day by day. I was mentally preparing to paddle Lake Winnipeg and the mighty Hayes River and, in that moment, could not fathom life beyond the expedition.

LIVING THE DREAM, DOWNSTREAM

WHILE THE HEADWATERS of the Minnesota River are in Ortonville, the headwaters tributary, the Little Minnesota River, continues upstream for another seventy-one miles into South Dakota. This stretch of the Little Minnesota River is narrow with a quick current. It took us two and a half hours to paddle four miles upstream, all the while giving 90 percent and not speaking, until Heidi and Elaine unexpectedly appeared onshore around a river bend.

"Ladies! Take out here!" they yelled and signaled us to pull over onshore. We pulled over, thinking it was just a quick pit stop. But their excitement continued to surprise us: they had packed us a picnic lunch and brought a few family and friends. After lunch we said our farewells, portaged over to Lake Traverse, and paddled the first third of the lake (more like a liver: lake and river combined) before setting up camp for the night.

The next morning, we finished paddling Lake Traverse and portaged around a small dam into Mud Lake. We slowly zigzagged along the shore to navigate the wind and large waves. It almost made me miss upstream paddling, when at least we were protected by the river's steep banks. Eighty-one years earlier, Eric Sevareid and Walter Port got miserably lost trying to navigate the islands and reeds on Mud Lake. Sevareid recalls slogging through the muddy marsh in search of the river as one of their toughest days, almost weeping with relief when they finally found the channel. We had similar struggles on Marsh Lake, but the route through Mud Lake was straightforward.

We arrived at White Rock Dam after paddling Mud Lake to find families fishing and enjoying the lake and river. It was a beautiful, warm, sunny day, and Ann and I were in high spirits as we ate lunch and watched the excited faces of people reeling in fish. I leaned back on the picnic table (back support was a luxury) and for a moment felt pure bliss. A short portage around the dam brought us to the Bois de Sioux River. Downstream at last. No more lakes (at least for now), no more pulling over for lunch or holding on to a tree if we wanted to take a picture. We could just float and enjoy the day! Not that we would do so too often, of course, because we weren't on this trip to relax.

When we were planning the trip, I struggled with how to tell my parents that I was going to live in a canoe instead of getting a job after graduation. When I finally called home to tell my mother what Ann and I were plotting, she was silent on the phone and then said calmly, "You can't do that, your sister is getting married in July." Not going on a three-month expedition because I was needed somewhere for three days didn't make any sense to me. I told her that, no matter what, I would make it to my sister's wedding in Philadelphia on July 2. After my expeditions at Menogyn and a two-month solo backpacking trip through Europe that I took when I was nineteen, my parents were not surprised by my postcollege summer plans. But "not surprised" did not mean "not worried." They eventually warmed up to the idea of the canoe expedition but stuck to their ultimatum: Wedding. Philadelphia. July 2. Ann and I had been pacing ourselves to arrive in Fargo by the end of June so I could catch my flight.

The Bois de Sioux forms the state boundary between Minnesota and the Dakotas before it meets up with the Otter Tail River to form the Red River of the North. We kept calling it the Bwah-de-soo, but the locals informed us that we were saying it wrong—it's called the Boys-de-soo. I could tell that Ann's studies in French made it difficult for her to seriously tell people that we were paddling the Boys ("You ladies out paddlin' da Boys?" we'd hear every now and then). When in Rome. Unlike the Minnesota, the Bois de Sioux current seemed to have no say on its flow or direction. The Lake Traverse Flood Control project, in which the Army Corps of Engineers dredged and dammed the river from 1936 until 1941, drastically changed the land and water here. It felt like we were paddling through a large man-made rain gutter. I was envious that Sevareid and Port got to see the once wild and narrow river, her waters flowing freely across the marshy landscape. As the sun went down we began looking for a place to camp. Once again there was nothing but farmland on either side of us, right up to the riverbank, and we didn't think a farmer would appreciate our tent in their crops. Throughout our trip, Ann and I tried to avoid situations where we were likely to draw attention, especially at night.

I was baffled by the lack of buffer zones in this area: areas of vegetation in between the agricultural fields and the river that provide habitat and improve water quality. During rain events, chemicals from the farm fields run off into the river, negatively impacting water quality and the ecosystem. Something as simple as a small area of grass, shrubs, and trees could significantly improve this problem by filtering out chemicals through root systems and allowing water to sink into the ground. But there has been significant pushback from farmers in the Midwest on buffer requirements. Area farmers are highly knowledgeable of their land and care deeply about the water, but unfortunately many farmers contribute to a system in which they get paid based on yield: the more crop they grow, the more money they make. But a well-run buffer zone program is vital to improving water quality.

Eventually we saw a farmhouse about a half mile off of the riverbank. We tied our boat and walked toward the small, old house amid a sea of corn and soybeans. We were used to asking for help by now, but something about this place seemed less friendly than our previous stops. Ann knocked on the front door. No response. I heard the faint hum of a motor nearby. We walked around back to see a very old man sitting on a lawn mower, meticulously mowing his backyard, one strip of grass at a time in a long diagonal. I walked toward him, but he didn't see me. Ann was worried we were going to give him a heart attack by sneaking up on him on his property—he clearly wasn't used to visitors. When I was about ten feet away he looked up from the mower with a surprised and confused expression.

His name was Milton Cross. His frail figure moved slowly and methodically through his musty home, as he pointed out old pictures of his farm and family. His wife had passed away, and now it was just him, the tractor, and the crops. It's amazing how you used to need an entire village to operate a farm. With the advancement in technology, one person can now farm thousands of acres of crops on their own, even someone as old as Milton Cross. Every motherly instinct in me wanted to clean his house and cook him a hearty dinner to regain some fat onto his skinny bones. I wondered who would tend the fields that had been in his family for generations when he was gone. Along with the exodus of people out of the small Minnesota river towns, family farms have been abandoned at an equal pace. Often when we stopped to ask farmers if we could camp on their land, we found completely empty houses and barns. It was spooky. The disappearance of family farms and the near ghost towns we paddled through made me see the real and current crisis of our food system. Will there be a new era of agricultural revival? Or will agriculture in places like Minnesota be controlled by megacorporations, run by a wealthy few?

We stood in silence with Milton looking out on the endless rows of corn and soybeans illuminated by the falling sun. Milton told us we could camp on his land by the river, pointing a shaky finger toward the sunken valley where our boat was beached out of sight in the mud. After setting up our tent right on top of soybeans, because there wasn't any crop-free land to camp on, we hitchhiked into Fairmont to get a pizza at the Cenex. A middle-aged man picked us up and said very little on our ride to town, occasionally looking at us strangely through his rearview mirror.

This made us feel uncomfortable. We were used to people asking us questions about our trip, curious about what two young women were doing alone in the middle of America's Corn Belt. But the driver just looked like he was thinking long and hard about something. A strange chill came over us despite the hot summer evening. Ann, who is more perceptive and skeptical of people's character than I am, memorized his license plate number and texted it to a friend. She was always on top of our safety, thank goodness. After the short ride into town we quickly hopped out of the vehicle and walked into the Cenex without looking back. Every now and then we would realize how lucky we were to come out on top of a potentially dangerous situation. (My mother met with a prayer group every week to pray for us on our journey. Ann and I aren't religious, but whenever we felt lucky we would say, "Score one for the prayer list!" and usually follow this with high fives.)

The waft of melted cheese and pepperoni upon entering the Cenex did not go unnoticed. After a long day on the river we decided to treat ourselves to a greasy, precooked meal with zero cleanup necessary. While we waited for our pizza, the people at the counter inquired what we were up to, probably because we looked so dirty and out of place. After telling them about our expedition, they said that two guys on the same trip had stopped there to get pizza years ago. From what we could tell, the Cenex was the only establishment in town besides a church and a few houses. Most everyone in Fairmont farmed corn and soybeans in the surrounding fields and had to trek out to a Walmart to buy food and supplies. I thought it was ironic that we were surrounded by farmland yet the only food for miles and miles was pizza at the Cenex. The first of three attacks on our food supply took place that evening, when a silent thief came in the night, nibbled his furry, masked face into our lunch bag, and consumed our ration of cheese for the week. Luckily, we were only a few days out from Fargo.

Back on the water the next morning, Ann and I started timing our miles: 5 miles per hour was our average when paddling downstream, compared to 1.5 to 2 miles per hour upstream. That day we experienced a sad exhibition of racoon karma. We knew that a raccoon had eaten our cheese the night before, but it came hungry and left happy before we even flitted our eyes open with the morning sun. As we paddled downstream, we saw a raccoon (out during the day, which isn't a good sign) climb down a tree, jump into the water, and try to swim across the river in front of us. About halfway across the river, we saw the raccoon give up and slowly sink, until we could see only small bubbles above the surface. It was strangely morbid to witness a raccoon drown, and Ann and I paddled silently on, deep in thought for some time. Had the cheese thief met its fate?

~~~~~~

AFTER FORTY-ONE MILES of paddling an unnatural, channelized chute, we finally reached the Red River of the North. We hopped out of our boat at a park and joyously took pictures with the Red River sign. Wahpeton was a bigger town than our usual stops, so we decided to take a look around. We moseyed aimlessly around town in our Muck Boots, caked in mud from the riverbank, eating delicious frozen concoctions from the local Dairy Queen. Sometimes we would try to hide our boat before entering into town, but this time we felt comfortable leaving our gear in the canoe, which we pulled up on a sandbank at the park. When we returned "home" to *Kawena Kinomaeta,* a small boy and his father were fishing by the shore. The boy told us that he had been keeping watch over our things. He had seen us pull up onshore and purposely fished by our boat just to keep it safe while we explored town. Not everyone on our trip was welcoming, and we were often greeted with suspicion, but encounters like this instilled in me a love and trust of all people, for better or for worse.

That day Ann and I paddled hard to Fort Abercrombie, North Dakota, and camped on a boat launch next to a sign that said "no camping." We had walked around the campground area, but due to a government shutdown everything in the park was closed until further notice. It felt like a movie set after all the actors and actresses had gone home for the day. We figured we'd go unnoticed regardless of where we set up camp, so we chose the spot with the quickest getaway for the morning.

I was exhausted from the long day and was almost asleep when a car pulled up by the boat launch. Its bright lights shone on the tent. Later on in the trip when the moon was full and bright on the shores of Lake Winnipeg, I realized that car lights and the moon created the same light inside the tent, and if I just imagined that one thing was like the other I could change how I perceived the situation. However the light looked was irrelevant in this circumstance—Ann and I tensed up inside our sleeping bags and looked at each other with fear in our eyes. I glanced at the shotgun lying in between us and wondered if I'd remember how to load it in a stressful situation. Whenever I heard unnatural activity outside of our tent, I reminded myself that no one knew there were two young women with travel guitars and granola bars inside the tent. I assumed that people outside were more afraid than we were when they spotted our tent, because we were two large hairy men with guns and chewing tobacco, clearly up to no good. Who else would be camping at a closed park next to a "no camping" sign at night?

I gave myself this silent pep talk until the muffled voices from the car grew louder and closer. Ann and I continued to look at each other in the darkness, our heads peeking out of our sleeping bags, communicating with our eyes. I knew Ann was thinking something epic, like how she would drop-kick someone if they even touched our tent. My mind ventured into the dark realm of "what-ifs," which was not as productive or as helpful as Ann's strategic planning. Already cozy in my sleeping bag, I half hoped that I could witness Ann in battle and half hoped that no one would bother us. Ann and I locked eyes again. She whispered the first audible communication of the night into the humid air,

"Should we scope it out?" I shook my head no. Ann didn't look satisfied with that answer, so I whispered back, "Ann, it's okay, it's gonna be fine." This unhelpful utterance was my defense mechanism night after night when Ann was concerned about sounds outside of the tent and I would respond, "It's probably fine." Our different reactions to potential danger—Ann's urge to investigate and my response to casually ignore it (even if I felt afraid, too)—would soon lead to a tipping point on the desolate shores of Lake Winnipeg. The car drove off and I quickly fell into a deep sleep.

The next morning we ate a quick breakfast of granola bars and pushed off into the fast current. Ann and I paddled with our sights set on the muddy banks of Fargo, North Dakota. We had given up trying to wash the thick, dry mud off of our clothes, gear, and boat—we were desperately looking forward to a shower (or two!) that evening at a hotel. About an hour out from Fargo, the TV news station reporter called Ann's phone to say there would be a camera crew onshore to run a story on our trip as we paddled in. She told us to paddle slowly and at an angle to "get the best shot." We giggled at this recurrent and unexpected theatrical component of our journey. When we saw the film crew on the riverbank, we staged our smiles and paddled slowly, at an angle, like the good paddling puppets we were.

"What did *you* do after college?" we heard the news station's anchorwoman say to transition from the previous story. We sat on the edge of the bed in a hotel where we were relaxing with Ann's parents before going out for dinner. There we were on-screen, smiling, paddling slowly and at an angle. "Nailed it!" I said to Ann with a sarcastic smirk and a knowing wink. We high-fived and laughed at our fleeting fame before heading out to explore the fine dining in Fargo.

The next morning, Ann and her parents drove me to the airport in Fargo so that I could embark on a very different side journey: my sister's wedding in Philadelphia. I felt guilty leaving Ann to pack out for the rest of our expedition alone. My time in Philadelphia was a blur of spas, mimosas, and arm-wrestling matches with willing adversaries (my muscles were exceptionally strong after the few days off, and I felt physically invincible, even if the match didn't always end in my favor). I danced with family and friends whom I had not seen for some time but often thought about on trail. But after only a few days I felt an intense longing for the river. I had been away from my home too long. City sounds and social pleasantries were a far cry from the comfortable silence and river waves that had been my day-to-day. Phones, people shuffling around the city, the traffic—all of these things seemed foreign and unsettling to me. Meanwhile, Ann was resupplying in St. Paul, diligently preparing maps, gear, and food for the rest of our journey. I flew back to Fargo excited to reunite with her and our constant companion and caretaker: the water.

DANGER BEFORE THE BORDER

PREPARING TO GET BACK ON THE WATER always takes more time than expected. There is so much beyond just food and maps that pops into your mind as you are about to push off: Fill the water jugs. Check. Reload on lighters. Check. Did we repack granola bars? What about that little foghorn your mom gave us to scare away bears? Do we have flares packed? An ungodly amount of bland oatmeal?

Those worries instantly vanished as Ann and I dug our paddles back into the familiar water, shaking hands with our old friend the river. We paddled a long day, catching up on the previous week and sharing silly stories about our time away. I told her how my grandmother encouraged me to "hang around an Ivy League campus" to find a boyfriend. I briefly tried to mingle with some strapping Princeton men at the wedding, but after shoving cookies into my mouth and hastily spilling milk down my dress mid-conversation I returned to arm wrestling family and friends. I reminisced about crying so much during the ceremony that snot flew out of my nose and onto my sister's pretty white dress when I bent over to fix her train. We laughed and caught up as if we hadn't seen each other in a year.

Like the Minnesota River, we found the Red River to be very flooded. It is a long, windy river that snakes around farmland in between the Dakotas and Minnesota. At its most windy reaches, we could paddle ten miles and only travel about four miles north. Because of the high water level, Ann and I took shortcuts straight over cornfields to avoid the bends in the river. We paddled through the muddy waters and disturbed the tops of corn plants as they sat underwater in perfectly aligned rows, silently waiting for the season to pass and hoping for better luck next year.

By evening, I could see no viable place to stop, and we were too far from the town of Climax, Minnesota, to make it there before nightfall. Sometimes it would take us over an hour to find a suitable camping spot. We decided to look for a farmhouse and were hopeful that a farmer would let us camp on their field. All of a sudden, around a river bend on our left, huge houses with beautiful lawns appeared out of nowhere. There was no town on the map, yet we were looking at a cul-de-sac of very modern, beautiful homes, engulfed by endless fields of corn and soybeans.

We speculated about which house had the nicest lawn before pulling over onto the green grass of one lucky private property owner. We smirked as we walked toward the house. We had perfected a spiel of who we were, what we were doing, and what we needed help with, complete with some jokes—a little peek into our goofy partnership. Within the first thirty seconds, people were usually confused and skeptical. Within the first minute, they would offer us a spot in their yard to camp. If the conversation went on for two minutes, we were usually offered a bed in their house. At three minutes we were being invited back for the holidays. Ann and I joked that we received such nice hospitality solely because our spiel was so good (even though it was), when in reality, the people we met are the most generous people you will ever find, and they are ready and willing to contribute to any adventure on their river. They have a deep care for the water. We always had that in common with our hosts.

A lovely middle-aged couple at the door listened to our spiel for a dangerous two minutes and invited us to stay in their vacant basement apartment. Ann organized our gear and perused the host's movie collection while I cooked mac 'n' cheese on the stove. When she showed me a series of videos about the rapture, we stared at each other, unsure of what we had gotten ourselves into this time.

After dinner, the couple came downstairs to visit with us and hear more about our trip. Almost immediately the woman asked about our religious and personal backgrounds, while the man sat quietly and listened. We felt uncomfortable talking about religion. When prompted, I said that I was raised Presbyterian and Ann said she had attended Catholic school. The woman was well groomed with soft eyes and a commanding hairstyle. She was kind and personable and told us at length about their children and activities at the local church. After not speaking for almost an hour, the man rose up, put his hands on us, and prayed over us in a loud, deep, confident voice. After sitting in silence for so long, his loud voice and newfound confidence took us by surprise. I wondered if he would have prayed over us in that way if we were two men? They said goodnight and retired upstairs.

The next morning, the woman invited us upstairs for breakfast. Ann and I always looked forward to meals that were different from our day-to-day oatmeal and granola on the trail. We excitedly looked at each other as if she had announced, "Come upstairs for bacon and eggs and bagels and coffee and fruit and yogurt and all of the things you wish you could eat every day but can't because you live in a canoe, haha!" We settled in at the dining room table, eagerly awaiting the breakfast extravaganza. I looked over at Ann, who didn't seem as excited as I was; her face suggested that she knew something. The woman swooped in behind me to ladle a heap of oatmeal into my bowl. I smiled at Ann knowingly. She shrugged and smiled back.

~~~~~

THAT AFTERNOON, two men joined our paddle for a fifteen-mile stretch of the river. They were with the International Water Institute, a river advocacy and education group that works in towns like Climax, Minnesota, where we planned to stay that night. We enjoyed the company on the water and were amused by their reaction to the bald eagles overhead. We saw eagles every day and had become very good at spotting them from a great distance. Every time the two men spotted an eagle they would stop paddling and take their cameras out. Their actions made me realize how familiar I had become with the natural environment over the past month on the river.

After passing through so many "ghost towns" and agricultural communities with decreasing populations, it was refreshing to stay in Climax for the night with vibrant, passionate community members. The local historical society had a barbecue for us at a rebuilt cabin and let us spend the night in their "artist's apartment" in town. (During dinner, our new friends told a story of a woman from the neighboring town of Fertile, Minnesota, who was murdered. The headline the next day read, "Fertile Woman Dies in Climax.")

The International Water Institute works to get people out paddling on the Red River and interacting with the water from a different perspective. It exemplifies the idea that experiencing the river allows people to build a relationship with the water, which, in turn, positively impacts policy, ecosystem health, standard of living, and the economy. The conversations we had with the people of Climax, as well as those in other river communities, really got me thinking about the opportunities that exist for ecotourism and the benefits that come from creating access to waterways. The potential to diversify the economies of these small river towns is enormous, and it can all start by simply putting a paddle in the water.

After experiencing the great hospitality of yet another river town, Ann and I wondered if we would ever camp again. We sometimes felt guilty that we were so pampered by "river angels" in the communities along our route. Early on, we had to reconceptualize the first half of our expedition: if we did not stop in these towns and interact with their community members, we would miss a large piece of the puzzle. Urban water trails were more complex than I had anticipated, and we had already learned more from community members than we ever could have accomplished on our own. We didn't mind all the cupcakes, either.

When we returned to the water the next morning, it was a beautiful summer day. We sang songs to the trees and reveled in being alone before that night's homestay in Grand Forks. We had arranged to stay with a farmer and his family along the river, just north of town. With several miles to go, we passed the time working through our entire musical repertoire to refine our harmonies. Ann usually sang the melody, and I had spent weeks trying to find the best harmonies or countermelodies to sing with her. We started practicing "Swing Low, Sweet Chariot."

Mid-song, a crack of thunder broke from the seemingly clear sky. I glanced behind the boat to see a black cloud rapidly approaching. Within minutes, hail began falling. The sound echoed through our boat as the ice hit the Kevlar in a constant, percussive manner that could have fit well with our music. But we were not singing anymore. We were frantically paddling through golf ball–sized ice toward the shelter of the riverbank. Since the river was still flooded, we were able to paddle into the forest with ease. Nestled in the woods, Ann and I crouched at the bottom of the boat, trying to protect ourselves from the painful hail. The ice hit hard against our bodies and began to fill our canoe. I moved my arms over my head to protect myself from any serious blows. We waited in silence, listening to the pounding of the ice on the trees, the water, and our boat. If it weren't for the pain I was in, I would have thought it was rather beautiful.

Minutes felt like hours as our boat filled with ice. Finally, the storm moved on, and Ann and I emerged from our crouched positions. Without words, we glanced at each other with the same wild look in our eyes that communicated our shared amusement at the sudden weather. After the shock of the hailstorm wore off, we went back to the music, determined to get the harmonies just right.

~~~~~~

THE DAYS AFTER WE LEFT GRAND FORKS, the last "big" city we would paddle through until we reached Winnipeg, were a green-brown blur of wooded riverbanks and murky waters. The Red River twisted and turned until we finally reached Pembina, North Dakota, just south of the Canadian border. The next morning we pushed off around 7:00 a.m. with hopes of reaching the border by 9:00 a.m. Would there be a sign pointing to the underused river that announced, "Welcome to Canada!"? I was worried we might accidently paddle right under the border patrol's noses and begin our time in Canada as wanted criminals. We didn't talk much in anticipation of the border crossing. Ann, who thinks of everything, called the border station before our trip, faxed over our passports, and let them know we were bringing a 12-gauge shotgun into Canada. She requested that they meet us by the river to avoid the mile-long portage to and from the station with all of our gear. They agreed but gave little insight into what to expect.

We turned the corner and saw a bridge with two huge black SUVs awaiting our arrival. The sun was out in full force. I squinted at the bright red and blue flashing lights as the border patrol vehicles drove down to the riverbank. I wanted to laugh at getting "pulled over" on the Red River, but the lights peppered my thoughts with fear. We paddled river left until our boat got stuck in the mud. After paddling the flooded river for weeks, we must have looked like wild rats: caked mud decorated the inside of our boat, covered our legs, and speckled our hair. We hopped out of the canoe and attempted to drag it over the mud to shore. There we were, slopping around in the mud while trying not to sink into the river as six border patrol agents in full uniform got out of their cars to watch and wait. "Front-row seats to see two women purportedly paddling to Hudson Bay barely able to pull their boat to shore! Come one, come all!"

Ann and I retired the boat about thirty feet from solid ground and used a quick-step technique (so as not to sink into the earth) to reach the border agents. None of them seemed amused despite the comical show they just witnessed. They looked us up and down. Our muddy boots, hairy legs, sunburned arms, and wild unbrushed hair. Our quick breaths after flailing around in the mud. I followed their eyes to our boat. Same assessment: wild, dirty, harmless.

One of the men's eyes lingered on the mud bank separating us and the boat. "Go get your gun and bring it here. We're not gonna walk over there through that mud," he said.

Three of the agents took Ann to the border patrol station to sign a waiver and pay a fee for the gun (around twenty-five dollars). I stayed with the other three to watch the boat. Ann turns red when she is nervous. She told me later that she still had her life jacket on at the station and felt hot and uncomfortable. Halfway through filling out the gun waiver, she was accused of acting "suspiciously" and had to go through another series of questions about our trip.

Time moved slowly on the banks of the rushing river while I waited for Ann. I pride myself in having good to above-average social skills, but I still could not get a conversation going with the agents. "Do you like your job?" Yes. "What does your tattoo mean?" No answer. I conceded to standing in silence while looking out at the water, longing to be back in the boat and on our way. Forty-five minutes later the other vehicle showed up and Ann hopped out. She looked as I did—desperate to get going. We thanked the agents and ungracefully made our way back to the boat. They watched us closely until we disappeared around the corner. The river was smooth sailing, and Ann and I were in high spirits. It felt like we were entering the promised land. Everything was so much greener, the bird calls even sounded happier, and where we expected to see a large agricultural field on the banks of the river, there was a large wind farm. We were sold! Next election to "go wrong" in the United States and we'd be back in the canoe on our way to Canada.

For many weeks, Ann and I had been musing about poutine. As a South Florida girl, this French-Canadian delicacy of fries, gravy, and cheese curds seemed like a beautiful (and unnecessary) meal of the gods. But burning thousands of calories a day had shifted my feelings from "unnecessary" to "essential." After eating poutine, there is no way you will want to eat anything ever again. And that's exactly the type of "full" we hadn't felt in months. We were on the hunt for poutine when we made it to the little French town of St. Jean Baptiste. As we got out of our boat we were stopped by a man named Richard with a thick French accent. He told us we had to eat Manitoba's best poutine at Yahooz Bar down the street. He said it was free pool night, too. Then he disappeared into the evening light. A god? A fairy? A wizard? We could only speculate. But thank you for your wisdom, almighty Richard, whoever you are.

We popped into the bar and eagerly inquired about the poutine situation. Sure enough, the bartender confirmed they have the *best* in all of Manitoba. A huge plate of poutine and a few beers later, Ann and I were basking in the glory of free pool night and chumming it up with the locals. Perhaps it was the adrenaline from crossing the border, the Canadian beer, or the carbo-loading that had just occurred, but for some reason Ann and I agreed it would be a *great* idea to paddle 160 kilometers to Winnipeg, overnight. Why in the world did we decide to do that? We were pumped up—ready to go!

This is the beauty of traveling with just one other person, as two like-minded people. I have been on expeditions with bigger groups, but it was difficult to agree on even simple things, like what to make for dinner. Deciding unexpectedly to paddle all night, through chilly, muddy waters, without sleep for more than twenty-four hours, is something very special in an expedition relationship and in a friendship. It quietly says, "I trust you, I feel safe with you, and I know we can do this"—behind the mask of "Yeah, why not? It will be fun!"

Ann is always good for a story. She came up to me one Friday after classes at St. Olaf and went on a rant about how we should go somewhere, anywhere, for the weekend. I recall her specifically saying, "Who knows, maybe we'll accidently hit a moose with our car or a tree will fall on top of us!" It was classic Ann Raiho, exercising her adventure muscle whenever possible. But deeper than that is her understanding that everything that happens, good or bad, is a story. And life is just a string of stories that we collect, over time, and we might as well make them good ones.

We made enough coffee to last us the night and set off on the rolling Red River. The moon was full and the wind was calm, although the temperature was crisp and getting crisper. There were no more obstacles in our way, or so we thought. Just 160 kilometers of flowing river to the city of Winnipeg. Moon shadows danced around our boat as we sang Cat Stevens's "Moonshadow," but, alas, we only knew one verse. So we repeated it over and over again until it was clearly time to move on. Usually Ann was ready to move on first. It takes me a while to realize that something isn't actually fun, which makes me a great babysitter. We passed the time talking about superpowers. Ann's would be an "ice cream out of nowhere spell," and mine would be to know the lyrics to any song we wanted to sing.

We talked, didn't talk, sang songs, drank coffee, shoved granola bars into our mouths, slowed down, sped up, and on and on. I nestled my head into the nook between my life jacket and my neck and entered a state of light sleep while my paddle continued to move on autopilot. I was jolted awake by a sharp pain in my wrist. During our trip I had learned how doing one activity for so long can fluctuate quickly from moments of pure bliss, laughter, and songs to feelings of exhaustion, helplessness, and unbearable physical pain. It felt like a whole year's emotions were shoved into twenty-four hours.

In mid-July, the days are long and the nights are very short. The darkness was about to lull us to sleep when a soft light appeared on the horizon, around 4:30 a.m. It awakened what energy was left inside of us. We were paddling eight kilometers an hour and only had twenty-four kilometers to go until we reached Winnipeg. That meant we only had three hours left and a beautiful sunrise to accompany us. Our spirits perked up with the sun, and we excitedly conversed about sleeping in a bed and going out to dinner with Ann's parents, who would be meeting us there. I had been slowly, over the course of the two weeks leading up to Winnipeg, trying to convince Ann that we needed to see the premiere of the final *Harry Potter* movie. I slyly talked about the movie in small increments over time without expressing any real emotion or opinion on whether or not we should actually see it in Winnipeg, our last chance before entering true wilderness. Now I had ninety minutes to really sell the idea.

I was explaining to Ann that we definitely had time to go to the movies in Winnipeg if we went to the midnight showing that night when she said, "What's that all about?" She was more engaged than I had expected! I began explaining the plot of the last book in the *Harry Potter* series when Ann interrupted.

"No, you goof, what is *that* all about?" She pointed to a large sign on the riverbank that displayed one word in bright orange letters: DANGER.

"Ummmm. No clue." My mind wandered to whatever meeting must have been held with authorities in Winnipeg to discuss some sort of danger:

"But how will we tell people about the danger?"

"I know! Let's put a sign out that says DANGER!"

"Great idea, meeting adjourned! Bill, go put a danger sign by the river near the danger."

BUT WHAT DANGER?

Ann directed our canoe toward the unhelpful sign. It was the only thing in sight and was intentionally facing the river, clearly meant for those traveling by water. I figured that we would just keep paddling to see what the danger was. But that's the main difference between me and Ann. I'm more of a laissez-faire, "let's see what unfolds" type of gal. Ann is a "let's figure this out now" kind of woman.

Ann rammed the boat into the mud, hopped out, and beelined for the sign. I sat in the canoe drifting in and out of sleep in the bright sun, trying to chase the shapes and colors dancing beneath my eyelids before they disappeared. Twenty-four hours ago I was just waking up. Perhaps I would have slept in longer had I known that it would be the only sleep I'd get in thirty hours.

The river was still very flooded, and the current was quick. I lay back in my seat and looked up at the bright blue, cloudless sky. Blue, green, brown. That's all we were used to these days. The orange letters on the sign were a foreign sight to my eyes, and they stuck out in an impertinent, almost insulting way. My vision had adjusted to the outdoor world, and now I could spot anything bright or human-made from a great distance. I thought back to a few summers earlier when I visited my sister in Washington, D.C., immediately after spending thirty days in the Ontario wilderness. I broke down on the street in Dupont Circle, wholly overwhelmed by the busyness of the city.

"Hi! We're paddling the Red River just south of Winnipeg, and there is a sign onshore that just says 'Danger.' Do you know what it means? No? Okay, thank you . . ."

I listened to Ann call random authority figures in Winnipeg trying figure out what was so dangerous. The thought crossed my mind to go help her, or at least to pretend to care, but I knew that we were going to continue on the river either way. She came back to the canoe defeated and clearly irritated with how relaxed I must have looked lying back in my seat staring up at the sky.

"Let's go," she said.

We pushed off the mud and continued downstream. As we turned the bend, the danger suddenly appeared. A large white structure. A dam. Not just any dam, but a huge dam with a control tower and rushing whitewater at its intake. And we were heading straight for it.

"Ann, I found the danger," I said. My attempt to lighten the mood failed. This was no time to joke around. If we were unable to paddle away from the intake, we could die.

We agreed to paddle over to river left to see if there was a path or portage around the dam. If we kept moving forward we risked getting sucked into the fierce water cycling through the dam. We turned the boat upstream and forward ferried across. There was no path on river left. Just large boulders leading up to a road at the top of the dam. We ferried over to river right to find the same thing. I'm willing to bet there were no paddlers at the table when they planned this dam. We looked helplessly at the steep hill of boulders in front of us. It looked like pure hell. But there was no other way. "Ann, promise to take it easy, okay?" I said in a motherly tone, remembering that she had torn her ACL during an ultimate Frisbee tournament the previous May.

"I always do!" she replied with a sassy smirk.

We ambitiously loaded our gear onto our backs and began our independent routes up the steep boulders. I created a mental map of where I accidently dropped a paddle and a water bottle, preparing for a lackluster scavenger hunt on my journey back. I kept a close eye on Ann to make sure her knee survived the tricky rocks while trying to hide my concern for her. For a moment I forgot about my growing frustrations with her.

It took both of us three trips to carry all of our gear over to the other side of the dam. My stomach finally woke up and started punching and twisting my insides, demanding food on the third trip across. While we were crossing the road, about two hours into our portage, an older man came out of the control tower with a steaming cup of coffee and a goofy smile. "Well heya, ladies! Where are y'all off to?"

Sometimes when you are hungry, tired, and frustrated, seeing someone leisurely drink hot coffee and look joyful is the WORST. This dude was the last guy we wanted to talk to right now.

Ann's body language was pretty clear—I'd have to step it up.

My concern over Ann's knee was quickly interrupted by this new pet peeve. I felt frustrated that I always had to be the one to engage with strangers, which usually ended with my being talked at by older men. I mumbled something about Hudson Bay and canoeing and kept walking with the last of our gear. The man grunted, as if surprised that two young women could be so foul and unwelcoming. I saw Ann abruptly stop in her tracks and turn to face him. Her face was bright red.

"Did *you* put that sign out there?" she asked angrily.

"Yeah, you betcha. Just letting you ladies know that the floodgates are open," he responded with a hint of pride.

Ann yelled, "YOU NEED TO PUT A NUMBER ON THAT SIGN!" She turned around and continued the portage without saying another word.

AT HOME ON THE BIG LAKE

CAN ALWAYS TELL when we have overstayed our welcome on land when I start to feel stir-crazy and anxious to return to the river. The water was our true home, and any pit stop we took was for the sole purpose of rejuvenating ourselves enough to continue with greater strength. Winnipeg provided a perfect respite and release for our minds and bodies. It was lunchtime when we arrived at a dock near the hotel where we planned to stay the night with Ann's parents. After twenty-eight hours without sleep, we were drawn to the bright white fluffy beds in the hotel room, which appeared before us like angels beckoning us into a dream world. Hypnotized and awestruck, we fell into bed without changing our clothes or brushing our teeth, like two gargoyles with no choice but to turn to stone at the first sign of light.

"Ladies! It's time to wake up!" Ann's mom whispered excitedly, eager both to say hello and to let us catch up on sleep: a true mother's dilemma. Pam Raiho's voice knocked on the door of my dream world. I slowly blinked my eyes open to see her silhouette in the doorway, and her excited smile somehow broke through the darkness in the room.

Pam and Ray Raiho are like parents to me. I spent many holidays with them, most notably Mother's Day. The four of us would all road-trip out to Lanesboro, Minnesota, each May to bike along the Root River to Whalen, a town with only thirteen permanent residents. At the local pie shop, we would each get a different flavor of pie to share and peruse the small store's eclectic book collection. Pam and Ray have seen me cry and laugh; they have watched me navigate through my many heartbreaks and meltdowns, achievements and good fortunes. They even coaxed me to stay at their house when I had the flu so they could watch over me. The Raihos were always there to deliver kettle corn and drop off the occasional Target sports bra or pair of socks, just in case. I was almost as excited as Ann to see them again.

According to Pam, we had already slept for eight hours. I could have used another eight, but my stomach was awake and, once again, demanding food at a rate that I could barely keep up with. We groaned as our aches and pains from paddling and portaging came back to life. Deciding to shower later, we threw on our cleanest trail clothes and hit the town.

At dinner we consumed twice as much food as any normal person would. I took advantage of our full stomachs, rested bodies, and all-around jolly moods to convince Ann that we should see the midnight premiere of *Harry Potter and the Deathly Hallows* before socially hiding under a rock for at least the next month and a half. She obliged. As we entered the packed theater I was overwhelmed by the unfamiliar smell of deodorant and perfumes wafting around us. I wondered if the people in the theater could smell us, too.

The next day we explored Winnipeg with the Raihos, stopping by the wharf where the Assiniboine River flows into the Red River. Much of the public park, a popular tourist destination, was shut down due to flooding. We were told the Assiniboine was experiencing a once-in-three-hundred-years flood due to high rainfall. I couldn't help but think about what our mileage would have been during peak flood stage. Weeks earlier, the Red River had crested twenty feet above normal, just downstream of the confluence where we were currently enjoying lunch.

"I'll have the IPA, please. And the nachos. And a burger," I told the waitress as she scribbled down my surprisingly large order. She didn't ID me for the beer. I had been of drinking age for a year and a half now, and the novelty had yet to wear off.

Ann followed suit. "I'll have the IPA as well. And . . ." But she was quickly interrupted.

"Can I see your ID, please?" requested the waitress.

I held my breath to keep from bursting out laughing. We all teased her for the rest of the day for having a baby face, but in the long run the joke is on us. Ann will have the skin of a fifteen-year-old when she is fifty.

We spent the rest of the afternoon grocery shopping and packing out for the rest of the trip. The Raihos had brought our second food drop with them from St. Paul, along with new gear that we needed for the more remote and potentially colder part of our expedition. The new gear included a large "bear barrel" to store our food. No more dogs or raccoons would eat our cheese! Or so we thought. We now had warmer sleeping bags, warmer layers, and a funny kit that Pam had put together with flares and a tiny foghorn to scare away polar bears. I chuckled at the idea of us blasting a small foghorn at a bear approaching our camp. We packed the kit along with our shotgun, hoping we would never need to use either of them. There was a fearful voice inside of me that knew we would.

Ann was acting strangely quiet all day. Any touch of a normal life in a city—sleeping in beds, eating at restaurants, and calling our loved ones—brought back memories of our life before the river. It was like we were living two lives: one as individuals with separate interests and friends and another as a team, equally determined to reach a remote, faraway destination. The former tended to surface when we were not in our canoe, for better or for worse.

~~~~~

ON OUR LAST NIGHT IN WINNIPEG we met with Mike Muswagon, a Cree council member from Norway House, for dinner. Ann had been in communication with him before our trip about where to stay when we arrived at Norway House. Mike graciously offered us a room in his house and encouraged us to try our best to make it in time for the Treaty and York Boat Days festival. The whole community gathers for days to cook on the streets and paddle the rivers and lakes, culminating in a very competitive York boat race for a ten-thousand-dollar prize. As we wrapped up dinner Mike gave us more specific directions on how to get to his house—take the channel on the right and look for the house with the red porch.

The next morning we said our goodbyes to Pam and Ray and took off once more on the Red River. If everything went according to plan, this would be our last pampered stop until returning home. As I waited for Ann to say a final farewell to her parents, I pondered if my whole life would be a series of arrivals and departures, excited to get somewhere and, as soon as I arrive, eager to leave.

There was a small tailwind to aid the sixty-four-kilometer paddle to Selkirk, our last stop before Lake Winnipeg. If we were making good time, we planned to paddle on to a place called Breezy Point. I was in favor of camping there, but we had a lock and dam in front of us, just past downtown Winnipeg, and we were unsure how long it would take to pass it.

We pulled over just above the St. Andrews Lock and Dam to scope it out. The lockmaster walked out to greet us and told us the waves were too big for us to paddle. He suggested that we portage. Ann and I checked out the waves just downstream of the dam. We agreed that we could handle them and told the lockmaster that we would like to go through the lock. Disregarding our request, he insisted that we portage instead. We pushed back again and again, each time more aggressively than the last.

"Is it legal to go through the lock?" Ann asked, curious if his suggestion was really a suggestion or a requirement.

"Well, yes. Of course. That is how boaters get through. But I just don't think you should . . . ," he responded in a parental tone. Perhaps he had daughters around our age. The same question surfaced in my thoughts as it did time and time again when we were in a situation like this: Would this have been the same conversation if we were two men?

Eventually he realized he was not going to win. We signed waivers saying we were liable if anything went wrong—a piece of paper stating exactly how we already felt: no one was responsible for our decisions except us.

Returning to the canoe, we paddled toward the ominous concrete walls of the lock. The doors slowly creaked open, inviting us into an unwelcoming room, its old wet walls covered in algae. It smelled damp and moldy, like a back alley in a New York City summer. Trash floated along the sides of the lock, waiting, like us, to someday enjoy the white sand beaches of Lake Winnipeg.

"Go left. When we get out of here stay far left, okay?" Ann barked orders at me. I could tell she wished she was in the stern today. We had already discussed the route, and I definitely did not need a refresher. If only she knew that her orders made me feel less confident and more resentful of her lack of trust in my abilities to steer us. My mind went wild as the water level dropped several feet. The doors in front of us began to creep open, and the waves came into view. Clearly, now was not the time to express my frustrations with Ann.

I stayed silent and kept far left through the thrashing waves until we reached calmer water. We turned around to wave at the lockmaster, hoping he had watched our graceful maneuvering through the rough water. In my mind the wave was more of a middle finger.

Ann and I had been tiptoeing around a disagreement for a few weeks that finally needed to come to light. Camp Menogyn runs trips on a few rivers that flow into Lake Winnipeg. Ann's friend Megan was guiding a trip on the Berens River and was going to be camping at Gull Harbour on Hecla Island near the western shore of the lake around the same time we would be paddling up the east side of the south basin. Ann was determined to meet up with the Menogyn group. I was beyond irritated by this plan. She wanted to paddle two days out of our way, cutting across the middle of the lake from east to west and back again, to see them before we journeyed into the part of our expedition where we would not see any familiar faces until we returned home. There would be no more calling home to say hello. No more scheduled food drops with the Raihos. Just our canoe, each other, and the vast wilderness.

We received many accounts of Lake Winnipeg, including two stories from people who had lost loved ones to the unforgiving waves on the lake. In terms of surface area, Lake Winnipeg is the eleventh largest lake in the world, but it is also very shallow. Sevareid felt like it may well have been the Atlantic Ocean. Storms roll in quickly, and it only takes a little wind to kick up the waves. Sevareid and Port were helplessly windbound for almost two weeks on the lake. They finally resolved to get a tow for the entire north basin of the lake from one of the large steamboats. I was nervous for what lay ahead, to say the least, and I did not want to paddle out of our way to see the Menogyn group.

"Can't we just wait to see Megan when we get back to Winnipeg?" I suggested to Ann. I felt like I had no say in the matter. Megan was scheduled to pick us up at the train station in Winnipeg after the expedition. She was already going to be the first person we saw after the trip. I didn't want to risk paddling across a lake we knew could be unforgiving just to say hello.

As much as I wanted to say no and control our joint decision, I didn't know how to say it without causing more tension. If I didn't want to go off course and Ann did, who was right and who was wrong? What was the compromise? To paddle halfway there and call it a day? Either way, one of us was going to be upset. And, as usual, I feared it was going to be me.

When we arrived at Breezy Point it was clearly not the beautiful waterfront park we had imagined. Ann cleverly renamed it Sneezy Point. There was trash everywhere. Lovers and others sat in their cars into the wee hours of the night (like my grandmother used to say, "Nothing good happens after midnight"), trying to escape the public eye. If they were paying attention, they might have noticed a blue tent in their headlights, tucked behind the trees.

The next morning the sun pierced the tent like a needle,

abruptly waking us up. In less than an hour after sunrise the tent had become a sauna with visible steam rising from our sweaty bodies. We had both disregarded our sleeping bags in the middle of the night and now lay sprawled out in our sports bras and underwear, extremely uncomfortable but too lethargic from the heat to get up and unzip the tent. Finally, Ann made the first move and I followed suit, but the outside air did not provide any anticipated relief from the heat and humidity.

The sky was bright and cloudless. There was no wind or hint of a weather system coming through that day. We had learned that extremely hot weather typically leads to a few good storms down the line. But not today. Today we were going to finish the Red River. Our speedy but monotonous journey through the muddy river valley would soon be behind us, joining the slow and strenuous Minnesota River as a distant memory. We were getting somewhere, but the end was still a far cry from our trashy campsite on Sneezy Point. Our biggest challenges still lay ahead.

~~~~~

WHEN RIVERS FLOW INTO LAKES or oceans they slow down, widen, and disperse like fingers stretching out in different directions. Sometimes it felt as though Ann and I were like the water molecules in a river delta. From the moment we set off, we flowed together with the current, following the slope of the land and the twists and turns of the riverbank. Some days we experienced the remedies of the natural environment, emerging clear-minded, cleansed, and more mindful than before. Other days, when the wind howled and the rain pounded on the water, we were thrown over and over into the murky unknown, collecting polluted thoughts and attaching negative feelings to ourselves, each other, and our surroundings. Back and forth, clean and clear to confused and dirty, constant puppets of the land and weather.

At the end of the Red River, we funneled into fingers that couldn't seem to agree on the fastest route to the lake. We were unsure whether to celebrate or fear the daunting endeavor in front of us—paddling 416 kilometers on Lake Winnipeg. We took the far right channel of the delta, weaving through small islands and the occasional marshy dead end. A man in a motorboat puttered up to our canoe, intrigued by the words "Hudson Bay Bound" written on the side, to inquire about our expedition.

"You know," he said, "there is nowhere to get food after this point." Again, the assumption that we didn't know what we were doing. When did advice become so insulting? We told him about our extensive food supply that would get us to Norway House, where we would pick up our third food drop, mentioning that we were already halfway to Hudson Bay and knew what we were doing.

"Halfway to Hudson Bay!" he laughed. "You're not halfway to Hudson Bay!" We had failed to mention where we started. Distance is relative. Once he understood more about our trip he told us he wrote for the *Winnipeg Free Press* and was interested in featuring our expedition. We exchanged contact information and paddled on, unaware if we would see him again.

We turned a small bend, and suddenly the channel opened into a seemingly endless space. The water was glass, with not even one ripple, reaching into the horizon and reflecting the blue sky and bright sun like a mirror. It felt like we were paddling into an oil painting. The Red River had finally pushed us into the southeastern corner of Lake Winnipeg. I reached for the handheld voice recorder in my life jacket pocket and hit play on the party mix we had recorded before leaving. Electronic dance music reverberated off the sides of our canoe, providing a soundtrack to our glorious arrival on Lake Winnipeg.

"I thought Lake Winnipeg was supposed to be big and scary—this is a breeze!" Ann laughed. After strategizing for weeks about how we would remain within two kilometers of the shore, we suddenly found ourselves five kilometers out, enjoying a floating lunch, already getting way too comfortable with the big lake. For days we would travel on flat water, thinking somehow we had escaped the throes of Lake Winnipeg's fearsome reputation.

Throughout our expedition we were frequently contacted by strangers offering a free meal or place to stay along our route. The Johnstons from Beaconia had offered their home along the southeastern shore of Lake Winnipeg as a rest stop once we arrived. Floating lazily on the lake, thinking we had all the time in the world, Ann called Penny Johnston to let her know we were near Beaconia and would love to stop in. In a few more days we wouldn't have cell service. We were told that our phone would be good until about Black Island, one of the large islands just before the narrow strait marking the boundary between the south and north basins. Ann got off the phone. Penny Johnston would be expecting us by her dock in an hour. We took off toward the shores of Beaconia.

From a distance we could see people dotting the sandy shore. It reminded me of South Beach in Miami. Growing up, my family had a sailboat that we would take out to explore the islands just east of the city. On our return trip, the mobs of people on the beach looked like stitches in a blanket covering the white sand, just as they did now. I thought it must be a Saturday, but the days of the week no longer meant anything to us.

As we paddled closer to shore, young people floated by in large rafts filled with beer, reminding us of what our summer could have been. They were bewildered at our arrival, seemingly out of nowhere, and shared their bounty of cheap beer with us while we swapped stories. In the corner of my eye I saw a woman frantically waving her arms by a dock. Her voice traveled across the still water, "Over here! Come over here!" It was Penny. But one of our new friends was telling a great story about a keg stand at a frat party and we didn't dare interrupt. Ann and I looked back and forth from Penny to the guy telling us the story like overexcited puppies. Finally Penny's movements became so frantic that we told the group we had to go.

Penny directed us to the dock and immediately asked us what we needed. We were pretty relaxed from our one beer and lacka-daisical paddle on the lake, so this question was hard to answer—we were doing great. The lake was calm, the vibes were good, and our canoe was fully loaded after our stop in Winnipeg. We didn't really *need* anything. We followed her up a steep wooden staircase to a very modern silver house behind the trees. The sun shone through the massive windows in her kitchen, filling every nook and cranny with light. Little trinkets from faraway places deco-rated the walls and shelves. I turned the corner and came face-to-face with a polar bear skin draped over the bookshelf. I jumped. Penny laughed.

Penny fed us noodles and pie and told us stories of paddling Arctic rivers in Canada. It didn't take me long to realize that she was a strong woman—the kind of woman who is taking down the patriarchy just by being her tough, confident self. She went on remote river expeditions like it was no big deal. We walked over to her neighbor's house on a winding path through the woods to check the weather for the week. A handful of people from all over the world (mostly Paraguay and Cuba) sat out on the porch drink-ing cocktails and wearing funny straw hats. It felt like we had stepped onto the set of a sitcom. "I technically retired, so if it is a nice day tomorrow, screw 'em, I'm not going into work!" one of them said, followed by a laugh.

They turned on the radio. We listened to a man with a thick Canadian accent announce an impending heat wave for the week. Briefly concerned about our travel through the hot, muggy days ahead, the group decided to sponsor our expedition with two comically large straw hats. They dramatically knighted our heads, sacrificing their sun protection for the rest of the day. This would mark the beginning of strangers giving us things we didn't really need or want to carry into the wilderness. We graciously accepted nonetheless. Their laughter echoed through the woods on our walk back to Penny's house.

To avoid the heat and higher wind speeds during the day, we resolved to paddle the lake at night whenever possible. Penny approved and offered us her guest bedroom to nap before our first night's paddle. We set our alarm for 10:00 p.m. I fell asleep almost immediately and entered into a restless dream in which I was running from a polar bear through a maze in a large house. I was unsure of where I was when I awoke to the familiar and ever-disappointing sound of our alarm. Ann was already bustling around the room, getting ready for our departure. It was time to go. I glared at the polar bear head and fur draped over the bookcase on our way out.

DON'T WAKE THE BEAST

MOONLIGHT ILLUMINATED THE PATH through the forest and trickled down the staircase to spotlight our loaded canoe by the dock. There were two moons that night, just as there would be two suns at every sunset on still days. The reflection on the lake was a constant reminder of the vast world above. We could've sworn there was a green glow in the sky to the north. I wanted so badly to see the northern lights that I started imagining hints of color beyond the blue-black blanket of stars. There would come a time when I would be unimpressed with a simple green hue in the night sky.

The trees outlined the lake with a pointed fringe, decorating the water's edge until they diminished into the horizon. It was incomprehensible to think we would have to paddle for at least two weeks to even get a glimpse of land on the north side. Small ripples from a light breeze started skirting across the glassy surface— a clue that we had not yet learned to read.

Within the hour we were navigating small waves, about a foot tall, and sticking conservatively close to shore. Paddling up the east side of the lake suggests a straight shot up the shore. In reality, it is a jagged outline of small bays separated by what we called "points," where the land shoots out into the lake to create an isthmus that separates the small bays. These points turned out to be great milestones for us, especially in the north basin, where the bays were often twenty to thirty kilometers long. There was a point ahead of us as we followed the curve of the land around the bend and into the next small bay. But the lake held another secret for us.

Scrrrrrraaaaaaaaaaaaape! Our bow hit a submerged rock waiting sneakily just below the surface, scraping the length of our canoe from bow to stern and causing a few visible scratches on the strong Kevlar. Ann and I took great pride in the condition of our boat. At a young age we both learned that canoes are only supposed to touch air or water. We were diligent to never hit bottom whenever launching from or arriving on land. We hit another rock and then another. Our conservative plan to stay close to shore was becoming more and more treacherous.

We made it out of the rock minefield and successfully rounded the point only to find larger waves and stronger winds in the next bay. An unnatural light from several lampposts illuminated a sandy beach up the shore. "Let's pull over," Ann suggested. I agreed. Ann, again, was the first to express concern about our safety.

Tacking back and forth along the shore was the only way to keep the boat somewhat perpendicular with the waves to prevent getting sideswept. Silhouettes of two men on the beach briefly made us rethink our stop until we noticed they were in uniform. They were as curious about the approaching canoe at 2:00 a.m. as we were about two strangers on a beach in the wee hours of the morning. They walked confidently toward us as we paddled hard to shore, letting our canoe ride out the small crashing waves until it beached on the sand. The policemen's bright eyes glistened in the lamplight as they scanned the situation: Two women. Packed canoe. Not dangerous. Our gun was tucked behind our pack out of sight.

"It doesn't look like you're here to cause trouble," one of the men said, a smile spread across his face. He was clearly unaware of our long-term goals to take down the patriarchy.

"We were thinking the same thing about you," I said, returning the smile. "Okay if we rest here for a while? We'll be gone before the sun."

"Sure. We patrol a few beaches around here, so we'll make sure no one bothers you," he replied. They walked back to their police car and took off.

Camping illegally on expeditions can be tricky in more populated areas. Ann and I often discussed whether we should call the police and let them know we were camping at a public boat launch or deal with the consequences if they found us first. Generally, we asked for forgiveness instead of permission (and got really good at hiding our tent behind trees). We pulled out our sleeping bags and left everything else loaded in the canoe. I began to wonder if our Winnipeg stop had been the last full night of rest we would get. Now we were subject to the wind—paddling whenever we could, day or night.

I couldn't sleep. I tucked my head into my sleeping bag and cinched the top as tightly as possible to keep the bugs out. But we now had warmer sleeping bags and I was heating up. Bugs or heat? I spent hours bouncing back and forth between the two evils. I convinced myself that the northern lights were out if I squinted just right into the night sky. My mind was racing. Ann hadn't talked about paddling over to Gull Harbour since we discussed it briefly after leaving Winnipeg. Maybe she no longer wanted to go now that we were on the lake and had a glimpse of the wind and waves. But what if she did? What mind game were we playing by not mentioning the elephant in the canoe?

A few hours later the wind died down enough for us to safely continue. Around the next point was Traverse Bay. Depending on the wind, we could either brave the fifteen-kilometer paddle straight across the bay or follow the shore for twice that distance, dedicating the entire day to a safe crossing. As the sun emerged from behind the trees, a thick layer of humidity poured over the surface of the cool water like hot fudge on ice cream. The heat slowed our strokes and made us feel lethargic. The wind had died down to almost nothing, and the waves had disappeared completely. We decided to cross.

Hitchhiking black flies joined our ship to shore. No matter where we were they somehow found us, even in the middle of a large bay. Our calves and arms were routinely bitten, taking us by surprise every time the sharp sting hit. About an hour into our paddle we couldn't see land in any direction. It was like trying to cross an ocean. At this point, if the waves picked up we were equidistant from shore whichever way we went. I suspected there were fires burning to the east. We floated in a smoky hot haze with no end in sight and no safe harbor from the shores we left behind.

Our new funny straw hats were surprisingly effective at keeping us cool, and I realized Penny's neighbors probably weren't wearing them as a joke after all. But no matter how helpful the hats were, there was no escaping the extreme heat of the afternoon sun. If the weather report we heard the day before was correct, it was in the upper nineties. The "chill mix" on the voice recorder we were listening to sent us into a meditative state. Our strokes slowed further. I was drifting in and out of consciousness when I saw the first glimpse of land: an island. We agreed to pull over and ate lunch in silence. Afterward I went for a swim to cool down, which apparently caught Ann off guard. Usually we ate as fast as possible and got back on the water.

"We don't have time to swim, Natalie. We have to go if we're going to make it to Gull Harbour," she yelled from on top of a rock.

My mind went wild. *Excuse me?!* I thought as I swam back to the rocky shore. How did we get from talking about maybe paddling to Gull Harbour on Hecla Island, a good two days out of our way, to definitely paddling over there without me knowing? I was livid. But so was Ann.

"Sometimes you make decisions without consulting me. I didn't want to go swimming. I wanted to keep going," she expressed.

"*I* make decisions without consulting *you*? Au, contraire!" I thought before restraining myself. What was the point in arguing? If Ann wanted to see the Menogyn group so badly then we would do it, whether I put up a fight or not. It was better to move on. After moments of playing out different scenarios in my head (in one I scream and yell, and in another I dramatically jump back into the lake), I finally responded, "Okay. Let's go."

I felt like a total pushover. But Ann felt like I didn't understand her or respect what she wanted. We managed to not blow up at each other as we paddled away from the island and found the eastern shore once more. It might have been better if we had fought to break down all the tension building between us. But that time had passed, and now we had a new mission: cross the lake.

A few hours into our paddle we agreed to pull over and cook a big dinner. We needed to fuel up on real food, not just granola bars and trail mix. As we paddled toward what looked like a good spot to make dinner we saw a black bear patrolling the beach. Continuing another kilometer or so would put a sufficient distance between us and the bear. Another beach presented a good alternative, but as we paddled toward it two eagles flew out of a nearby tree, marking their territory. They screeched in disapproval as we arrived. Another dinner spot already reserved. We settled for a small, unoccupied beach a little farther down shore and made Gouda mac 'n' cheese. Ann poured water into a bottle and mixed in Gatorade powder, announcing that we'd be drinking "Ragerade" to get us through the night. We pretended that Ragerade gave us super strength and flexed our strong arms on the beach after each sip before launching. Food and drink lifted our spirits. For a few hours we laughed and sang, enjoying another beautiful sunset paddle on Lake Winnipeg, briefly forgetting our anger with each other. But then everything went dark.

~~~~~

THE SHORELINE ABRUPTLY DISAPPEARED. The last ray of light had sunk beneath the horizon, and a veil of darkness fell over our eyes.

"I could have sworn the moon would be out. It was out last night," reasoned Ann. We would never have paddled at night without moonlight to guide the way. But where was it?

While we were singing, dark clouds quietly entered the night

sky. Where there once had been bright stars was now only darkness. The jagged outlines of the trees that we so faithfully followed up the eastern shore were now gone. Everything was still
and quiet. We could only hear the soft buzz of mayflies dancing
above the water. The hair rose on the back of my neck like warning flags. The air lay thick against our skin, now speckled with
goosebumps. Something was coming. We had been too busy
talking and laughing to notice the signs. We agreed to find shelter. And quick.

As we directed the canoe toward the invisible shore we luckily crash-landed on a sand beach. Our grand scheme to cross the
lake would have to wait until tomorrow. I was looking forward
to catching up on sleep, but Ann announced we were just going
to nap until the storm passed. I felt like a constant slave to Ann's
plan, but she was right. We had to move with the weather.

The winds picked up just as we zipped our tent closed. They
howled through the trees, and soon an orange sky replaced the
complete darkness. Lighting struck like bright swords stabbing the lake from the heavens. The sound of the crashing waves
seemed to move closer and closer to our tent as the night wore on.
We assured ourselves, like we had to often, that the lake was not
the ocean: it did not have a tide effect. We were not going to wake
up in water. Even so, as I began to drift into dreams, Ann woke
me up to help pull the boat even deeper into the woods. Why was
she always so concerned? I obliged, half-awake, then quickly fell
asleep again.

Scratchhhh . . . scrattcchhhh . . . I opened my eyes. Large hands
were pushing against the side of the tent right above my face. Was
I awake? I blinked and looked again. Sure enough, I saw sharp
claws gently scraping across the thin, vulnerable nylon walls of
our home. I jolted upward and jumped to the other side of the
tent, slamming my leg on the travel guitar.

"Ann! Bear! Bear!" I screamed, now fully awake. Ann sprang
into action.

"The bear kit!" she remembered out loud. "Get the foghorn!"

Pam Raiho, probably sleeping comfortably in her bed at this hour, would not be excited to hear about our bear encounter but would be very pleased that she provided something useful for our journey. I honestly never thought we would use it.

"Got it!" exclaimed Ann. She pushed it triumphantly.

Waaaaaaa waaaa waaaaaa ... A thin, whiny sound came from the trumpetlike head of the foghorn, sounding more like a sad trombone than something that would scare away a bear. I would have laughed if I wasn't already so scared.

We knew that it was just a black bear. Perhaps the same one we saw earlier onshore. It wasn't aggressive and seemed curious about our tent. Still, it needed to go. Black bears scare easily (with or without a tiny foghorn). They are really more like large raccoons compared to the carnivorous polar bears we could cross paths with later.

We counted together. "One. Two. Three." We unzipped the tent and ran out, making as much noise as possible. I flailed my arms in the air to look bigger and scarier. The bear ran into the woods, likely terrified by the beasts that had just emerged from the funny blue thing by the water. I looked up at the orange sky and then out to the lake where lightning continued to strike in the distance. There was very little rain, and the wind was constant but tolerable for us to comfortably fall back asleep. We tossed and turned for hours. It was the night that would never end. And it wasn't over. Lightning struck nearby. The loud crack, much closer than before, woke us both up in a panic. In the corner of my eye I noticed the tent slowly lifting along the sides. The wind speed had passed the "comfortable" threshold. The worst of the weather was here, and it was no longer safe to wait out the lightning. We grabbed our life jackets and followed the bear's path straight into the dark woods.

At camp Ann and I learned that when the weather gets rough you should sit on your life jacket in the woods, far away from each other. The last thing I wanted to do was to sit all alone in the middle of a storm with a bear nearby. We agreed to bend the rules a little and squat down on our life jackets near each other for company. But just as we settled into "lightning position," I looked up to see our tent whip into the air, its flat bottom flying like a kite in the sky, only rooted to the ground by one stake. It was as if our campsite had been completely turned upside down. We ran back and disassembled the poles. Keeping everything inside the tent, we threw it all—the lumpy mass of sleeping bags, journals, our gun, the travel guitar, and our personal gear—into the woods. Back on our life jackets surrounded by trees, we squatted down and watched the fireworks. The lightning exploded in the night sky, illuminating for brief moments the large crashing waves in front of us. I kept thinking about Eric Sevareid's experience on the shallow lake: when the waves get big they can pick you up and drop you right to the rocky bottom. I was thankful we were not out on the water.

Once the storm died down we set up our tent deeper into the woods for protection from the wind, which was still blowing strong from the west. The waves grew even taller and stronger while we slept.

The next morning the wind had not died down, and we knew there was no use waking up with the sun. The crashing waves sounded like a prerecorded audio clip created to lull us back to sleep. I was glad for the opportunity to catch up on rest, even if we were stranded against our will. Around 11:00 a.m. the wind still showed no sign of decreasing, which gave us an excuse to make some of the more labor-intensive meals buried at the bottom of the bear barrel. We whipped up some dehydrated eggs and rehydrated some vegetables to make delicious omelets for a relaxing brunch (substituting Ragerade for mimosas). The wind finally began to die and the diminishing waves looked promising for our journey to Hecla Island near the west shore.

"I can't believe this thing didn't work last night!" Ann laughed as she held the tiny blue foghorn in one hand, her breakfast in the other. "Who uses a foghorn to scare black bears anyway?"

"Ann! Bear! Get the foghorn!" I comically reenacted Ann's desperate demand for the foghorn from the night before.

Ann pretended to rummage around. "Found it!" She activated the foghorn (which was unfortunately pointed in my direction), fully expecting the sad whiny sound it had expelled just hours earlier.

BAAAAAAAAAAAAHHHH! A massive sound blasted forward and echoed through the woods. I quickly clamped my ears and glared at Ann, whose expression was somewhere between amusement and sympathy. "Go figure," she said with a shrug, casually tossing the horn onto the sandy beach.

An hour later the strong winds had ceased and the waves lightly lapped at the shore, a fraction of their previous size. It's strange how the same body of water can kick up into a fierce beast and then fall into a lull just hours later. We packed up and launched again onto the big lake. It felt like we were tiptoeing around a sleeping dragon guarding an ancient treasure. I paddled lightly. "Don't wake the beast," I thought.

WAITING FOR THE WIND

~~~~~~X~~~~~~

THE WEATHER SEEMED TO BE ON OUR SIDE for the twenty-kilometer crossing to Gull Harbour, and halfway to Black Island the wind began to gently push ol' Canoey north. A little tailwind is nice, but any wind has the potential to be too much. Luckily, we made it to the southern shore of Black Island and congratulated ourselves for avoiding any trouble in open water. Now, if a big wave hit our boat the wrong way, if we tipped, we could feasibly swim to land and live out our days on an island—maybe start a two-person village . . . or eat each other. At this point, eating each other wasn't too hard to imagine since we had been emotionally eating away at each other for weeks. I had too much time on the crossing to Gull Harbour to think about how I never wanted to do the crossing in the first place. It better be worth it. My resentful thoughts toward Ann grew until unexpected waves pulled me back into reality.

The channel in between Hecla and Black Islands creates bizarre and unpredictable wind and water. It feels similar to walking into a mall in the summer: you get smacked with aggressive air conditioning (hold your skirts!), but then a few steps in everything feels normal. We had just opened the door and taken our first step into the channel when the waves swelled and the wind changed direction in what seemed like a matter of seconds.

Water hit our boat from every direction and jostled us like a rubber duck in a bathtub. Finally, a few steps in, the waves and wind agreed on a tailwind—the biggest we had encountered. My heart skipped a beat every time I looked back from the stern at the massive waves forcing us north. I ruddered hard to keep the boat straight and directed our canoe toward a lighthouse in the distance. But as it came into full view, I noticed that it was surrounded by what looked like a brick wall, with waves crashing into it, smashing everything in their wake against the hard surface.

It was impossible to turn. We had to keep the canoe perpendicular to the massive waves or else they would crash over our gunwales. Or sideswipe us. Either way, we would tip and lose everything to the beast. Slamming straight into a brick wall didn't seem like a good option. We couldn't hear each other over the waves, and there was nowhere to pull over to strategize a way out. As we got closer, what clearly had been a vertical wall now looked like a very steep sandy slope. Our landing would have to be strategic, but for the first time we had an escape plan that did not involve our canoe sinking to the bottom of Lake Winnipeg. The moment we beached at such a steep angle a large wave would surely crash over us. I glanced at the loose items in the boat: the voice recorder sat on top of the bear barrel, slowly rocking with the boat, awaiting its fate. At least everything else was tucked into the sides of the canoe. If we moved fast enough we could come out unscathed.

Five waves to go. Four waves. Our canoe began to surf the crest of the waves, threatening to spin wildly. I ruddered hard and responded to the unpredictable turning of the boat. We had lost what little control we had. What came next was a blur, similar to someone punching you in the face (I would imagine), where you can't quite pinpoint the beginning or end of the blow.

CRRAASSHHH!

We crashed headfirst into the sand wall. Our bow followed the steep contour of the shore, angling up and up until we were successfully lodged into the bank at a 45-degree angle.

Ann scrambled out of the boat and tried to pull the bow up higher onto the steep sandy slope with all her might. I jumped out, slamming my shin on the gunnel, and pushed from the stern. A wave crashed over us. The voice recorder teetered, winked goodbye, and tumbled into the lake. "Shit!" I yelled. Months of daily accounts of our journey—gone. Our only music to get us through the long days was now underwater. We timed our pushing and pulling with the next wave and successfully lugged the loaded canoe up to safer ground.

I took a moment to look out at the lake while unloading the canoe. Those same fierce waves from the night before were there again, but this time we were out in them. I thought again about my mom's prayer group back in Florida.

"Score one for the prayer list, huh?" I broke the nervous silence, trying to lift the mood. Ann smirked and rolled her eyes. We knew we were lucky to be standing on solid ground with almost all of our gear (RIP, voice recorder) still intact.

At a loss for what to do next, we hiked over to the bay on the other side of the peninsula. It looked like a completely different body of water. The waves were calm, and there was just a hint of wind. It was the type of summer day where families could have been lounging on the sandy beach and swimming in the lake, but just a hundred feet away was literal doomsday.

In the distance, on the other end of the bay, we could see our destination: Gull Harbour. There was a hotel with a well-landscaped lawn, a pavilion, and a sandy beach adjacent to a long dock in the water. It looked like a great vacation spot, but I worried what the staff might think when two canoeing vagabonds washed up onshore. Megan and her Menogyn group would have arrived here the day before and set up camp at the nearby campground. Ann was very excited to see them and, I admit, now that we were here, I was also excited.

With our boat pulled safely onto shore, we took off for the campground with renewed energy. RVs and tents were tucked away in their wooded spots. I felt lucky to have had such secluded and pristine waterfront camping spots on the lake so far. The sounds of sticks breaking for campfires and pots and pans rattling in anticipation of dinner could be heard throughout the grounds.

We peeked into every campsite to look for the Menogyn campers. With only a few unexplored campsites left, we began to question if we were in the right spot.

We resolved to calling out, "Megan! Menogyn!" We walked around for two hours. No response. A nice woman named Yvonne joined our search party and biked around the campground to speed up our efforts. They were nowhere to be found.

Did we get the dates wrong? Ann was sure they were supposed to be here tonight. We began to worry. Could something have happened on their trip? And then it hit me: we paddled all the way here for nothing. For no one. And I was pissed.

Later we discovered that the wind was too strong at the mouth of the Berens River, where the group was supposed to take a ferry to Gull Harbour. They were windbound on the east shore.

We returned to the lake to set up camp. In the real world, people reserve campsites or stay in hotels or resorts. In our world, we camped wherever necessary for the night, preferably close to the water for a quick escape in the morning. Eyeing the darkening sky, we decided to set up our tent in the pavilion by the beach. To us it was a normal decision, but it must have seemed highly questionable to paying tourists to see two random women with *lots* of gear camping for free in plain sight.

The next morning the wind howled relentlessly from the northeast. We decided to pop into the little restaurant at the inn for breakfast. It was miserably overpriced, but then again, we were not used to pulling out our wallets for anything these days. Within the first few minutes of sitting down we agreed that the owners of the inn, an older couple, were in fact the *worst*. The woman was nice, although she looked depressed, as if she had expected more from the romantic dream of opening a restaurant on Lake Winnipeg with her husband. But the man was cranky and far too sure of himself or, rather, unsure of everyone else.

"What are you ladies up to?" he asked. I could tell he was slightly perturbed by the surprise siege of his pavilion.

"We're paddling to Hudson Bay. Hoping to get there by early September!" Ann said conversationally.

"HA HA HA! Yeah right! I bet you a keg of Bud Light Lime that you won't make it there 'til October!" He walked away.

We were perplexed. First, can you get Bud Light Lime in a keg? Was that even a reward? Couldn't he have offered up better beer? Second, we were stunned by his skepticism. Usually people said things like "cool" or "sounds fun" or "good luck" when we shared our journey with them. We weren't prepared to be laughed at and told we couldn't meet our goal. I had an inkling that the conversation would have gone differently if we were two burly outdoorsmen.

Ann's phone began to vibrate wildly on the wooden table during breakfast. The owner glared at us from behind the counter for disturbing the peace. I wondered if he had stayed up all night feeling angry that we had the nerve to move into his pavilion. Ann got the hint and quickly ran outside to take the call. I stayed at the table, shuffling cards and practicing my game face for our upcoming cribbage match.

"It's David Squire," she announced when she returned, as if I was supposed to know who that was.

"Who's that?" I said, unnecessarily shuffling the deck of cards for the tenth time.

Ann sighed and explained, "That guy in the boat at the mouth of the Red River. You remember? He wants to meet up and get an interview. He'll be here tomorrow morning."

She sat down and cleared her plate to prepare for our cribbage showdown.

"I told him we were camped under the pavilion. He laughed and asked if he could sponsor Hudson Bay Bound with a room here. Looks like we'll be sleeping inside tonight!"

"Well, that's just lovely!" I said in a Cockney accent. Ann was not amused. "The weather is supposed to be gnarly tonight," I said, now in my normal voice, shifting my eyes from the breakfast table turned game table to the large waves crashing on the beach outside. The flag on the flagpole was whipping wildly in the wind with an ominous backdrop of dark storm clouds. We were frustrated that we struck out trying to find the Menogyn group and now were stranded. At least we had a deck of cards. I dealt the first hand. Back in college, Ann and I played an epic game of chess that resulted in our not speaking to each other for two days. I had trash-talked throughout the entire game and then over-celebrated my victory. I knew playing games on our expedition was dangerous, especially with tensions running high already, but we had to pass the time somehow. We were windbound all day, and the forecast was not promising.

We played cribbage at the restaurant for hours, transitioning from morning coffee to afternoon beers. The owners of the inn tolerated us because of the new business we afforded them when David called to pay for our room for the night. Watching us hunker down was probably less painful for them now that they were getting something in return.

The day disappeared. We went for a sunset walk out to the point just north of Gull Harbour and sat on a swing set looking over the lake.

"Do you think we'll ever be able to leave?" I asked Ann jokingly.

"I don't know," she responded in a serious tone. And for a moment I didn't know, either. We could be here for days. We could be here for weeks. Eric Sevareid and Walter Port were windbound on Lake Winnipeg for nearly two weeks until they hitched a ride north on a big boat. Would that, too, be our fate? It was not impossible to imagine. We swung in silence, staring at the distant storms and dark expanse of endless turbulent water.

It was nice to sleep in a bed that night. Although Ann felt anxious about the gear we left under the pavilion, especially with the onslaught of the storm. I'm sure to her I seemed not to care. I did care, but if we weren't going to do anything about it I wasn't going to lose sleep over it. I started to wonder if my nonchalant demeanor was hurting more than it was helping.

The next morning was once again too windy to launch. We walked to the pavilion to discover that our gear was fine but the tree next to our tent had been struck by lightning and now had a huge crack down the middle. We were thankful to have been indoors when that occurred.

"Another prayer list win, huh?" I said as we surveyed the damage.

"Any more joking about the prayer list and we're going straight to hell, you know," Ann responded jokingly, mustering up a little sass.

I looked out at the large waves and the constant flapping of the flag by the pavilion. "I'm pretty sure this *is* hell. Hell Harbour. Gull Hell-ber. What's this place called again?" My joking around was a little too close to the truth to be funny.

We mused about the other visitors to Gull Harbour. They had probably saved up money and taken time off from work to travel here and relax by the lake. Their vacation spot had become our prison.

David Squire arrived right on time for breakfast, bringing doughnuts and fresh fruit. What were the chances we would run into someone on the Red River who wrote for the *Winnipeg Free Press* and who would graciously house and feed us during a trying time? I wondered what would have happened if he hadn't asked us about our trip. Or if he had been on the other side of our canoe and hadn't seen "Hudson Bay Bound" spray-painted on the side. Fate was clearly at play here, I thought as I shoved doughnuts into my mouth like a ravenous teenager. Our list of "river angels" was expanding.

He interviewed us about our journey, but we lacked the exuberance that we normally would have had on a good day. The lake was wearing us down already, and we hadn't even gotten to the infamously windy and fickle north basin.

David wanted a few pictures for the article and asked if we'd be willing to paddle around by the dock, close to shore. We reluctantly agreed. The waves were too large by the beach, but perhaps by the dock we would be able to paddle out and back without too much trouble. I felt slight PTSD from the lighthouse waves while cautiously getting into the canoe.

Struggling to push off from the dock, we plowed through the headwind into deeper waters where the waves were like large ocean swells. I glanced back to force a smile at the camera. The short paddle reaffirmed our decision—it was still too dangerous to leave. After the brief photo shoot, we said our farewells and thank-yous to David, who set off on the two-hour drive to Winnipeg.

Back at our favorite loitering spot in the restaurant, Ann and I continued our never-ending cribbage competition. Instead of keeping score with a traditional cribbage board, we were rapidly filling pages of my journal with small tally marks. We agreed it was safe to play cribbage for the rest of the trip only if we ended on a tie so no one lost (or, more importantly, so no one won).

The owner stopped by to chat us up again. His name was Marvin, but because we didn't like him we decided to call him Milton. After all, there are few things more insulting than getting someone's name wrong after several interactions. It was a small consolation for his skepticism. However, he was in higher spirits today and had warmed to the idea that we were probably never going to leave his inn.

"You ladies want to work in the kitchen today? If you do, lunch is on me," he said. I hated how he acted like he was doing us a favor.

So this was it? This was our new life on Gull Harbour? I could see the headline now: "Hudson Bay Bound Women Stuck on Lake Winnipeg, Become Amateur Cooks at Resort." We were assigned the very important role of making cinnamon buns for the week. It was hard to resist eating the dough while we baked, like I normally would do at home.

We set the dough to rise and went for a walk to the lighthouse. Desperate to leave that evening, we wanted to see what the waves were like on the other side of the peninsula. Maybe they'd be manageable enough to paddle back to the islands and skip back to the east shore. We emerged from the protected woods onto the exposed point with the lighthouse. I looked down at the large bruises on my legs, remembering our dramatic landing days earlier.

When we reached the point, hot air blasted our faces. It reminded me of the wind before a hurricane back home in Miami. Before a big storm, my family and I would stand in the backyard and see who could lean the farthest into the wind before inevitably toppling backward. It was troubling that these winds reminded me of a hurricane. No matter how badly we wanted to escape, even just to the other side of the channel, it once again wasn't in the cards. I could see the defeat on Ann's face as we turned to walk back to our duties in the kitchen.

"Our stuff is everywhere. I don't know where anything is!" Ann vented on our walk back.

I agreed. Our things had exploded all over the pavilion and the hotel room where we were staying now. But no matter what I said to comfort Ann, it felt like nothing could make her relax about our situation. I often play devil's advocate and try to represent the other person's views or strive to articulate a silver lining when people are upset about something. But sometimes people just need affirmation that the situation does, in fact, totally suck. I decided to give that technique a try because repeating the phrase "It's fine, it is going to be fine" was clearly not helping. Ann didn't respond well to that approach either, and I felt like no matter how I tried to console her, she only snapped back at me.

We returned to the inn in silence.

ESCAPE FROM GULL HARBOUR

THE 5:00 A.M. ALARM WENT OFF and we didn't dare push snooze. Our desire to launch was much greater than our desire to be well rested. Today was the day we would leave Gull Harbour—I could feel it. Packing would be a challenge because our gear was still scattered everywhere, but we managed to wrangle everything together in the dim light of dawn.

With a fully loaded canoe waiting for us by the water, we zipped up our life jackets and gazed over the lake into the sunrise. Rays of light hit the tops of the waves before disappearing into the shadow of their crests. The beast had not slept for days and showed little sign of slowing down, but we were determined to leave despite the unwavering weather. Staying at Gull Harbour for a fourth full day was simply not an option.

It was still too dangerous to launch, but we did it anyway, without expressing any concern to each other. Our homemade spray skirt was attached, but I didn't trust it to keep out the big waves. We pushed off the shore and battled the initial crash. The first one surged over the spray skirt in the bow and seemed to roll off the side. So did the second, third, and fourth ones. But some water from each wave leaked down to the bottom of the canoe. I could feel the standing water slosh around my feet. I lowered myself to my knees to center my weight below the gunwales. My hips and abs worked hard to keep us from tipping. My stomach lurched and my heart dropped as I looked out into the dark dangerous abyss of water ahead.

"I'm turning around!" Ann yelled. Even though she was just feet behind me I could barely hear her above the wind and waves.

I nodded. In the moment, I was thankful for Ann's constant concern for our safety. Turning around in a headwind is no easy task. There is inevitably a moment when the boat is parallel with the waves, and in large waves that moment has to be well timed. Ann maneuvered gracefully in the water, considering the conditions, and directed our canoe back to shore.

Back by the familiar pavilion, we devised a new plan to escape "Hell Harbour." We thought the waves might be more manageable in the northern bay. But before we could commit to portaging our gear a kilometer north, we needed to scope it out. We pulled Canoey up onto shore where we thought she would be safe and abandoned her to scout the bay to the north. No luck: bigger waves, stronger winds, more open water. We wouldn't have dilly-dallied sulking on the swings if we had known what was slowly happening to our canoe back on the beach.

Ann saw it first on our walk back. "Shit!" She took off running toward the shore. My eyes followed Ann and then saw what had upset her. I launched into a run, too. My heavy Muck Boots scraped the gravel road and kicked up dust behind me. Not for the first or last time, my mind went into survival mode, running solely on instinct, with no time to process or reflect. Just action, and fast.

The canoe was in the water on its side, parallel with the waves, getting smacked by each crashing blow. Our gear was slowly venturing out to the belly of the beast, who apparently didn't want it because she kept pushing it back to shore with sharp watery claws and crested white fingernails. Everything we owned, everything we needed for our expedition, was in jeopardy.

Ann arrived at the scene first. Her body showed no reaction as she ran into the icy water after our runaway gear. We delegated tasks without speaking. I ran to the canoe and tried to push it upright, but it was too full of water to budge. It made an unnerving crunching sound each time a wave crashed over it. Unable to right the boat, I ran into deeper water to help Ann gather gear. Water rushed into my boots, turning my feet into sandbags. My veins tightened and my blood slowed in the cold. Adrenaline took over as we successfully gathered our gear. Back onshore, we teamed up to save the canoe, which now had a small shallow crack in its hull, running lengthwise from bow to stern. Fortunately, the crack was just visible on the outside of the canoe and was not deep enough to let water in.

Luckily for our pride it was still very early and most people were comfortably asleep in their beds at the inn. Too bad, because it would have been a great show to watch through the window, perhaps while Marvin chimed in with some skeptical comments. I could see him pouring coffee and saying, "Those ladies think they're gonna make it to Hudson Bay! They can't even keep their boat out of the water!" We sat and stared at the water and accepted our defeat. The sun had risen high above the horizon and warmed our shivering bodies, a silver lining to our challenging morning.

People began to stir around the dock, and morning sounds filled the air. A man drove his trailer into the water at the boat launch and unloaded a motorboat. He moved gracefully like a dancer performing an old routine. An elderly couple emerged from their sailboat, where they had slept for the night. Their boat was large and steady. It seemed to mock our canoe's size and ability to handle what I now assumed was common weather on the big lake. Then a light bulb went on in my head.

"Ann, what if . . . what if we could get back to the east shore today after all?" I said, nervous to suggest what I was thinking.

"I know. I've been thinking the same thing. But do you think anyone would take us?" She was staring at the big boats bouncing around in the waves by the dock, too. I was thankful that we were on the same page.

"If we can get back east, the wind won't be so bad, you know? We could paddle again," she said.

"Well I s'pose it's time to be social, then! Let's get outta here," I responded with a wink and a smile.

I stood up, wiped the dirt off my hands, and considered our

marketability: two sunburned young women with wet, knotted hair, drenched clothes, and Muck Boots that squeaked with each step (despite our having emptied them many times), in desperate need to get off the island. Who wouldn't want to change their vacation plans to help us get back east?

Apparently most people, especially in this weather. But Yanx and Barbara, the elderly couple on the sailboat, were not most people.

Barbara was eighty-one and Yanx was eighty-five, but they showed no sign of slowing down. Originally from Germany, they had four children and now lived in Winnipeg, where Yanx had been a professor for many years. They had traveled the world together, and it was immediately obvious that sailing on Lake Winnipeg was second nature to them. Yanx showed us handmade maps on aged paper with chicken scratches that revealed the lake depth, outlines of the shore and islands, and their favorite spots. Their memories sang of sunny days while swimming with family and romantic sunsets on their boat by private rock quarries. Through their stories, I could tell they loved each other and loved this lake.

"We can take you as far as the southeast side of Black Island. Will that work?" Barbara might well have been revealing that we had won the lottery.

"Will that work?! Anything to get us off this island is a godsend," I thought. "Yes, that'd be great!" I replied. For the first time in days Ann and I were grinning from ear to ear.

I ran into the restaurant and bought two of the largest cinnamon buns for our journey. It felt funny to purchase baked goods that we ourselves had made the day before.

"Hey Milton! I mean Marvin, sorry. We'll call you first thing when we finish our trip, okay? And you can send us that keg of Bud Light Lime."

"Sure you will," he responded sarcastically. "Isn't it cheating to get a tow?" He turned around and went back into the kitchen.

I smiled at the space behind the register where he had just stood and shrugged off a brief moment of nostalgia for our time at Gull Harbour. Marvin couldn't get me down this morning. If anything, he had really motivated us. Just think—a whole keg of cheap beer!

We loaded our gear onto Barbara and Yanx's sailboat and tied the canoe across the back. Our bow and stern stuck out on either side. They quickly joined the ranks of our river angels.

The sun disappeared behind what looked like a day's worth of cloud cover as we pushed off from the dock. Ann and I settled in by our canoe and looked back at Gull Harbour slowly slipping away in the distance, closing another chapter of our journey. The waves still seemed threatening from on top of the sailboat. We pretended our cinnamon rolls were glasses of champagne as we hit them together and laughed at our grand escape. Little did we know we had exchanged one prison for another—the shackles of hospitality.

"Lunch is ready, ladies!" called Barbara from inside. We scrambled down into the galley, where food was laid out and a little table had been set for lunch. Barbara and Yanx were very curious about our trip and prompted good discussion about things like agriculture and politics. It was the most intense conversation we had had since college, perhaps due to Yanx's background as a professor. Talking with him and Barbara made me realize how much we had learned and how so many of our experiences told a bigger story about the social, environmental, and economic state of the region we were paddling through. We shared our thoughts on farmers and water quality, small-town economies, and access to rivers and recreation in the communities we had visited. Before we knew it, lunch was over and Yanx was excitedly diving into his detailed lake maps, explaining snippets of history and the state of the lake today while he hunched over old papers in the small cabin. He pointed out where they were going to anchor for the night and the best route for us to cross from Black Island back to the east shore.

Paddling again sounded like a dream. Four days ago we were traveling the opposite direction along the south side of Black Island. Soon we would be back to where we had crossed over from the east shore, with little gained but lost time and a new desperation to get going.

Yanx told us that Lake Winnipeg is a remnant reservoir of the great glacial Lake Agassiz. Lake Agassiz drained in a few directions, one through the glacial River Warren, the parent river to the Minnesota River. He warned us that as we entered the north basin we may feel hemmed in by water all on sides. He described the east shore as lined with swamps (or muskegs, as the locals call them), leaving very little room for camping or exploration beyond the water's edge. While the beautiful white sand beaches in the south basin lured tourists from around the world, the north basin was a rugged wilderness where fewer people dared to travel.

"Tell them about the slime, Yanx!" Barbara exclaimed as she prepared tea.

"Oooooo, yes, of course. Thank you, Barbara! You ladies are in for a treat!" he responded. They bounced back and forth like this for every new topic, excited to share their expertise with newcomers.

Apparently an unavoidable challenge for us would be paddling through green slime that sometimes stretches hundreds of kilometers across the lake. The water rushing through the agricultural areas of America's Corn Belt carries with it large amounts of nitrogen and phosphorus, which, when finally settling in Lake Winnipeg, causes toxic algal blooms so immense you can see them from space. This negatively impacts the fishing and recreation industries on the lake. Yanx stressed that the algal blooms were going to be especially bad this year due to the flooding from the Red and Assiniboine Rivers, which were rapidly draining the Midwest into Manitoba.

"When you are paddling through the water, it will look like a green shaggy rug that fell into a pool. Sometimes you can see bits of it peeking above the water, but most of its gelatinous body is just below the surface. It'll probably get stuck on your paddle, too. So, good luck!"

Yanx and Barbara shared a chuckle. Their knowledge of the lake continued to astound us. Going over maps and learning about the lake quickly rolled into teatime.

"We'll be there in about half an hour, girls!" announced Yanx. We were thrilled to get on the water and were already brainstorming how far we could paddle before sunset. The waves and wind had calmed down for the first time in days.

But when we arrived and Yanx anchored, he would not let us leave. "You need dinner first. Stay for dinner." They had been so gracious to give us a tow back east that we felt obliged to stay, even though our itch to get on the water intensified with every moment we sat "relaxing" with Yanx and Barbara on the boat. As usual, I hid my frustration well, but Ann could not. She was clearly anxious to get going and was not looking to extend our little teatime much longer. At long last dinner was ready, but it was hard to engage in conversation like we had over lunch. We just wanted to hurry things along so we could paddle again. But during dinner, Yanx announced that we would be camping on the island that night and pointed out the small circular window where he thought would be a good spot.

"Thanks for the suggestion, but we're going to paddle back to the east shore tonight," Ann said nicely.

"No, no. You can't paddle tonight! The waves are still too big. Wait until tomorrow. The weather will be better tomorrow," responded Yanx.

We didn't push back.

After dinner, Yanx said he would take us to our campsite on the island, just around the bend. He was adamant that we not paddle the waves, which to us seemed like ripples compared to what we had already experienced. We watched as he tied one end of a rope onto the bow of our canoe and the other end to a small motorized boat he had just put in the water. He then instructed us to load our gear.

I didn't want to cause trouble after they had been so generous to us, but this was *ridiculous*. Yanx wanted to tow our loaded canoe (with us in it) to the island but didn't want us to paddle. We were supposed to just sit and be pulled "safely" to shore.

What did he think we had been doing this entire time? Only paddling when the water was like glass? I imagined he would not like hearing about the hailstorm on the Red River or our maneuvers above the dam before Winnipeg. Or perhaps the tailwind we had paddled to Hecla Island just days before. Having someone else dictate our schedule and route was obnoxious even if it did come from a sincere concern for our safety. Any attempt we made to suggest a different plan was shot down. Yet here we were, about to sit in a canoe while an elderly man in a motorboat pulled us through the waves to shore. That sounded like a safety hazard in itself.

Reluctantly we went along with the plan. The rope tying our canoe to the motorboat tightened quickly as we jolted forward at an alarming pace. We were not perpendicular with the waves, as we would have been if we were paddling to ensure water didn't get into our boat. Ann grabbed her paddle and started paddling even though there was little we could do to change the direction of the boat. A wave smacked us from the side, and water rolled over the gunwales into the canoe. This was Ann's breaking point.

"Stop! Stop! Let us go! Untie us!" she yelled in Yanx's direction. He was taken aback by the urgency and fear in Ann's voice. Perhaps that's what he needed to get the message, to understand what we'd been trying to say this whole time: let us go. And at last, he did.

Ann untied the rope from the bow and began to paddle. I grabbed my paddle, sank it deep into the oncoming waves, and felt a rush of energy and a sense of home flow over me.

Around the bend on Black Island, Yanx pointed out the spot where we should camp. "We'll bring you breakfast in the morning, around eight. Get some good sleep tonight," he said. Then he was off.

Once the tiny motorboat was out of sight, Ann looked back with a look of annoyance and relief. "Let's get outta here, yeah?" she said. Again, we were on the same page. It seemed like all we did lately was escape.

I redirected the canoe to the northeast, and we set off once more. Barbara and Yanx would bring us breakfast the next morning, only to discover that we were not there. They would wonder what happened to those two young women they helped on Lake Winnipeg. I couldn't articulate why I was annoyed. Neither could Ann. Strangers had taken us in, done us a huge favor, and fed and taken care of us. They were loving and kind people. It wasn't that we were ungrateful; rather, it was that somewhere, mixed in with their abundant generosity, we had lost control. We had lost our freedom to choose.

Ten kilometers into our evening paddle we found a large granite rock that seemed like a heavenly place to set up camp. We were back on the east side of the lake, at last. Our quick detour to see the Menogyn group had turned into a multiday unexpected side adventure. The lake was beginning to teach us a thing or two about patience, but our time at Gull Harbour was only a glimpse of the strong winds, massive waves, and debilitating isolation we would soon experience.

Ecstatic to be on the move again after several days of sitting and waiting, we celebrated with a delicious dinner of chili and cheese and opened up the bag of chips that David Squire had given us during his short visit to Gull Harbour. The next day we would paddle out of the south basin of Lake Winnipeg and into the infamous north basin, completing another milestone in our journey. We toasted our progress with the chips just like we had the cinnamon buns earlier that day (who knows what we would do with actual champagne). "Onward!" we said, as we crunched our chips together in the air. After a few games of cribbage and a lullaby on the travel guitar, we fell fast asleep, feeling at home back in our tent on the east shore.

〰〰〰

THE NORTH BASIN OF LAKE WINNIPEG is vast and desolate. The lake resembles a large fish, with its tail to the south and its body narrowing before opening up to the north. We had traversed the tail, had progressed through the narrowing body, and now were entering the ribcage—the unforgiving belly of the beast. Eric and Walter got a tow for this part of the journey because it was getting late in the season and they didn't know how long it would take them to complete the lake. Back then, the lake was home to a booming fishing industry, so it was easier to get a ride on a steamship or fishing boat from Berens River to Norway House. As we learned from Yanx and Barbara, the fishing industry had diminished, due partly to the algal blooms in the lake. Now there are only a few active fishing towns left on the north basin. We had calculated that we could paddle the entire lake, 416 kilometers as the crow flies, in twelve days, but with our most recent detour we were just entering the north basin on day eight. It would take us twelve more days to reach the Nelson River at Warren's Landing. Ann liked to say it felt like three months.

The next morning we paddled Loon Straits, the narrow four-kilometer-wide channel separating the south and north basins. There was a soft south wind and sunny skies. At last, the lake let up and let us really paddle. The shoreline changed from white sand beaches to large granite outcroppings and small islands. When we popped into Granite Quarry Cove to eat lunch and explore the old site, we surprised a family on their sailboat. They, like Yanx and Barbara, had their own special spots on the lake. We gave a small wave in between paddle strokes and continued to shore.

A dark cloud came into view above the tall granite cliffs. Another day, another storm on the lake. We decided it was time to go. Paddling past the sailboat on our way out of the inlet, Ann yelled, "Could you give us the weather forecast?"

The woman nodded, disappeared into the cabin, and emerged with a large radio. We paddled closer so we could hear.

In between spurts of white noise a man's nasally voice read the weather forecast: wind speed (in knots), temperature (in Celsius), and precipitation (in millimeters).

"Khhhh . . . Wind at . . . khhh . . . knots from . . . khhh . . . the southwest . . ." We listened until the weather report started from the beginning again. It was forecasted to rain that night, but we would get a strong tailwind in the morning. I looked out at the gentle water and dramatic granite cliffs around me. Even if there was a storm coming in, at least we weren't sitting in an office watching the clock tick.

We thanked the woman and grabbed our paddles to continue on our way. I stopped and looked up at her with one last request.

"If you meet a couple named Barbara and Yanx, will you tell them that we are alive and well?" I asked. It must have been a strange departing comment because the woman squinted her eyes and nodded slowly. Perhaps she thought we had run away from home.

Until now, the western winds had masked any smell of smoke from the fires to the east (which were likely started by the lightning storm on the night of the bear scare). The air smelled like a campfire the entire day and into the night.

We reached the southern point of Bloodvein Bay and set up camp. If the forecast on the radio was correct, the winds would be in our favor the next day to guide us thirteen kilometers across the bay. In the middle of the crossing, we would be at least six kilometers away from land in any direction. If the wind was not on our side, we would take the safer route and trace the shore, even though it would double our travel time.

In the tent that night we pored over the maps and agreed that the quicker route would be best, if possible. We had to compensate for lost time.

A TALE OF TINY BOATS

~~~~~~~✕~~~~~~~

I AWOKE TO AN UNFAMILIAR SILENCE. Our tent was not flapping in the wind, and the sounds of people rummaging about in the early morning were absent. A bird call broke the stillness, as if to say, "Wake up! Today is going to be a good day!" I hopped into my morning routine with a sense of urgency. Always a sense of urgency. That's how Ann and I were "raised" at camp.

By now we had developed an unwavering morning routine. First, I'd pull the plug on the Therm-a-Rest. If Ann was not already awake, or vice versa, the sound of air rushing out of a sleeping pad was a passive-aggressive way of saying, "Get the heck outta bed, you lazy bum." This signaled the true beginning of the day. Then I would stuff my sleeping bag into its compression sack to eliminate any temptation of crawling back into it.

Whenever possible, I would sleep in my "day clothes" so I wouldn't waste time getting dressed in the morning. Then I would shove everything into my purple compression dry bag, push out all of the air, roll it up, and clip it shut. Next, I would unzip the tent, throw everything out, run out, and zip it behind me as fast as possible to keep out any bugs looking to hitch a ride for the day. At this point, whoever was out of the tent first started smugly unstaking it. This says, "Uh-oh! Too slow!" to the person scrambling to get their things out. One time on a thirty-day canoe trip through Wabakimi Provincial Park in Ontario, my friends actually did collapse the entire tent on me because I was moving too slowly. Never again!

Once out of the tent, I would start making breakfast and coffee. One of our favorite items on trail was a brown-camo plastic French press mug. It looked cheap (it was) but could quickly make enough coffee for two people and was durable enough to survive being thrown around the canoe all day. We would usually make two rounds of coffee, one for the morning and one for the day. The ugly camo mug was one of the items that never found a permanent home in our canoe or packs. It lived like we did—just floating around. While I prepared breakfast, Ann would pack up the rest of our gear and bring the canoe to the lake or the river, half in the water and half out, and load everything that was ready.

Then we'd play the hurry up and wait game. Getting out of the tent and packing up as quickly and efficiently as possible was vital to get a good start on the day. But so was casually eating breakfast. This is what we referred to as the "danger zone" of packing out. It didn't matter how quickly we moved before breakfast if we relaxed too much during morning coffee. Sometimes we would linger too long over our bowls of mushy oatmeal and then have to rush to leave camp. But that feeling of finally pushing off from shore was unbeatable. It was like reliving the day we pushed off from Fort Snelling, day after day.

We pushed off that morning with our eyes set on Bloodvein Bay. Conditions were perfect for the thirteen-kilometer crossing to Princess Harbour. A light tailwind pushed us on our way, but the push soon became a shove. We were kilometers from land in any direction. If we needed to get off the water it would be challenging. If we turned any other direction than north we wouldn't be going with the waves, which put us at risk of getting sideswiped. The wind didn't make us decide just yet, though. We still had time to paddle comfortably. But as time went by, I noticed that Ann stopped being chatty and I began to sing old jazz standards—the telltale signs of fear.

The wind shifted direction twice within the hour. We were only halfway across the bay. The swells grew. The beast was taking bigger breaths beneath us.

"Stop singing!" Ann yelled from the bow. I obliged. I was singing to calm my nerves, but it stressed Ann out.

"Turn in," she said definitively. I agreed that the waves were too large (and getting larger) to continue north. Even if I had wanted to protest, it was unlikely that we'd be able to hear each other over the wind.

The beast's claws scraped at the sky from the water below. The large swells grew taller and sharper, threatening to crest and crash with each peak. If we swamped here we would be in trouble. We would lose everything and have to swim ten kilometers to shore. I was confident that we would survive if we tipped, but our canoe and everything in it would surely sink to the bottom of the lake. I distracted myself by thinking about how we would somehow find another canoe. Ending the trip was not an option. I didn't know why, but it felt like our destiny to paddle to Hudson Bay.

We directed Canoey toward an island ahead, about three kilometers out from the east shore, which would provide a safe place to wait out the wind. We paddled hard to our new destination, not noticing the plane flying low just behind us. "Watch out!" I yelled, but Ann could not hear me over the wind and waves. All of a sudden, like an eagle diving from the sky to catch a fish, the plane dove in between us and the island to scoop up water from the lake and then flew back into the sky and headed east. We were only a football field away from being scooped into the large bucket on the bottom of the plane. I wasn't convinced they saw us, a seventeen-foot canoe in open water. I thought the plane must have been collecting water to put out the fires to the east. Fear overcame me and I instinctively began to sing, this time under my breath so Ann could not hear. We were almost to the island. But we needed to maneuver some big waves to get there.

We circled the island and beached the canoe where the water was calm and protected from the west wind. After hours of sitting and waiting, making biscuits, and playing cribbage, the waves and wind calmed down and the weather turned dark and curiously calm. This was our window. We launched once more to cross Bloodvein Bay, this time sticking much closer to the shore.

Threatening dark clouds broke open halfway to Princess Harbour. Rain poured from the sky so heavy and hard that we could no longer see anything in front of us. We had to trust that the direction we were paddling would get us to Princess Harbour. I nervously watched the growing water puddle on the bottom of the canoe.

"See that dock? Let's pull out there!" Ann yelled. It was hard to hear anything with the rain and with my jacket cinched tight around my head. Luckily I saw the dock, too. Little houses came into view along the shore. Generally, we avoided camping near buildings or signs of people, but the rain was too much. Any longer and it would fill our boat to the brim with water. Plus, it was already 9:30 p.m. It had taken the entire day to cross Bloodvein Bay. We pulled up on the dock, emptied the water out of our canoe, and dragged our wet gear onto the shores of Princess Harbour.

The town looked abandoned. The grass was tall, the dock needed some fixing up, and it was pitch-black inside the windows of the little houses nearby. We looked closer and saw two houses farther up the shore with lights on.

"Better ask permission, whaddya think?" I asked Ann. We hadn't had a problem settling into Gull Harbour without asking, but something about this place felt different.

"Yeah, let's split up. You take that house. I'll take the other," Ann said as we marched off.

I arrived at my house first and knocked on the door. An elderly woman named Brenda answered. I thought she had to be over eighty years old, and I wondered if she lived here all by herself. I jumped into my spiel: Hudson Bay, women, paddlers, storm, waves, camp by the boat launch, yada yada. She got the idea and gave us her blessing to camp by the dock before retreating back into her home.

Not a minute later, Ann knocked on the door a little farther up the shore. An elderly couple in their pajamas opened it and smiled.

"We know why you're here. Of course you can stay," said Frank.

His wife, Myrtle, winked in agreement with a look of admiration on her face. They, too, must have been over eighty years old. Apparently, Brenda had already called and given them the news. Ann was confused, but we learned quickly that word travels fast in Princess Harbour.

Back at the dock, we set up camp in the dark and peeled off our wet clothes in the tent, exchanging our day clothes for our dry night clothes before cozying into our sleeping bags. I felt like I could face any weather during the day if we had warm, dry sleeping bags waiting for us at night. We fell asleep to the light pitter-patter of the dissipating rain against our nylon home until a strange sound woke us up the next morning.

SNIFF SNIFF SNIFF. Someone was outside of our tent. A big four-legged someone, whose nose was gently pushing against the rain fly. Remembering our bear incident, I awoke abruptly to investigate.

"Rufus! C'mon now. Leave the ladies alone," said Frank from outside.

We popped our heads out of the tent to see a big brown dog sniffing our gear, checking out the new company. Frank was on an ATV by the dock.

"Well, now that you ladies are up, Myrtle wanted me to tell you that breakfast is ready!" He rode off toward the houses, with Rufus trailing behind.

At breakfast we learned that Princess Harbour was once a vibrant fishing community and home to hundreds of people. The town is on a peninsula that juts out into the northern end of Bloodvein Bay and is only accessible by boat. Only ten people lived there now, and population growth didn't look promising: six out of the ten residents were over the age of eighty, and two others were a gay couple who moved there from Winnipeg. And most of them were related. We heard about their family tree while shoveling eggs and bacon into our mouths: Frank was married to Myrtle, and Frank's brother was Ed, Brenda's husband, whose son and his husband lived in the modern home by the dock.

I felt a wave of peace and safety sitting and chatting with Frank, Myrtle, Ed, and Brenda. They were like wizards or mages of the lake, living in a small village and using their magic powers to garden and spread joy to everyone who crossed their path. There was something almost beyond human about them. When we told them about our expedition, they showed no skepticism or confusion. They understood what we were doing and wholeheartedly encouraged and supported our journey.

After breakfast, Frank said, "I'd like to show you something, if that's all right?" He was refreshingly sensitive to our time and schedule. I glanced out the window at the waves crashing onto shore. It was obvious we had time to kill. And for some reason it felt like we were supposed to be here.

The smell of freshly shaven wood and glue wafted into our nostrils as Frank opened the door to a small room. Light flooded through the windows so bright that I could see the dust stirring in the air. There was no need to flip the light switch to see the masterpieces in front of us. Small intricate ships lined the walls on misshapen wooden shelves. My eyes traveled from boat to boat, taking in every detail—the names perfectly painted on the sides, the small windows, the lookout towers, even the safety boats and their pulley systems. Then I looked at Frank. He grinned wildly with watery eyes. I realized he probably didn't get to share his life's work with people very often. He had handcrafted every boat that had sailed on Lake Winnipeg.

"The SS *Colvile* had its heyday in the late 1800s," Frank explained as he pointed at one of his meticulously built models. "It was built for the Hudson's Bay Company and generally traveled in between the Red River and the Saskatchewan River." He moved from one to the other, sharing their history and purpose on the lake. We spotted the SS *Wolverine,* the passenger and cargo boat that carried Eric Sevareid and Walter Port across the north basin of Lake Winnipeg.

"Queen Elizabeth II was a passenger on this beauty," Frank said as he pointed at the largest ship in his collection. The MS *Lord Selkirk II* carried thousands of passengers on multiday excursions to Lake Winnipeg, complete with dining rooms, cabins, lounges, and other amenities. She sailed for seventeen years before retiring in 1970. "They used her for scrap metal in the end," explained Frank, a little disheartened. How something so fancy and fabulous with such rich history could be turned into scrap metal was understandably sorrowful. He was especially proud to bring that boat back to life through his work.

He walked over to a cabinet and pulled out two handmade wooden birds painted with the words "Princess Harbour" across the top.

"Take these with you to remember us," he said. There was something sad in his tone, as if he knew that he was near the end of his life, that they were *all* nearing the end, and Princess Harbour was not going to live on once they passed away. It would become just another ghost town like so many other once vibrant waterfront communities.

We left the model ships and joined everyone in the living room to watch the daily news. Once we heard the weather—it would be a calm night—I could feel Ann's itch to get going.

"We're going to go check out the lake and see if we can leave soon," I announced, breaking everyone's silent contemplation of a world outside of their own.

"Have Rufus keep you company!" said Myrtle, still looking at the television. The big brown dog popped up from behind the couch, as if he had been eagerly waiting to hear his name amid the noise. He followed us out the door.

Ann and I walked, with Rufus in tow, across an old airstrip that transects the peninsula to scout the waves on the exposed waters to the north. They were even larger than those on the other end. We were windbound again.

On our walk back we talked about how free we felt here. Unlike with the old German couple and the owner at Gull Harbour, we felt like we could do whatever we wanted to here without offending our new friends. Usually we'd be distraught to be windbound. But our weather worries faded when we realized we'd get to spend the day with warm and interesting people. They felt like our own grandparents. We walked back into the house to find that everyone had moved from the living room back to the kitchen to play games. The cards were out and the coffee and tea were flowing. Our kind of people.

Continuing the tradition of sharing music with our hosts (which is about all we could offer in return for their hospitality), we pulled out the travel guitar and ukulele to entertain them while they played cards.

Over tea we learned more about the history of the lake and Princess Harbour. Freighters used to come through with fish shipments and boats would anchor in the harbor, sometimes for the whole summer. The population in 1985 was a whopping twenty-three people. They explained that traffic had gone down over the years because of gas prices, but I couldn't help but think that the algal blooms Yanx told us about were partly to blame. In turn, we shared stories from our travels, and the hours flew by.

Around 7:00 p.m. Ann noticed that the waves had gone down. "How do you feel about another night paddle?" she asked.

"Let's do it. Dinner first, though?" I responded. Myrtle and Frank were cooking in the kitchen. It would be advantageous for us to start the night paddle with full stomachs. And part of me never wanted to leave Princess Harbour.

After dinner we packed up our tent and gear and loaded our canoe.

"Phone us from Berens River. We'll be thinking of you!" they said as we pushed off the dock.

Ready for adventure!

The flooded Minnesota River has claimed many victims, including this Chevrolet.

Approaching a generating station on the Minnesota River

Portaging the dam at Minnesota Falls

Pelican crossing, downstream on the channelized Bois de Sioux River

A sign of uncertain danger on the Red River

We played *a lot* of cribbage in the tent.

Ann sings a lullaby on the travel guitar.

Kawena Kinomaeta set free on the shores of Lake Winnipeg

Hopelessly windbound as another storm moves in on Lake Winnipeg

Yanx and his sailboat save us from a dull fate at Gull Harbour on Lake Winnipeg.

We explore a quarry inlet along the east shore of Lake Winnipeg.

The sleepy village of Princess Harbour on Lake Winnipeg

The immense expanse of Lake Winnipeg

Treaty and York Boat Days at Norway House

Myhan in her natural habitat

A tricky rapid set on the Hayes River

Hudson Bay Bound Spring Break on Lake Opiminegoka

Cooking dinner at last light near Knife Rapids on the Hayes River

Branding our paddles at York Factory

Exploring the Hudson's Bay Company outpost at York Factory

Our fierce protector settles into her new life as a canoe dog.

We were sorry to say goodbye to our new friends. Ann expressed that she wanted to retire there. But we both knew the sad truth: Princess Harbour would probably not exist very long into the future. At least not in the way it seemed to us now. Indeed, the 2016 census would show a population of zero in the once beloved town.

~~~~~~

WE DEPARTED AS THE LAST RAYS OF SUN nestled beyond the horizon. There were touches of pink and purple in the cloudless sky, and the wind had danced off to another lake, for now. The remaining light slowly gave way to darkness, and the stars multiplied across the night sky. The lake was completely flat, like black glass that graciously gave way to our canoe and perfectly mirrored the sky. Every shining constellation was both above us and below us. It looked and felt like we were paddling through space.

I was in the stern. I always felt Ann's hesitance when I took the stern, which I did every other day, just like we agreed. Was it a need to be in control? Or maybe she thought I was incompetent in the stern? I couldn't be sure. I aimed my sights and the canoe at a faraway point across the horizon. The gift of a still night was not lost on me. We could make thirty or forty kilometers on a night like this. And who knew what the wind would bring tomorrow.

Ann was uncomfortable with our distance from shore. We were three or four kilometers away from land in the middle of the night on the eleventh-largest lake in the world, which had already shown us its unforgiving strength and unpredictable behavior. A few hours into the crossing, she asked if I could point the canoe a little closer to shore. I could tell from the way she asked that she had been thinking about it for quite some time. I could also tell that it was not a question but a demand. I obliged, or at least thought I obliged, and angled the boat slightly closer to shore. It saddened me to turn away from the quickest route. After some time, Ann spoke up again. She wanted to get even closer to shore. Once again, I thought I had fixed the problem. Apparently not.

Ann blew up. She blew up like she had wanted to since the beginning of the trip. How come she had to be the fun police all the time, she asked. How come I never took responsibility for our safety? Why did it always have to be her job?

Ugh, I hate conflict. HATE IT! I remember in middle school sitting on a bus next to my first "boyfriend," trying to break up with him. He was crying on my shoulder. I was silent for a long time while I thought about all of the awesome things I could tell him to make the situation better. He is a great person and has lots of friends and is going to be fine! It is important for us to move on and be happy. After all of my brilliant brainstorming, I finally opened my mouth and said, "Just get over it." I stood up and walked away.

That's exactly how I felt now with Ann yelling at me. I'm going to have to say words, and they are going to have to be good. The truth was, the way I cope with fear is by being chill. The more Ann stressed out, the more it made me relax. The more I relaxed, the more Ann stressed.

After lots of internal back and forth, I finally spoke: "There's nothing I can do, Ann. It's just my personality."

What Ann heard, however, must have been, "Sorry, can't help you." As if a stranger had just asked me for change on the street. "Sorry, not my problem." She responded that I never tried to be there for our relationship. Whenever I found something bright and shiny to play with, I was off, at the expense of everyone around me. She wasn't completely wrong.

Years and years of pent-up frustrations with each other came out. Like pulling weeds from a neglected garden bed. We started from the beginning and eventually came to the trip, to our current frustrations. We were loosening the soil with each weed we pulled, which makes it slightly easier to tackle the big stuff. Slightly. Ann elaborated on how she didn't trust me because I didn't put our safety first. She said I was compromising our relationship because I was always thinking about the fastest or most fun way to do things.

What perfect combination of words could I orchestrate to make this better? My ego was damaged beyond repair. I had done some serious destruction, too. I could tell Ann was still boiling by just looking at the back of her head. I wanted her to know that I loved her and that everything was going to be fine. But I also wanted to tell her that I was pissed at her, too, because I felt like she always had to be in charge, like my opinions didn't matter because we were going to do whatever she wanted to do in the end. But there was nothing to say. So we paddled in unresolved silence. I pointed the canoe much closer to shore to keep sparks from flying as we moved forward.

Unbeknownst to us during our fight, the northern lights had appeared in the night sky, as if trying to get our attention while we were blindly yelling at each other. It was the very first time I had ever seen them. The sky lit up with green dancing strings and reflected on the lake, as small ripples frolicked on top of the previously still water. I wanted so badly to tell Ann that this was the most magnificent moment of my life and I was thrilled to experience this with her. But then I remembered I wasn't talking to her.

Here I was in a canoe with my best friend watching the northern lights for the first time. I finally had someone, someone I loved dearly, to share a magical moment with. Someone to turn to and say, "How cool is this?" But we continued our silent brigade.

As Ann had requested, our canoe was now much closer to shore. The northern lights had subdued, and darkness once again reigned over the lake in the wee hours of the morning. It was difficult to see where the water ended and the shore began, but I had an inkling that we were *too* close to shore. I was overcompensating.

When I opened my mouth to speak, it was dry. I was nervous to say anything at all. We hadn't spoken for hours. But Ann had an epic headlamp, much brighter than mine, so I asked if she would shine her light toward shore so I could better gauge where we were. She silently obliged. Two huge green eyes reflected in the light, staring at us from about thirty yards away. A giant bull moose had been watching us this whole time. "Yep," Ann said, briefly breaking her silence. "We're too close to shore." For a brief moment I wanted to laugh.

I redirected away from the moose. The ripples in the lake were growing stronger in response to the new breeze that seemed to whisper, "I'm coming." A gentle warning. We adhered to the signs and pulled over on a nearby peninsula to camp. Just as we slithered inside our sleeping bags for the night, the wind howled and rain began to patter on our tent. A gentle applause for our wonderful decision making.

A few hours later, I awoke to find that the wind was still blowing steadily on the sides of the tent and the sun was just coming up. Ann was wide awake. She thought she heard something walking around outside. For the first time on our trip, I pretended to be concerned. I, not Ann, got out of my sleeping bag and went outside to see if there was anything, a bear or moose, wandering around our camp. I did a thorough job, too, narrating to Ann what I was seeing, walking around a bit, assuring her that everything looked normal. It was such a small thing to do, but in that moment I understood how I needed to fix our relationship. I had to pretend to care about little sounds in the night. I had to pretend to deliberate over the waves and wind each morning. I had to pretend to step up and be the person responsible for our every move. Just by pretending, I would actually *be* that person, allowing Ann to relax a bit and renounce her role as "the fun police." I at least owed it to her to try.

I climbed back into the tent feeling like a warrior returning from battle only to find Ann looking unamused. For a moment, I forgot we were fighting. It was going to take more than simply checking on camp to fix this mess, and I was too restless to fall asleep. Ann snoozed off again. She looked mad at me even in her sleep. I rummaged through our bag of trail notes and opened one from my older brother:

Natalie and Ann,

You two are doing the coolest thing imaginable after graduation. All I did was cook fish and smoke pot for a year. This blows that out of the water. Good luck and safe travels. Natalie, I am so unbelievably proud of you. You have more guts than anyone I know, and you are using them to the fullest. Don't listen to anyone who does not recognize your form of ambition. I love you very much and can't wait to see what you will do next.

Love, your brother,
Tim

His words reminded me of the real reason we were doing this expedition. Tears flowed down my cheeks as I flipped to an empty page in my journal. For me, writing has always been easier than talking. So I grabbed my pen in hopes that it would help me articulate my heart and mind.

Ann,

We knew that doing this trip would take lots of planning and time spent with each other. I think that the fact we wanted to do the trip together is a testament to how much we value our relationship. Even though this trip may be difficult, we will come out strong. I'm sorry if I've seemed careless—in a way I thought if I kept my cool maybe we could counterbalance each other. I know you think I view you as an anxious person, and I think you view me as a careless person, but we should work to change that before any more resentment builds.

Last night was a spectacular paddle and I was happy you were there to share the night sky with me. I have really enjoyed our trip so far, every windbound day and every rainstorm. In fact, I just felt a raindrop! We should play cribbage. I think the main thing I wanted to say was that we are sisters. Like sisters, we accept the other for their differences, fight occasionally, and recognize that our friendship is forever.

P.S. This lake is HUGE.

I handed Ann the letter when she woke up. The wind was too strong and the waves were too large to paddle. I lay on my back, watching the side of the tent cave in and push out, swaying back and forth in the wind.

Ann looked up from the note. "Want to play cribbage?"

WINDBOUND TO NORWAY HOUSE

THE WIND FINALLY DIED DOWN enough for us to push off from shore without getting too much water in our boat. Our relationship was on the upswing, and it felt like our friendship woes were somehow tied to our windbound days—the weather and the challenges we faced afflicted our moods as well. Now that we were rebuilding our friendship, it felt like nothing could go wrong. But by midday the weather picked up again. The transition of the water from manageable to dangerous was gradual, like the almost imperceptible movement of the sun across the afternoon sky. Our conversation waned as we began to notice how the waves had snuck up on us. Somehow we had missed all the warning signs.

Before long, I was looking down on Ann from the crest of a wave and instinctively began to sing the usual jazz standards. Remembering that Ann doesn't like it when I sing in stressful situations and that I was supposed to care more about our safety, I instead broke the ice: "The waves are getting pretty big. Let's pull over." I congratulated myself for stepping up as the safety police for once. Ann made no comment.

When people spoke to us of Lake Winnipeg before our trip, they described its beautiful long white sand beaches. What we were seeing was something very different. Manitoba Hydro, the hydroelectric power company in Manitoba, manages the water level on the lake. The once wild lake is now a large reservoir. And this summer the water level was eight feet above normal, which meant that instead of white sand beaches we had, on one side, small beaches next to a berm and, on the other side, a literal swamp. Needless to say, our camping options were limited.

Sometimes we had to camp uncomfortably close to the water to find flat and solid ground. The crashing waves so close to us at night sounded like cars passing on a highway. It reminded me of the time on the Minnesota River when I pretended the light shining on our tent from the headlights of a car was really the light from a bright full moon.

We crash-landed on a small beach, luckily with no damage to the boat or ourselves. It was only midafternoon. I began setting up the "kitchen" (a burner connected to a gas canister) and dug around for food in the bear barrel. Typically for lunch we would hastily consume cold salami and cheese burritos on the side of the lake, hyperaware of the time we were wasting while the weather was on our side. I looked up to see that our hammock had been expertly tied between two trees, frantically dancing in the wind. Ann must have thought we'd be here for a while. I looked out at the lake. The large swells in the distance turned into whitecaps that eventually crashed onto the beach like mighty ocean waves. The force of the water and the endless horizon made me forget momentarily that we were on a lake.

"Chef Natalie, at your service, madam! Tonight, we are serving pancakes with rehydrated blueberry compote!" I said in a British accent as I put a burned pancake into Ann's metal bowl and covered it with blue slime. Ann's courteous chuckle turned into a loud shriek.

I responded, "Oh c'mon, it's not *that* bad, AnnnooooOOOHHH MY GOD!" There was a snake just feet away from her.

I'd like to say that we didn't overreact. In truth, it was Ann who remained calm while I ran into the tent and zipped it up. I'm not proud of it. I poked my head out of the tent door to see Ann in a fencing position with a long stick as her foil. While I was scurrying for safety she had tossed a stick at the snake to scare it away but, in doing so, had managed to lodge the snake between two sticks. Now it was doing that head up, mouth open, tongue out thing that snakes do in movies. God dammit!

"Just free it, Ann! Lift up that stick with your stick!" I yelled from my bunker.

"But it's freaking out!" Ann was still holding her fencing stance. I wondered what other things she had learned at private Catholic school.

"You can do it!" I yelled, suddenly having turned into a confident spectator.

In one fell swoop Ann plunged her stick into the space below the stick holding the snake. The stick flew into the air, and the snake quickly slithered away into a pile of branches by the berm, about ten feet away from where we were eating lunch. "My hero!" I exclaimed as I exited the tent. Ann the warrior stood victorious with her sword now resting at her side.

We continued eating. "Ann, your resume is going to look awesome after this trip. 'Stick fencing and snake capture and rescue, 2011 to present.' It'll look way cooler than 'summer intern at nature center'!"

Just then another snake came by. And then another. Our concern grew with each passing snake. I glanced over at the pile of branches. Then I looked closer. Tangled in the pile were dozens of snakes. It was hard to tell where the sticks began and the snakes ended. Ann saw this, too, and we reached an immediate nonverbal agreement—it was time to go, immediately.

We later learned that the inner-lake region of Manitoba is home to the largest concentration of snakes in the world, most notably the red-sided garter snake. The Narcisse Snake Dens, where tens of thousands of garter snakes overwinter in huge limestone cracks below the frost line, was only 145 kilometers to the southwest of where we were stranded.

We hurriedly packed everything up and loaded our canoe. I tucked the gun along the side of the boat next to one of our packs. Almost every morning for six weeks we had been tearing down camp and expertly packing out (even though it probably looked like an unorganized mess to anyone else). We were in default mode. After zipping up our life jackets and loading water bottles under our canoe seats, we looked out at the crashing waves. Our spirits sank. There was no way we could push off in these conditions. We took up the only unoccupied real estate on the beach and crouched down by the canoe. Trapped between snakes and waves, we waited for our chance to escape.

When the wind finally let up, we guided the canoe into the lake, letting it ride the waves as we walked out with it until the water was up to our knees. We tacked up and down the shoreline, cutting the waves as they came toward us and riding them back to the shore before turning around, cutting through, and riding them back again, until we saw open space that would make for a good campsite.

Our canoe was like a surfboard as we ruddered wildly to remain on course, ever at the mercy of the large waves. When we landed I looked back in the direction we had come from and could still see the snake-infested beach. On an expedition, there is nothing more demoralizing than being able to see your previous campsite from your current one. Something about it is worse than not moving at all. Which, unbeknownst to us, was our next big challenge.

Ann put rocks and logs on top of the tent stakes to make sure our home didn't fly away. The wind was persistent and showed no sign of flagging. It howled from the west for three straight days. The days we spent on that small beach on the east shore of Lake Winnipeg blurred together like a movie filmed all on one set.

On the first day we caught up on sleep. The sun shone bright on our blue tent and created a calming light inside. The wind caused the sides of our tent to flutter and dance around us while we napped. I closed my eyes and imagined I was resting on a beach in Jamaica or Hawaii. But the comforting sun, warm breeze, and lull of crashing waves somehow felt less relaxing on the east shore of Lake Winnipeg.

I went through phases of sleeping, waking, and then falling back into dreams. Ann, too, was tucked into her sleeping bag for most of the day. Our bodies had been active for so long that they seemed happy for the opportunity to shut down completely.

It was 9:30 a.m. on the second day. Ann was still asleep and the wind still howled from the west. Windbound again. We were in purgatory—desperate to move on but unable to proceed. Our priorities shifted: Cribbage. Guitar. Sleep. Eat. Cribbage. Sleep. Monitor the sky. A storm was coming. Hunker down. Wait it out. Restake the tent. Make sure the canoe doesn't fly away.

I sank into a deep depression. Day turned into night, but time had lost all meaning. There was no one to see and nowhere to go. I felt like we would never leave this beach we had learned to hate. How long could the wind persist? It answered our question with the same song the next morning. We didn't debate whether or not to paddle this time. We didn't even bother to talk.

Ann walked off along the beach, while I meandered on the berm. Something caught my eye. It was a bush that had what looked like pea pods hanging just above the sand. I picked one and opened it. It was empty. I opened one after another to find that they were all empty, probably past their prime for the season.

My journey from one bush to the next led me closer to the beach, where I found a small, intricate piece of driftwood. It reminded me of the sticks and snakes at our previous campsite. It seemed like weeks ago that we had come across them. I collected the driftwood and stacked it into different shapes: a bear, a canoe, a woman. My eyes traced the beach for more washed-up treasure and landed on Ann in the distance, fully engaged in drawing pictures in the sand with her finger.

Something about today was different. We saw everything around us in a new light. Instead of feeling trapped or anxious about waiting, Ann and I had entered a new state of mind. We felt like five-year-olds playing in a sandbox. Entertainment was everywhere, from the plants and shrubs to the driftwood on the sandy beach. I spent five hours trying to whittle a recorder out of a long piece of driftwood (it didn't work) and enjoyed every moment of it—from the sound the knife made scratching against the moist wood to the sight of the twisted shrivels of bark that fell around my feet before blowing away in the wind. I closed my eyes and took slow, deep breaths in rhythm with the crashing waves. The air was the perfect temperature. I reflected on why I put myself through the turmoil of these long journeys.

Suddenly, something unnatural sparkled in the distance. Ann saw it, too. We reunited on the beach and broke the silence to discuss what it could be. The glimmer came and went methodically like a flashing streetlight. Like a paddle reflecting the sun's bright rays in between strokes.

"It's a canoe," Ann said under her breath, slowly getting used to using her voice again.

And with that, we snapped back into reality.

"Ann . . . if they can paddle, that means we can paddle, too!" I thought out loud. She was way ahead of me and was already taking down the tent.

The canoer must have seen us, too, because the boat was aimed straight for our campsite. Ann took a closer look and whispered, "No freaking way . . . it can't be . . ."

Months earlier, when we were packing out for the trip, we realized that we had forgotten to buy yoke pads for our canoe. While we wouldn't have many portages, the few we did have would be much less painful with cushions in between our shoulders and the hard wood of the canoe's yoke.

Ann ran out to an outdoor store in Minneapolis called Midwest Mountaineering, where a very helpful employee named Bear helped her find the right yoke pads. Bear was memorable: a tall, lanky, outgoing character with a great name who was very excited about our journey. Ann rushed home and threw the pads in our "Winnipeg drop" bag.

The glittering canoe came closer. Sure enough, it was Bear, soloing a Pakboat up and down the waves. He somehow managed to keep his boat straight while waving a friendly hello in our direction.

We were shocked to see anyone at all. But to see someone who knew our home and community was a special treat. The three of us stood together on the beach looking out at the waves, swapping stories and musing at our chance encounter. Bear eventually announced that he should be on his way. He ungracefully pushed his boat into the crashing waves and took off. It felt as if we had just run into each other on a city street walking opposite directions and now had to get back to our own lives. Our brief encounter with Bear on the beach fueled us with the energy we needed to move forward. We were free from the shackles of our isolation and windbound days. Somehow the waves looked less foreboding now, too. It was time to go.

Our water supply was running low after three days, and my throat had become dry and scratchy. The last of the supply sloshing in the Nalgene at my feet enticed me, but I did not indulge for fear that it would be awhile before we could locate fresh water. In an emergency, we could use our water filter to refill our dromedaries. While the water looked clear and clean in some places, it was hard to forget the Red River's murky polluted water that emptied into Lake Winnipeg. We weren't that desperate, yet.

The sun was quickly setting as we approached the mouth of the Poplar River. We camped just outside of the Poplar River First Nation reservation and waited until morning to venture into town. At 5:00 a.m. we paddled into the Poplar River against a strong headwind. We mused about the day ahead—it was early for the wind to be awake. Three hours later we pulled onto shore. It felt like we had arrived early to a movie set, before all of the actors and directors crowded the empty streets and abandoned buildings.

Ann stayed back with the boat while I walked around. I found the Northern Store without too much trouble, but it wasn't open until 10:00 a.m. There was a very clean and modern house next to it that seemed completely out of place with its surroundings. I saw a young man walking around and inquired where I could refill our water supply. He, too, was a visitor and had just arrived to meet with the manager of the store. We joined forces and become a search party of two.

An old woman appeared from a nearby house to smoke a cigarette. "Did you know?" she shouted in our direction. "Cigarettes here are eighteen bucks a pack. Expensive habit!"

"Do you know where we can find the owner of the Northern Store?" I responded, ignoring her comment. We were still a good distance away from her.

She pointed to the nice house behind us, put out her cigarette, and went back inside. This, too, felt like a scene in a movie. Perhaps the lack of water was getting to me.

We knocked on the door several times. No answer. I turned away to continue my search for water elsewhere when a large shirtless man appeared in the doorway with sleepy eyes and a grumpy tone in his voice. "Whaddaya want?"

He said I could refill our water in his sink. I slipped inside, unknowingly bringing in sneaky spiders hitchhiking on the dromedary bags. No one seemed interested in chatting. I made quick work of refilling our water and dipped out of the house to catch back up with Ann. Even for this short time, it felt strange to be away from her.

I grinned when Ann came into sight. Not because I was excited to be reunited again, but because she had a hilariously annoyed expression on her face, which was clearly the upshot of being talked at by some man on the dock. In this moment I admired Ann's "stank face." It was an expression I could not replicate.

Back in the canoe with our water resupplied, the waves were pushing us toward the northeast shore. But along with the support came smoke from fires burning in Ontario. It was difficult to see the shore or any oncoming obstacles. The thick smoke blanketed the water, rocks, and trees around us.

Each wave seemed to swell higher than the one before. Ann prefers headwinds. They are more predictable, giving us more control over the boat. But I prefer tailwinds. I like to get where we are going quickly, enjoying the ride and occasionally surfing the scary waves. Or at least that is how I felt before what happened next.

The shoreline briefly showed itself through the smoke. A peninsula was coming up. We would be protected from the wind around the next bend, for a while at least. Smoke enveloped us once more.

We were like two kids on a teeter-totter. One person sat on top of the wave while the other dipped to the bottom. Up and down, up and down, over and over. Ann screamed something from the bow, but I couldn't hear her through the howling wind and crashing waves. And I did not need to—I saw it, too. But it was too late. We were paddling straight into a minefield of large rocks that were mostly underwater. But at the dip of the waves, the dark, slimy, impenetrable stones emerged like ancient pillars rising from the sea, only to disappear again, engulfed by the unruly water.

Ann rose above me. I could not see ahead. She rode the wave down, and the unsettling prospect briefly came into view. As Ann rode the next wave down, two huge boulders appeared on either side of our canoe, so close we could have reached out and touched them. If we had been only a foot to one side or the other, our canoe would have crashed into rock and our fate left to the unforgiving waters of Lake Winnipeg. But our compass wasn't so fortunate. It was sitting out on the map case near the gunwales and toppled into the lake.

Whether it was fate, luck, skill, or a combination, we came out the other side curiously unscathed. Around the bend, the waves and wind abated. We floated across the still, smoky water. Everything was quiet, except the audible pounding of my heart from inside my life jacket. There was nothing to say. Our bodies were in shock, and for once I had no impulse to lighten the mood. Could we have died? We pulled the boat onto shore and sat by the water, hugging our knees to our chests. I stared at the water, replaying in my mind what had just happened. Once our bodies had recovered, we returned to the water again.

As we continued through the smoky haze, a maze of islands appeared, providing landmarks to help pinpoint our location on the map. The map showed small islands in two places. Perhaps in desperation to get off the lake, we agreed we must be at the northernmost location and could make it to Warren's Landing that evening.

"What is that smell? Is that you?" I asked Ann, half-jokingly. Something really did smell awful, but far worse than any scent Ann could exude.

"Ah. We found it. The infamous algal blooms Yanx told us about!" Ann pointed toward what looked like a green carpet floating just below the surface of the water up ahead, the result of agricultural runoff on the Red River. We paddled hard through the green slime to reach the next big point on the map, which was a bend about thirty kilometers up the shore. Around that bend, we hoped to find the mouth of the Nelson River at Warren's Landing.

Our spirits lifted for the first time since we saw Bear approaching our deserted island beach. Were we really just hours away from finishing Lake Winnipeg? It was too good to be true. As it turned out, it wasn't true.

"This is it. This has to be it," Ann spoke more to herself than to me. We had been on the water for fourteen hours since we left camp, and if this was not the mouth of the Nelson River, then we were clearly the victims of some sort of reality show prank. We were at our limit, emotionally and physically.

I offered a half-hearted congratulations, like wishing someone a happy birthday when you're unsure of the exact day. We turned the bend to find more shore. More trees. More water. More of the same, with no end in sight.

In denial, we paddled into every inlet, searching for the mouth of the Nelson River. Later I would laugh at this attempt, because the real mouth of the Nelson River is impossible to miss. All hope of finishing the lake that day was lost. We set up camp, like we always did, like any other day. According to the map, if we were where we thought we were now, there was still a full day of paddling ahead—another thirty kilometers to Warren's Landing. We were crushed, but knew we could get there the next day. When we woke up the next morning, however, the wind once again had other plans.

"What if we walk the boat out to those rocks in the distance? It looks shallow enough," I said without conviction. It was a terrible idea, and we both knew it.

"Yeah, maybe. Or the wind might die down in the afternoon. We could wait," responded Ann, tactfully dodging my questionable suggestion.

The waves came crashing onto the sandy beach like ocean waves slamming into the coast. It was shallow, though, and they started to crest and crash far offshore. If we could get past the whitecaps, then we could feasibly ride the big swells in deeper water, but we weren't willing to risk it after our close call the day before. The finish line was within reach, but we were windbound again. A feeling of hopelessness descended over us.

We soon decided that hopelessness had run its course. It was bad enough that we thought we were going to finish the lake the night before, but to feel bad about our challenging situation just seemed useless. In the tent, listening to the familiar flapping of the vestibule in the wind, I journaled about a Buddhist parable I had read in college called "The Second Arrow." In the story, the Buddha explains that in life we cannot avoid getting hit by the first arrow, which represents painful things that are beyond our control. But the second arrow is our reaction to the first, and it can be avoided. Pain is inevitable, but we can, to a certain extent, control our suffering and assuage the feelings of disappointment, guilt, shame, and insecurities that arise from the painful event itself.

I popped my head out of the tent to see Ann running buck naked into the crashing waves. I paused, laughed, and went to join her. We spent the rest of the day swimming, playing games, and watching the sunset on the horizon.

~~~~~

ON AUGUST 3, our eighteenth day on Lake Winnipeg, we arrived at the mouth of the Nelson River at Warren's Landing. We turned to see two tall electrical towers on either side of the mouth of the river with several wires running between them. This was it. I looked back at Ann with the biggest grin I could muster and broke into tears. We bawled and sang and laughed out loud as a perfect tailwind propelled us into the Nelson River and on to our next challenge: the maze of Playgreen Lake, where Eric Sevareid and Walter Port, too, got miserably lost looking for Norway House.

Everyone gets lost on Playgreen Lake. In *Canoeing with the Cree,* Sevareid wrote about all the islands on the lake looking the same and of feeling like they were paddling in circles. The shape of Playgreen Lake creates the illusion that it is a dead end, even though it has at least five channels flowing out of it. We looked across the water but could not find a break in the trees. There were islands sprinkled everywhere, masking the true outline of the lake. We set up camp on an island next to an old, run-down fishing co-op building and fell asleep.

The next morning we paddled against a strong headwind toward a dark, looming sky with streaking rain heading our way. Finishing Lake Winnipeg made me believe that we were somehow done with challenging weather. Mother Nature reminded us, as she did again and again, that she was still in charge, no matter where we were. We pulled over on an island to make coffee and wait out the storm. After a thrilling game of "Name the Three People You Would Never Want to Be Stuck in a Room With," in which we laughed and reminisced about college mishaps, a fishing boat suddenly appeared like a beacon, showing us the way. We hopped in our canoe and followed its path until we came to an unassuming channel. It was the passage to Norway House.

YORK BOATS AND DOG DAYS

$$\sim\!\!\sim\!\!\sim\!\!\sim\!\!\sim\!\!\times\!\!\sim\!\!\sim\!\!\sim\!\!\sim\!\!\sim$$

W E ARRIVED AT NORWAY HOUSE just in time for Treaty and York Boat Days, a festival celebrating the history of the Cree First Nation people who were forced to settle there in 1875. Located just north of Lake Winnipeg and nestled on the banks of the Nelson River, Norway House was historically a transportation hub and an important site of the fur trade between the Cree and the Hudson's Bay Company. The Cree were nomadic people for thousands of years before settling at Norway House, living off the land and surviving the frigid winters of central Manitoba in the same woods and waters that Ann and I now traversed. Paddling through these blue waters and beautiful lands, we were just beginning to understand this complex environment and the communities that settled here. It was powerful to realize that people had survived here for so long, living sustainably and symbiotically with the natural world.

In 1875, the Norway House Cree Nation agreed to the terms of a treaty (known as Treaty 5) with the federal government, with the intention of sharing the land to sustain their livelihood. For the Cree people, the true intentions of this treaty lay in the spoken words exchanged during negotiations, not in what was written down. Though the treaty provided some benefits to the community, including free education and health services for members of the First Nation, the Cree were essentially forced to settle on muskeg (swamp), rock, and water—largely undevelopable land with little economic potential.

Transitioning to a confined reservation inevitably changed the lifestyle of the Cree First Nation people, as it did for other

indigenous peoples throughout North America. The land reserved for them in Treaty 5, an eighteen-by-five-kilometer plot,
was not suited for subsistence farming or development like they
had hoped. To make matters worse, Manitoba Hydro, the electric
and natural gas utility, started damming the Nelson River in the
late 1960s. The company dredged two channels through the reservation (without consent) to transport water more efficiently
from Lake Winnipeg to the Nelson River. The two channels, one
that is three kilometers long and the other thirteen, caused severe flooding to Cree traditional lands. Fluctuating water levels
eroded the shoreline and contaminated the water with silt and
minerals, disrupting the natural balance of land, water, wildlife,
and the aboriginal people. After almost fifty years of contami-
nation, erosion, and debris from hydro projects, it has become
nearly impossible for Cree First Nation people to rely solely on
their surrounding natural resources for survival, as their ances-
tors before them had.

Before we left on our expedition, people told us not to stop
at indigenous communities along the route. Someone even told
us that if we did stop, all of our gear would be stolen. Ann and I
knew that connecting with these communities was essential to
our journey. We were eager to learn more about their history, culture, and relationship with the land and water. As we paddled the
channel into Norway House, we remembered Cree council member Mike Muswagon's directions: "Look for the house with the
red porch."

Red porches happened to be in vogue that season at Norway
House. We comically paddled downstream, then upstream, and
then back down again, in a failed effort to find Mike's house, all
while people from the community watched with amusement. A
motorboat idled by, filled with people taking pictures of us paddling in circles. Finally, a woman flagged us down: "It's this one!
Come this way!"

As we pulled our boat onto Mike's backyard, we were warmly

greeted by Crystal, Mike's daughter. We went inside to meet the rest of the family, who immediately made us feel welcome and at home.

Ann and I spent the rest of the day walking around Norway House. The entire community was out in full force, cooking food in the streets, playing games, and singing songs to celebrate Treaty and York Boat Days. There were stray dogs running rampant near the lake, where teams of paddlers were practicing for the big York boat race later that day. York boats are large boats that were used by the Hudson's Bay Company to carry furs and trade goods along inland waterways from Hudson Bay to the eastern slopes of the Rocky Mountains. The boats were manufactured in York Factory on Hudson Bay, and the winning team of the boat race gets a lofty prize of ten thousand dollars—approximately half the average annual household income in Norway House.

We were easy to pick out of the crowd, two white women walking around a Cree reservation. But people were excited to talk to us and hear about our adventure. Unlike the strangers we encountered in the United States, the people at Norway House took very little time to warm up and build close relationships. They had no hesitations about touching, hugging, teasing, laughing, and loving each other and anyone who came along, including us. It was strange to think that people told us not to stop here.

As the sun began to set we noticed a curious long line of people waiting nearby, while others walked back to their homes in the waning light. We hopped in Crystal's car for a quick tour of the town. She brought us to a place by the water called RCMP Point, where the Royal Canadian Mounted Police were stationed. This is where a group of American canoers that summer had camped for the night and loudly talked about how they never went through the border station when they paddled into Canada. The Canadian police were waiting for them when their float plane landed at the end of their trip. Life lesson: always go through border patrol.

I hopped out of the car and immediately lost my breath. It felt like the time I jumped into Lake Superior in November—it knocked the wind out of me. Except this time it wasn't cold water. It was a masterpiece of light and color encompassing the entire night sky. The northern lights danced in a way that made our previous sighting on Lake Winnipeg seem like nothing. A river of green and pink horizontal stripes flowed through the dark canvas above. Ann and I stood still, contemplating the vastness of the universe. Crystal seemed unamused. I gave her a glance, as if to say, "This is the most beautiful thing I have ever experienced." She understood my look and laughed, "I see this almost every day in the winter."

Back at the house, Mike Muswagon and his wife, Janice, told us more about their community, a more serious side than what we had experienced earlier that day. Roughly 85 percent of community members rely on government assistance, and very few jobs are available. The Canadian government created Treaty and York Boat Days, the event of the year at Norway House, to "celebrate" the day Treaty 5 was signed and the Cree people lost their land and livelihoods. When we asked about the long line in town earlier that day, Mike explained that the Department of Indian Affairs sets up a booth every year during the event to give every resident of the Norway House First Nation a crisp five-dollar bill. Cree First Nation people line up to receive this token payment in return for their forced settlement and the unjust taking of their traditional lands.

I was hesitant, like it wasn't my place, to express the outrage I felt about what seemed like an insult to the Cree people. How could an annual payment of five dollars per person help the community recover from losing their lands? Ann and I had to constantly remind ourselves that we were two white American women on Cree land. It was not our place to identify problems and brainstorm solutions. Neither of us knew much about the Cree or the land and water we were traveling. We were there to learn as much as possible and to seek out opportunities to tell others of the challenges that communities like Norway House face.

We stayed up late into the night. Mike and Janice talked about food justice and health issues in the community. The Cree people used to the live off the land, foraging and hunting for food and medicine, but now most people get everything they need from a local grocery store (which is outposted from Winnipeg). The cheapest food is processed food, and for a community in which 85 percent of their population is on government assistance, the cheapest option is often the best option. As a result, Norway House Cree Nation people, like many Native people in the United States, are experiencing significant health challenges associated with obesity (diabetes and heart disease, to name two) due to this drastic change in diet.

Mike and Janice also mentioned that Norway House has a lot of stray dogs but no humane society. In the winter, the hungry dogs pack together like wolves and attack people. For safety reasons, Norway House began allowing dog hunting to help manage the population of strays. Though Ann and I were fascinated by all that we were learning about this community, we were looking forward to a full night of rest and were fading quickly. That was until Mike said something so startling that it knocked the sleep right out of my eyes.

"Ladies, you're going into polar bear country. You need a dog. If a polar bear comes, it will eat your dog first, and you'll have time to load your gun."

Ann and I both paused before breaking into laughter at Mike's joke. But I noticed that Mike was not laughing. In fact, he looked very concerned. We fell asleep that night bouncing our reactions to Mike's advice back and forth from one twin bed to the other in the dark. "Crazy, right?" "Yeah, seriously! No way, man!" "Can you imagine us taking care of a dog? We can barely remember to brush our teeth in the morning!"

Giggles faded into silence, and I heard Ann's breath deepen.

She had fallen asleep, but my mind kept spinning. It was out-
rageous to think we could pick up a stray dog and carry it in
our canoe for the next month. We didn't live anywhere, and we
weren't making any money. How were we supposed to take care
of a dog? All the same, I was afraid of what lay ahead, and Mike's
logic made sense. A dog would either alert us of a polar bear or
meet an unhappy ending while we prepared for battle.

The next morning the Muswagons took us to see the famed
York boat race that everyone was talking about. We followed the
racers in a motorboat while shouting words of encouragement
through a megaphone. I felt lazy watching the paddlers put so
much effort into each stroke while we coasted alongside. We had
lingered in this comfortable place for too long, and it was time to
get back on the water.

The second event that day was a unique cultural experience for
us, but not one we were expecting. The music portion of Treaty
and York Boat Days included Elvis impersonations, country sing-
ers, and Justin Bieber merchandise. I was smacked in the face by
how commercial it all seemed, even here in the middle of the
Canadian wilderness. We stopped to watch an outdoor event
called the "Strongest Person Contest," where women were flipping
huge tires back and forth on the pavement. I felt envious of their
strong bodies and flexed my biceps to see how they were coming
along. I cared about my body image in a different way than most
women in their early twenties. Before the trip, Ann and I would
sometimes say, "We're gonna get HUGE!" and high-five each other.
If I feel strong and in shape, I'm a happy camper.

Crystal disappeared on a "secret mission" around lunchtime,
so Ann and I putzed around town and carbo-loaded for our departure the next morning. I began to see the stray dogs in a new
light, like I was window-shopping for something I knew I wasn't
going to buy. "That one is a great size," I'd say with a wink, nudg-
ing Ann. She'd respond, "Yeah, but its coloring could be better,
you know."

That night Mike and Janice threw a barbecue at their house in our honor. When Crystal arrived, she announced that she had found the perfect new member for our expedition. A small white husky puppy with one bright blue eye appeared in the doorway. As it limped toward the picnic table, clearly injured, everyone cheered for the new addition to our expedition team. I gave Ann a look that said, "Oh hell no," which she readily returned. The pup was no more than ten or fifteen pounds and was, from what I could tell, only a few weeks old. It was blind in one eye.

Here we were, in Manitoba, Canada, far from home, away from our "real" lives. This family had taken us in as their own and had probably searched all day for a dog we could take on our journey to protect us in the wild, to watch over us when they could not. I looked down at the helpless, adorable ball of fluff limping around and then glanced over at Ann. She looked concerned and amused, like she had just received a terrible birthday present from a well-meaning but clueless grandparent. We tried to smile and show our thanks, but we had something completely different in mind. Perhaps a sturdier dog that would both love us and ward off polar bears? The thought of this little puppy defending us (let alone itself) in the wilderness was laughable. So laughable that our fake smiles turned into real laughs.

Sometimes when I get too "inside my own head" I try to simplify my surroundings. Where once I may have been thinking, "Holy crap, I don't want this dog. I feel bad telling this amazing family that there is no way we are going to take this fragile fluff ball on trail," I transitioned to thinking, "I am a woman on a canoe trip, currently in Norway House, Manitoba. A family that I've never met before is trying to convince me and my best friend to take a stray dog on a big journey." That exercise, usually paired with a deep breath, reminds me that I am both painfully insignificant and extremely lucky to be alive. That nothing matters but everything needs caring for. And that it is okay to tell the Muswagons there is no flipping way we are taking this dog out on the river!

In the end, the Muswagons weren't hurt that we didn't want the injured puppy in our canoe for the next month through intense rapid sets, potential wildlife encounters, and rapidly decreasing temperatures. But regardless, Mike's words rang true: a dog would be an extra defense against polar bears. And we were nervous to enter polar bear country. I thought about how people often act out of fear and isolate themselves from anything that might harm them. And sometimes they pick up dogs as live bait in foreign lands! That night we told Crystal that we had changed our minds. We did want a dog. Not a little helpless pup, but a medium-sized, middle-aged dog that would fit in our canoe and not need too much babysitting. She was excited to help us find one. Without a second thought, we jumped in her car and went touring around the reservation.

We drove slowly through the dark night on dusty dirt roads. We caught glimpses and shadows of dogs running in and out of range of the headlights and streetlamps, moving in packs through the sleepy town. The streets were empty. An older woman glanced apprehensively out her window in our direction and then quickly closed her blinds. It probably looked like we were up to no good.

We pulled into the parking lot of the movie theater and saw the silhouette of a dog, all alone, licking the remains of ketchup packets off the asphalt. "That's it. That's the one," I said. There was little discussion or deliberation. Ann had a hesitant look about her, as if she were considering all of the diseases the dog might have, but I knew that if we were going to act it had to be now. I ran out of the car, swooped the dog into my arms, and threw her in the back seat. For better or for worse, our team of two became three.

We sat around the Muswagons' cozy living room trying to pick a name for our newly acquired adventure dog. I realized it was the last time that we'd get to lounge comfortably on their couch, laughing with our new friends, before launching into the most dangerous part of our journey. We planned to depart the next morning for the last leg of our expedition: the wild, whitewater rivers that flow from boreal forests into taiga and cold, barren tundra.

Mike thankfully snapped me out of my thoughts. "What about live bait? Janice—what is 'live bait' in Cree?" he chuckled. Now that the dog was with us, looking at us with her two deep golden eyes, it was impossible to think of her as live bait.

There was something about her that made us feel brave. She was small boned but had a very thick black and brown coat that made her look twice her actual size. Tough and scrappy from her time as a stray, she was solemn, like someone who was forced to grow up too fast. We speculated she was an older dog because of her calm demeanor and the light gray hair speckled across her nose. She looked wise. Like a wolf. Ann must have been thinking the same thing.

"Mike, what is 'wolf' in Cree?" Ann asked.

Mike thought for a second and then responded, "Myheehan."

Myheehan. That would be a fun one to say to every person walking down the street drilling us about our dog's name and breed (assuming she didn't get eaten before we got back to the "real world").

But when the trip was over—then what? Who would keep the dog? That question spiraled into a series of others: Who would keep the tent? The GoPro? We hadn't figured out any of the logistics beyond getting a float plane out of York Factory and a train back to Winnipeg. Would the dog be able to come with us on those travels, too? It seemed too soon to plan for the end.

I couldn't conceptualize the finality of our journey. In many ways, it felt like it would never end. I would continue to wake up, pack out, and paddle all day toward an arbitrary, faraway final destination. If we only focused on the finish line we might lose sight of where we were and what we needed to do to move forward that day, right now. If we had thought only about Hudson Bay, we never would have persevered through the painfully slow Minnesota River or the throes of traversing Lake Winnipeg.

There were many what-ifs in the back of our minds, but we had more pressing matters at hand. Far more important than figuring out the logistics of picking up a dog was choosing a proper name for our new teammate. We thought Myheehan was a bit out there for a dog name, so Ann and I agreed to abbreviate Myheehan to Myhan. The Muswagons gave us their blessing—Myhan the wolf dog was a fitting name for our fluffy, fierce warrior. Little did she know the journey we were about to go on together.

INTO THE WILD

"Pᴇʀꜱᴏɴᴀʟ ɢᴇᴀʀ?" Ann asked. She looked like a teacher going through a checklist before a class field trip.

"Check!" I responded cheerfully. After days at Norway House we were itching to get back on the water. It was sunny with little wind—perfect conditions for our upcoming paddle across Little Playgreen Lake back to the Nelson River. From this point on we had to keep an eye on the maps since we would only be on the Nelson one more day before peeling off onto the Echimamish River. It would be easy to miss our turn, and we did *not* want to backtrack. Our upstream days were over.

"Even your toothbrush?" Ann was determined not to leave anything behind. I pulled out my wet dirty toothbrush from my life jacket pocket and shrugged. "What's left of it, at least!" Any dentist (or anyone, really) would be appalled at the state of our discolored toothbrushes. But they still got the job done.

"One dog?" Ann said with wide eyes and a big smile that suggested we were brilliantly insane for picking up our newest member. I looked over at Myhan, who was lying in the Muswagons' backyard hesitantly glancing our way. She had no clue what her life was about to become. Neither did we. Would she stay in the canoe? Would she run away at night? Would she bite us? Would we get rabies in the wilderness, far away from medical attention? Would a polar bear actually eat her instead of us? Time would tell.

Ann had mailed our third food drop of nonperishable foods to Norway House months prior to our arrival. After packing out the gear and dry foods, we visited the Northern Store to restock on cheese, salami, and tortillas and to pick up our new heaviest item: dog food (just in time for the portage-heavy part of our trip). To date, we had collected big funny straw hats from Penny's friends, two wooden birds from Princess Harbour, new Norway House jackets from the Muswagons, and now a large bag of dog food and a dog who, we hoped, could carry herself across long portages. I wondered whether we would regret taking on so many mementos. Every pound counts when carrying gear through the woods. The only other community we would visit was at Oxford House, about a week's paddle from Norway House. The stretch from Oxford House to York Factory would take about two weeks, weather and wildlife permitting.

Ann's checklist turned into a joke list of items that we either didn't need or didn't have, like the two straw hats (check!) and the voice recorder (no check, sadly). After we assumed everything was loaded, it was time for the dreaded goodbyes. The Muswagons lined up by the canoe to say farewell.

"You ladies watch out for the Sasquatch, okay?" Mike warned as he hugged us goodbye.

Janice told us a story about a man from Norway House who looked Sasquatch in the eyes, and, as a result, his life began to slowly deteriorate until he had nothing but poor health.

"The danger is not crossing paths with the Sasquatch. He won't harm you physically. Rather, it's what happens *after* you see him that should scare you," Janice explained. "Look for straight lines cut through the forests. That's a sign he's been there."

"And remember to leave him an offering whenever you can," followed Crystal.

"And don't look him in the eyes," chimed in one of the grandkids.

A new checklist was forming in my mind. A list of things to avoid at all costs:

1. Polar bears
2. The Sasquatch
3. Getting rabies from our new dog

I looked over to see Ann tearing up. I thought about telling her that we probably wouldn't encounter the Sasquatch if we left little peace offerings at our campsites—there was nothing to fear! Luckily before I opened my mouth to console her I realized she was crying because it was sad to say goodbye, which made more sense. Ann almost always cries at goodbyes, and whenever she cries, I cry, too. We were in danger of turning into a hot sobbing mess of love.

Not wanting to linger any longer, Ann picked up Myhan, our final cargo, and placed her on top of one of the packs in the middle of the canoe. She settled in easily, maybe because she was exhausted from her life as a stray. Or perhaps because she was destined to be a canoe dog and was finally home. We hoped for the latter. I felt the familiar thrill of using my arms the way they were meant to be used, one paddle stroke at a time, as we pushed off from shore and onto the next leg of our journey: the Arctic rivers.

We paddled away from Norway House in our loaded canoe with a new furry companion, a gun, and concerns about threats to our lives beyond bears and rapids. We must have been a spectacle to the community, including the Muswagons, who were still waving goodbye from their red porch as we disappeared around the bend in the channel.

Usually after days off the water we had more energy to get rolling on the river. But the visit to Norway House was different. Our minds were spinning. We had socialized nonstop, and what we learned about the injustices to the indigenous people was too heavy to simply paddle away from. We were just beginning to process what we had learned about their history, the ongoing struggles of the people who had been our friends and caretakers these last few days.

~~~~~

"LUNCHTIME?" I ASKED ANN. We had reached a patch of islands at the end of Little Playgreen Lake, where the Nelson River narrows, quickens, and continues north.

"Yeah. I think the lunch bag is over by you," she responded.

"Nope, it's gotta be up there." This back and forth went on for several minutes. We pulled over and dug through all of our packs in search of the food bag. If Myhan could talk she would have told us that her stray dog friends say thank you for the delicious salami and cheese we carelessly left behind in the Muswagons' backyard. Instead, Mike left a voicemail on Ann's phone describing the lunch bag as "gruesomely demolished" by a pack of dogs. Our perishable food for the next three weeks was gone.

The idea of paddling back to Norway House, returning to the grocery store, repacking, and relaunching sounded awful, like the movie *Groundhog Day,* where Bill Murray just keeps waking up and living the exact same day over and over again. We were unwilling to enter into that nightmare of reliving the day again. We had new snacks, tons of granola bars, and enough food for breakfast and dinner. If we were just launching on a three-week trip, then we might have gone back to get it. But this was the last leg of a three-month journey. Three weeks now seemed like a long weekend in the big scheme of things. Probably to the dismay of dietitians everywhere, we agreed to survive on Bisquick, rice, noodles, oatmeal, and granola bars for the rest of the expedition—a carb-only diet.

Myhan stretched her legs on Hope Island while we sat by the water chowing down on our granola bars. For the first time in weeks there was a real current in the water. After Lake Winnipeg, we had only paddled channelized waterways. Now the Nelson River, or what was left of it after all the dams went up, was kicking back into gear. The water rushed over the rocks near shore, gently hinting at the waterfalls and whitewater sets in our future. The river must have been a sight to see before Manitoba Hydro manipulated its flow and changed its natural floodplain. But our travels would soon take us off the controlled flow of the Nelson River to the faster currents of the Arctic Hayes River, where humans had yet to leave a permanent scar on the landscape.

Nestled on the shores of the Nelson, we made dinner, played cribbage, and fell asleep to the trickling sound of flowing water. We agreed that Myhan would sleep outside. Part of us still expected her to turn into a vampire dog, bite us, take all the food, and run into the wild. So far she had just slept in the boat all day and looked at us lovingly. But we weren't buying her adorable puppy eyes—she was clearly playing us like a travel guitar.

The next morning I awoke to the familiar rat-a-tat of rain on the tent. Myhan was running around in the woods nearby, her body rustling against the low bushes and branches. It was calming to hear sounds we could actually identify outside the tent now. Before, a rustling in the woods was a bear, or a squirrel, or a crazy ax murderer. But now it was just Myhan (and definitely not the Sasquatch). I curled up in my sleeping bag and looked out at the raindrops collecting before they overflowed in streaks down the sides of the tent. If I moved, Ann would move, and I desperately wanted to sleep in and wait out the rain. The sound of Ann's deflating Therm-a-Rest would truly be a disappointing end to a cozy rainy morning in the tent. I didn't know Ann was awake, too, thinking the same thing about my Therm-a-Rest. We played cat and mouse for a while until it was obvious we were both waiting for the other person to make the first move. Finally a truce was called: we agreed to sleep until the rain stopped.

The smell of the wet forest and the narrow river was different than what we were used to. Lake Winnipeg smelled like open air, sweat, and sunscreen, like a sunny day on the beach. The river smells were more complex. The rain kicked up new aromas—

hints of fresh soil, wet wood, and moss-covered rocks, complete wilderness and isolation.

Our sense of urgency was different on the river, too. Because paddleable conditions were a rarity on the lake, we had to take advantage of ideal weather, day or night. But now I felt a new relaxation: the freedom to choose when we traveled and how far. But the river's powerful current would require us to be far more technical with our paddling and conservative in our decision making. A flipped boat meant our gear would float downstream for polar bears to find on the shores of Hudson Bay. A severely cracked or damaged boat meant possible evacuation. An accidental joyride down a class V ledge could mean something far worse than losing our gear or damaging our canoe. And we could almost feel the creatures that Myhan either attracted or scared away lurking in the woods, watching us paddle from behind the trees. Whether it was our newfound lack of urgency, delaying our inevitable travels through polar bear country, or the soothing tapping of the rain on the tent, we decided to take an impromptu layover day. This was something we would do often now that the weather was less inhibiting and we could accurately determine mileage for each day.

Before we left Norway House, Mike had equipped us with a fishing pole and lures for the rest of the journey. "Catch your dinners whenever you can," he advised. Fishing was more enticing now with our lack of fresh food. We unsuccessfully fished the day away, eventually retiring to continue our ongoing cribbage competition. We fell asleep to the comforting sound of Myhan patrolling the surrounding forest for food, friends, or foes.

The next day we awoke early with no desire to linger any longer. Our Therm-a-Rests exhaled deeply as we rushed to get out of the tent and onto the river. A beautiful morning fog floated above the calm waters of the Nelson but was quickly pulled away by the bright rays of the rising sun. We gracefully maneuvered the river, twisting and turning, riding the small swifts through narrow passages between islands into wider channels outlined with majestic granite bluffs. In and out and around we went until we reached a vital fork in the river. Watching the maps carefully, we turned right and entered into a confusing weave of channels and islands.

"Okay. We can't miss it if we only take rights," said Ann. It was her turn to navigate. "Take every possible right, and we should be in the clear."

"What's that? Is that oil?" I asked, stunned by what I saw in the water. A thick, black channel appeared to our right. My heart sank. I immediately thought an underground pipeline must have burst nearby.

"It's a right. We have to take it," said Ann hesitantly.

The water beneath us transitioned from a blueish brown to pitch-black. To my surprise, I looked down to discover I could see my entire paddle as it dug into the darkness. It wasn't oil at all. The water was so clear it was reflecting the dark soil at the bottom, creating an illusion of black water. It was the clearest water we had encountered yet on our way to the Arctic Hayes, where we would soon be able to drink straight from the river without filtering our water.

This marked the beginning of the Echimamish River, formerly known as Blackwater Creek. The Muswagons told us that "Echimamish" in Cree means "river that flows both ways" and warned that sometimes the current would be with us and other times against us. While many rivers flow from lakes to oceans or other rivers, the Echimamish curiously flows sixty kilometers from one river system to another, from the Nelson to the Hayes. It was like the river couldn't decide which way to go.

Fish lurking in the vegetation beneath the surface scattered when they felt our presence. The water was so clear we could see every scale on their glistening bodies. I made a note to drop a line in when we got to camp. The river was calm for the most part, except in those moments when the current shifted beneath us.

Several small creeks flow into the Echimamish, making it difficult at times to tell where the main channel is. We rode its sharp twists and turns through boreal forests, swamps, and granite outcroppings all the way to Hairy Lake. It was appropriately named: large reeds covered the entire surface like hair. Ann pointed out a boulder in the water and said, "Look! A mole on ol' Hairy's skin!"

We directed the canoe toward a rocky spot on the shoreline that made for a good campsite. As we paddled to our home for the night, the abundant fish in the reeds teased us for not catching anything on the Nelson River, tempting me to try again. I trolled a line from the back of the canoe, secured the fishing pole between my legs, and continued paddling.

Tug. Tug. Tuuuuuuggggggg! The fishing pole almost jolted out of my thighs and into the water. Was the lure stuck on a reed? *TUUUGGGGG!!*

"Ann! Fish!" I exclaimed. It had been years since I last caught a fish. Myhan suddenly perked up from her usual sleeping spot on top of the pack as if to ask, "Dinner time?"

The force on the other end of the line suggested it was a big fish. There was no way we were going to reel it into the canoe with Myhan intently waiting to pounce. We paddled hard to our destination with the fish in tow. When we finally arrived, I hopped out of our boat with the pole and finished the job, reeling in the fish and stabbing it in the head with my camp knife until it stopped flopping around on the rocks. Myhan watched but stayed away, hopefully impressed with my skills. She acted like she knew she was cooler and more savvy in the wild than we were; I just wanted her to like me. I filleted the fish on a flat rock and threw the bones and guts back into the water (not wanting to attract any bears or wolves to our campsite) while Ann set up camp.

"Fish soup is on the menu tonight! All local, sustainable, and organic," I assured Ann.

"Protein!" she appropriately responded. We were already feeling the woes of our new carb-heavy diet.

Myhan, too, was thinking about protein as she skeptically eyed her processed dog food. She had other plans for dinner but would wait until we fell asleep to catch a real meal.

At dusk, with full stomachs, we dove into the tent to escape the onslaught of mosquitoes. The bugs were getting worse the farther north we traveled, especially in swampy and boggy areas. Every night after setting up our sleeping bags we'd turn on our headlamps and slaughter mosquitoes, sometimes squishing hundreds of them against the top of our bloodstained tent. Counting fallen mosquitoes became a fun ritual before bedtime and after our nightly game of cribbage. After slaughtering more than one hundred (Ann killed more than I did, so I felt the pressure to up my game moving forward), we fell asleep to the comforting sound of Myhan running through the woods on night watch.

Ann beat me out of the tent the next morning. I had lost at cribbage and bug killing the night before, and now I was last out of the tent. My ego was damaged, to say the least.

"Woahhh! What the . . ." Ann was halfway out of the tent when she came across something peculiar, something that had not been there the night before. I abandoned stuffing my sleeping bag into its dry sack and crawled over to the vestibule, where she was examining a mysterious item on the ground.

It was a furry and dark-brown hand with long discolored fingernails protruding from creepily curved, humanlike fingers.

"I think it's a beaver hand," explained Ann as she leaned in closer to examine it. I looked around. There was no beaver in sight and no other body parts scattered around our camp. My eyes settled on Myhan, who was watching us intently from under a nearby tree. Perhaps she found some protein to eat after all. But why would she leave a beaver hand behind? Her expression was one of gratitude, as if she had just given us a present, affirmation that we were truly a pack. She ran over to greet us with a new-found affection (or to ask for dog food to chase down her late-night beaver snack). Whatever her intentions, I was overwhelmed with the feeling that we were a real family. A misfit family of two best friends and a dog, but a family nonetheless.

~~~~~

WE WERE BACK ON THE WATER in no time after a delicious breakfast of chocolate twelve-grain hot cereal. The reeds on Hairy Lake were so thick we could barely see the water beneath us. There was no clear path through, so we periodically stood up in the canoe to figure out where we were going. It reminded me of navigating Marsh Lake back on the Minnesota River.

"Over there, to the right! There is a small black channel." I spotted the Echimamish again as it slithered away from the lake. Sometimes just a few feet of perspective helped us find our way. We crashed a path through the brush and broke free once more on the narrow black waters of the Echimamish.

We sang to pass the hours, improving our well-rehearsed harmonies on classics like "Red River Valley," "Blue Eyes Cryin' in the Rain," and many of the songs we had sung for our old friends at Princess Harbour. Thunderclouds rolled in behind us, adding a much-needed low end to our melodies. The storm only stayed for a song or two before skirting southwest, probably off to torment paddlers on Lake Winnipeg. We had been lucky with weather lately.

Our maps for this part of our journey were drawn by a man named Hap Wilson, best known for his numerous Canadian canoe route guides and books about life in the wilderness. We referred to them as "Hap Maps" and relied on them for navigation, information about whitewater sets, and important landmarks along the route. The landmark we were currently looking for was a "grassy, low-lying campsite" at a fork in the river where we were supposed to stay right. Everything around us was grassy and low-lying, and no "campsites" were marked or looked unique from any other potential stopping points.

We approached a fork in the river. To the left was a narrow channel with slightly stronger current flowing our way; it disappeared behind a large granite rock. As I glanced down that corridor, a gust of wind smelling of rocks, moss, and waterfalls traveled through the granite canyon and swirled around us. It felt like a spirit calling, beckoning us to enter the left channel. But we suspected the grassy low-lying land in front of us was the landmark we had been looking for. The Hap Maps said to go right. We denied the river sirens and paddled forward.

A marshy landscape opened before us, widening our view of the river valley and blue sky above. The river spilled outward onto the land, no longer confined by rock or slope. It did what all moving water wishes it could do: breathe into the landscape, slowly stretch into the woods before narrowing again, responding only to its natural surroundings, free of any human-made confinement.

Small beaver lodges appeared along the shore, and after about an hour of paddling an enormous beaver dam blocking the entire river came into view. I began to question if we had taken a wrong turn. Whether it was the sudden change in scenery, our hesitance to spend the rest of the day pulling the canoe over beaver lodges, or the sirens whispering in the wind, "Come back to the left channel where everything is magical and easy," we convinced ourselves we had taken a wrong turn despite the clear direction in the Hap Maps to "stay right." Our feelings irrationally overpowered the facts and maps. We traveled an hour back to the fork in the river and ventured up the alluring left channel.

The smell of the fresh air put us into a trance. Finally, we made it to the wilderness we had been inching closer to every day for two months. The air felt wet and refreshing, as if we were paddling through a cool, shaded rainforest. But here too something was not jibing with our previous experience on the Echimamish: the current. Water rushed toward us, moving faster and faster the farther we traveled up the enchanted valley. We quickly knew that we were no longer on the Echimamish River, which we were told was slow and swampy. No matter how much we wanted to avoid the marsh, mosquitoes, and beaver dams awaiting us, we knew we had to return to the right channel. And so we did. An hour later, we were face-to-face with the same beaver dam (a two-foot wall of sticks blocking the entire river) that had made us rethink our direction earlier that day. At least this time we knew we were on the right path.

Ann and I are notorious for avoiding portages at all costs, usually by coming up with ridiculous schemes to get around obstacles. Contemplating how to get around the wall in front of us, I thought back to the train bridge on the Minnesota River, where we climbed large wooden beams to pull the boat through a small passage in the fallen logs. Then I thought back further, to years earlier on our Menogyn trip on the Kazan River in Nunavut, Canada. Our group was in the middle of a five-kilometer portage over a hill covered in rocky, uneven tussocks through a strong wind that kept spinning the canoe around on people's shoulders—like a pinwheel in an open field. Ann and I were together, trading off the canoe and pack throughout the portage, when we saw a small lake on the other side of the hill. We came up with a plan to portage to the lake, paddle about a half kilometer, and then hop back on land to portage to the end. When we shared this plan with our guide she laughed and said no, because it was just a silly way to avoid portaging another thousand feet out of the more than fifteen thousand we had to walk already. To us, that thousand feet of paddling would have been worth it. Some might call it laziness, but I like to think of it as creative problem solving.

"Should we try to lift over it?" Ann presented an obvious solution that seemed feasible in theory, but our canoe was loaded to the brim (with straw hats, wooden birds, new jackets, and dog food), and we had determined that Myhan was afraid of water because she never let so much as a paw touch the river. We would have to lift our canoe with all of our gear and our dog up two feet while standing knee-deep in water. Ann joined me at the front of the canoe. I thought about exchanging my Chacos for my Muck Boots, but I was already knee-deep in the water. We gripped the gunwales at the front of the boat and counted, "One. Two. Three. Lift!" The bow raised about a foot in the air before falling back into the river with a splash. We would have to lift it twice as high to prop it on one of the sticks before raising it up and across from the stern. Myhan looked skeptical as she watched from her perch in the middle of the boat.

We tried again. And again. Time after time we'd inch closer to the top of the ledge but to no avail. By this time we could have been back on the water after a short portage, but Hudson Bay Bound must try everything possible before taking the easy way around! We agreed to try one more time. We grunted like weight lifters, pushing beyond our strength just long enough to lodge the bow on top of the ledge before letting go. This time it did not crash back into the water. We took a moment to catch our breath before sharing a perfect high five. I could feel something crawling on my feet. I had lingered too long in the marshy waters.

Once the boat was set on the ledge it wasn't difficult to slide it across the top of the slippery sticks—Myhan's first wilderness theme park ride. I climbed back into the bow after accomplishing a triumphant feat to find we had a much larger audience for our grand performance. Both of my feet were covered in tiny black leeches, writhing and sucking on my skin for sustenance. After a moment of shock all I could do was laugh while I pulled them off one by one.

"One! Ah ah ah . . . Two! Ah ah ah . . . Three!" I continued counting them slowly and dramatically, imitating the Count from Sesame Street. Ann was thoroughly grossed out when I came to the final number. "Sixty-six! Ah ah ah . . ." I felt loopy and goofy, perhaps because I had just lost sixty-six leeches' worth of blood.

"Well, Ann. At least I'm not afraid of leeches anymore," I said as I gathered my Muck Boots and put them nearby in case we had to get out of the boat again. Continuing on the river, we exited the canoe constantly to navigate over wayward sticks and branches. But none of the obstacles were as challenging as that first ledge, and our watertight footwear kept the leeches at bay for the rest of the day. Come dusk, leeches were the least of our problems in swampland.

The river grew into a bog with little resemblance to the black water we had paddled before. Mosquitoes appeared intermittently to warn us of what was to come as the sun sank below the horizon. We set up camp on dry grassy land while Myhan began her nightly run through the woods. Then the army arrived.

Black clouds of mosquitoes descended on our campsite as the last rays of light disappeared behind the spruce trees. We were speechless. Not because we were shocked by the number of mosquitoes but rather because neither of us wanted to be the first person to crack. Silence was strength. Our competitiveness led us to complain very little, if at all, and I was not going to be the first one to suggest that the situation was absolutely ridiculous and full-blown miserable. No chance.

Instead, we quietly ate our soup and avoided eye contact while swarms of tiny bloodsuckers took turns injecting their needlelike faces into our exposed skin. "Pain is mental. It only hurts if you let it hurt," I kept reminding myself while exuding a cool and composed facade. A second wave of mosquitoes flew in for backup. I wondered if they had planned to eat us alive and needed a full army to get the job done. How long had they been stalking us? What was worse, getting mauled by a polar bear or getting eaten alive by tens of thousands of mosquitoes?

"This is THE WORST!" I broke out into laughter. Thankfully Ann, too, had simultaneously cracked. We yelled and flailed around, swatting the mosquitoes with one hand while balancing our hot soup (now peppered with bugs) in the other before bolting into the tent. Ann speedily zipped the door closed behind us. It was the first and only night we would finish dinner "indoors." Mother nature had finally pushed us to the brink.

We settled in after our nightly routine of squishing juicy blood-filled pests against the nylon tent. Ann was worried about Myhan.

Sure, the beaver hand was a cute gesture, but if we had a domestic dog that had eaten a beaver, we would have taken them to the vet, concerned about bones and diseases. What would she hunt tonight? Where did she go when the woods went quiet? I tried to stay up to comfort Ann, but my eyes were failing me. I clicked off my headlamp.

"It'll be all right. You can go to bed," Ann said. She noticed I had been conversing with my eyes closed and kindly gave me an out. "You've got a big day tomorrow, remember? It's your birthday!" She smiled wide and pointed her headlamp on my face waiting for my reaction, like an adult trying to make a child excited about something totally normal. I grinned in the orange light, my heavy eyes still closed. Camaraderie and thoughtfulness were seeping back into our relationship after our fight on Lake Winnipeg. I felt a deep appreciation for our friendship in that moment. I had forgotten it was almost my "trail birthday"!

Before the expedition, we each picked a date for our fake trail birthdays (our real birthdays are in November and December) and decided how old we were going to turn on that day. Tomorrow I would be twenty-five years old: that sounded like prime time. I speculated that I would be wandering around less at the ripe age of twenty-five than I was in my early twenties. Maybe I'd actually live somewhere and have a life partner. Maybe I'd even have a career, which I was told I needed to figure out pretty soon. I drifted into dreams of my future while Ann stayed up listening for Myhan in the woods.

We packed up camp in record time the next morning to avoid any prolonged interactions with the mosquito army. Back on the river, we enjoyed a floating breakfast while poring over the maps for the day. We were only hours away from Painted Stone Portage, a short twenty-five-meter portage that marks the end of the Echimamish River and the beginning of our journey on the Hayes River.

After paddling through the peat bog and lifting up and over our final beaver dams, a sign marking the portage came into view. The river abruptly stopped at a large rock, with no water flowing over or around it. It was an absolute dead end. To our left was the short portage that would bring us to the Hayes River, the next leg of our journey. It was thrilling to be so close to a river that we had traveled so far to get to. Every upstream stroke, downstream push, and windbound anxiety had woven together to bring us to this fast and unforgiving river and soon to the vast waters of Hudson Bay.

PANCAKES AND PORTAGES

W E HAD READ IN THE HAP MAPS that the Hayes River is the largest naturally flowing river in Manitoba and drains the third-largest watershed in the province. It is one of Canada's most outstanding wilderness canoe routes and was a central artery for the Hudson's Bay Company's fur trade route between the late seventeenth and early twentieth centuries. The Hayes begins at Molson Lake, located just northeast of Norway House, and runs northeast. The Echimamish joins the flow just before Robinson Lake. The route we chose to paddle is referred to as the "Hayes River corridor," which stretches 600 kilometers from Lake Winnipeg—following the Nelson and Echimamish Rivers to Painted Stone Portage, where the river continues northward for 480 kilometers—to the river's mouth at Hudson Bay.

At this point in their journey, Eric Sevareid and Walter Port had already branched off onto the Gods River, which flows just south of the Hayes before the two rivers join and flow together for the last two hundred kilometers to the Bay. They had originally planned to take the Hayes River, but due to low water levels in 1930 they were redirected by locals to the Gods River instead. We chose to paddle their intended route.

Mike told us a little bit about Painted Stone Portage before we left Norway House. It is a spiritual place for Cree people and was a sacred meeting place for many years. The Hayes was a traditional source of food, spiritual renewal, and transportation long before European settlers arrived on the shores of Hudson Bay.

We decided to spend time at the portage before launching again to take a breath and celebrate our accomplishments. But fear of what was next—waterfalls and whitewater, polar bears and colder days—made it difficult to fully appreciate how far we'd come. This was the perfect spot for a coffee break. I sat on the jagged rock, fired up the stove, and waited for the water to boil while Ann made us peanut butter and jelly tortillas. I poured the hot water over the coffee grounds—it smelled like home. I closed my eyes and drifted back to a Saturday morning in Miami as my siblings and I crowded the futon watching cartoons while Dad fired up the old coffee maker. Wherever we were, no matter how remote, we still had familiar smells to trigger some connection to home.

"I'd totally hang out here," I said, passing the coffee for Ann to have the first sip. We started doing small but thoughtful gestures like this more often, and it was doing wonders for our relationship.

"Yeah, me too. It's so sad it was blown up," Ann replied. We admired the landscape in silence. There were sharp chunks of rock strewn about like the aftermath of a long-ago explosion. Someone at Norway House mentioned that settlers used dynamite on this site. Bright green and yellow mosses blanketed the rock portage, which was covered in tall thin logs pieced together to look like a railroad track. The wooden tracks bridged the Echimamish to the Hayes and were there to help people push and pull their loaded boats across without having to empty their gear. With the efforts we had previously shown to avoid portages, especially short ones, I was willing to bet we would have built that contraption if it wasn't already in place—taking an hour to avoid ten minutes.

Ann sang a perfectly strange rendition of "Happy Birthday" to me while Myhan pranced around the open rock face. We talked about our futures. Our hopes for partners and travels, our desires to feel both settled and free. To have all of our things in one spot while living adventurously, to mature and grow while making unpredictable and impulsive decisions to better ourselves and build character. Everything we wanted from life seemed contradictory, but we believed we could do it all.

After completing the short portage, we launched onto the Hayes River, and a decisive current shuttled our boat downstream. Immediately the scenery changed from swampy flatland to large exposed rocks covered in mossy vegetation. It felt strange to have reached the last river of our expedition. For every segment of the trip so far—whether upstream, downstream, or across a massive lake—there was always something to look forward to, always the next thing that was somehow going to be better or more beautiful than the thing before. But now that we had reached the Hayes, we knew that our time together on this journey was coming to a close. The end itself seemed blurry, almost impossible to imagine. It wasn't really a place to reach or a prize to win. It was just an arbitrary finish line floating in the future. I wasn't completely convinced I even wanted to arrive there.

As the river widened, the dramatic rocky scenery seemed to say, "I'm here to stay." I thought more about my fake twenty-fifth birthday. Were my twenties going to be like paddling upstream, fighting to prove to the world that I was a competent adult, worthy of a job, friends, and a partner? And if I did find a life partner, was marriage the dreamy downstream Red River that I would paddle until boredom struck? And kids, I thought. Would they be like Lake Winnipeg, stripping my ability to choose my own schedule or move freely, providing beauty I had never experienced before, coupled with dark clouds, unmanageable waves, and close calls? All the while, would I be looking forward to the Hayes River, a well-earned retirement that still had its curveballs and buggy nights? Near the end of my life, would polar bears haunt my dreams until I paddled into the hazy horizon of Hudson Bay, hopefully looking back over our route with gratitude and release?

"What do you think we should cook for dinner tonight?" Ann asked after a long silence, pulling me back into the present. Sometimes I had to remind myself that I was paddling an Arctic river in

Canada with my best friend and our new dog. We made it to Robinson Lake to find it was just as hairy as Hairy Lake, except much larger and longer. If Hairy Lake was someone's head speckled with hair, then Robinson Lake, where we set up camp for the night, was someone's long hairy leg. I looked down at my calf. "Yep, looks about right," I thought.

Ann graciously offered to cook a birthday dinner for me while I relaxed, so I took the canoe out by myself to fish. I felt strangely vulnerable paddling an empty canoe. I could feel the space beneath me, from the boat down to the bottom of the lake, as if I were carefully maneuvering across a swing bridge through a canyon. Even though the canoe had been my home for months, she felt much sturdier when filled with gear and responded better when both of us were paddling. I returned to camp empty-handed but with a new appreciation for my paddling partner. I walked up to Ann to tell her I had no luck fishing when she turned to me and said, "TAA-DAAA!! Happy birthday!" She revealed a scrambled and undercooked yellow cake sloppily covered in watery chocolate frosting. My perfect birthday cake. That night Ann did all of the dishes and even instigated a dance party in the tent before we fell asleep. It was one of the best trail birthdays I had ever had.

The next morning we paddled the rest of Robinson Lake in even more beautiful weather. Scott's journal from the 2005 expedition said that, at this point in their journey, it was very cold and wet. Reading about how miserable they were somehow made the sun feel even warmer and the sky even bluer for our morning paddle to Robinson Falls, a series of five waterfalls through a jagged granite canyon.

The Hayes River was an important transportation highway used by First Nation peoples in Manitoba long before the arrival of Europeans in North America. In 1684, the river was given its Anglo-European name for James Hayes, a member of the Hudson's Bay Company. That same year, the company established its North American headquarters at York Factory. The Hayes

River was the main trading route between Norway House and the mouth of the river at Hudson Bay. For me, it seemed like a gateway to the entire world. To the north, we could paddle the great expanse of Hudson Bay to the Arctic Ocean. To the south, we could paddle back to where we began at Fort Snelling and continue down the Mississippi River to the Gulf of Mexico. We could stop in and say hello to my family in Miami before paddling to Cuba or around the Florida Panhandle. The opportunities were endless—we could spend the rest of our lives in a canoe if we really wanted to.

Myhan eagerly jumped to shore before we beached the canoe at the portage. At first glance, it looked like a path that had been traveled for thousands of years but not maintained for a decade. We prepared for the portage like we always did—overcommitting to carrying too much. It was clear where we were supposed to go, but downed trees and overgrown brush covered the well-traveled soil around every turn. Myhan, used to sitting and sleeping in the canoe, was thankful for the opportunity to stretch her legs during the day (who knows what she did at night). We were thankful for her. She ran the path from beginning to end over and over again like a beacon announcing our presence to any wildlife that might otherwise be caught unawares.

"Check it out. What do you think it is?" I asked Ann, pointing at a pile of fresh scat near our gear as we piled on more than we could feasibly carry for the kilometer-long portage. Ann peered closer, leaning over as much as she could without toppling over with the fifty-pound pack on her back.

"Bear scat. It's really recent, too," she said with a hint of concern. Just then Myhan popped out of the trees, returning from her scouting mission as if to announce, "All clear ahead!" before taking off again. With our furry fearless protector by our side we felt safe venturing into the unfamiliar forest.

It was crazy to think our last real portage was exactly a month ago when we carried our gear over the dam into Winnipeg on

July 12. That portage was strenuous because it was unexpected and there was no path to follow. This portage around Robinson Falls, a series of class V ledges, was a kilometer long, the longest of our entire trip—impressive, considering we were paddling continuously for three solid months. We had been through far worse. Years earlier, Ann completed the Grand Portage trail in Minnesota (over eight miles long), and we had both portaged four miles across a great divide on an expedition in the Arctic.

I quickly recognized that our celebration may have been premature when I approached our first obstacle: a creek cut about five feet deep into the granite rock, with four thin branches laid across the narrow canyon, suggesting a precarious route (the only route) over the creek and back to the path on the other side. Imagine giants crossing the Grand Canyon by laying large logs from one rim to the other. Then shrink that so the Grand Canyon is only five feet deep and the logs are only skinny four-foot branches. Myhan ran across without hesitation and looked back at me, confused why I had stopped walking. She then ran ahead to catch up with Ann, who had successfully made it across with her fifty-pound pack, making me feel more confident that I could do the same.

At the end of the portage we celebrated with a large brunch of pancakes, dehydrated eggs, and dehydrated hash browns along with coffee. Since our lunch bag was literally left to the dogs we settled into a daily two-meal routine. We would launch in the morning without eating breakfast, find a good spot in the early afternoon to cook a big brunch, and then have the usual dinner at night. I was beginning to worry about our reliance on Bisquick for all of our meals and wondered how our bodies would fare after weeks of little calcium or protein. But with our first big whitewater set coming up, we had bigger things to worry about than nutrition.

~~~~~

THE HAYES RIVER IS WILD and free-flowing. People have not yet dammed its waters or hemmed it in with development. It is able to flow over the land in times of high water and trickle down to expose its jagged, rocky bottom during low water. It was the only water body on our expedition that we could drink from directly without filtering or boiling the water first. We had this luxury once before on the Kazan and Kunwak Rivers in Nunavut, Canada, four years prior. Instead of carrying large jugs of water to last us three or four days, we now clipped metal cups to our life jackets and dipped them into the water whenever we were thirsty. It was a small glimpse into a time before we used our waterways as dumpsters, polluting them with trash, applying chemicals to lawns and farmland, and covering natural filtration systems with concrete parking lots and riverfront properties. I wondered if my kids would ever have the simple pleasure of drinking straight from a river. A sadness sank in my stomach—somehow I knew they would not. Even remote rivers like the Hayes are being polluted from faraway industries through air particles that cross the land and settle on their waters. In the same way, I was born too late to experience drinking directly from the pristine Boundary Waters wilderness, as was the norm decades before I ever paddled a canoe.

The Nelson River, just north of the Hayes, had been severely dammed (starting in the 1950s) and stripped of its natural rapids and falls. But the Hayes was still free to flow naturally as it dropped 725 feet from source to sea, at times cascading down large rocks to form dramatic rapids and at others sliding smoothly over rocky terrain. So far we had only experienced the latter calm stretches of the river. But today we faced our first real rapid set. It had been four years since we maneuvered fast water sprinkled with obstacles. I was nervous we had somehow forgotten how.

Leaving Robinson Falls, the river widened into Logan Lake. The shore was covered in reeds and grasses, reminiscent of Hairy Lake, with pine trees set back far from the water's edge. A slight tailwind coupled with the downstream current quickly pushed us through the "liver" (our word for lakelike sections of the river) and back into the narrow and winding sections through large granite rock outcrops. We twisted around sharp bends similar to the zigzags on a heart-rate monitor until the familiar sound of rushing water hit my ears before my eyes could see the rapids. We paddled close to shore, ready to pull over at the first sign of white-water.

Ann and I had been trained to scout every rapid set before paddling it to determine a route and make sure no large rocks or pillows (mostly submerged boulders in the water that create small eddies) took us by surprise. This was something that we would do less and less as we became more familiar with the river. The Hap Maps described whitewater sets as easy or difficult on a scale of class I to class V rapids (based on the technique required to ma-neuver the rapids and the volume of the water). If a rapid set was classified as class I, II, or III *volume,* we would often run it with-out scouting first because it generally meant there were few real obstacles blocking our path. A class III *technical* meant that we would have to use whitewater paddling techniques to skirt around rocks and trees or to quickly cross from one side of the river to the other. We agreed not to run any rapids classified above class III technical with a loaded canoe. We didn't want to risk damaging our boat beyond repair or losing any necessary gear, especially when we were so close to the Bay. Hitting just one rock the wrong way could be enough to puncture our fragile Kevlar canoe. We had a repair kit with sheets of fiberglass and epoxy that we hoped never to use. (But that's also what we thought about the foghorn.) Around the next bend we saw the frothy white tops of rapids dancing excitedly as the river dropped quickly in elevation.

"Let's pull out on that boulder," Ann suggested. We were ner-vous to paddle the first rapid set of our trip and conservatively pulled out sooner than necessary to scout the river. There was a clear "V" (referring to the shape the rapids make, usually com-ing together to make a V shape at the end of a set). A little farther down was a small ledge to our left. We walked the length of the set and discussed strategy in great detail.

"Okay. Start river left, staying tight to the boulder until we pass that rock. Then backferry to river right before the ledge. Stay center right to avoid the rocks on far river right. Ride out the V at the end, moving right center to center, exiting just outside of the highest-volume waves at the end of the V." I summarized the plan. We repeated it over and over again. We could have spent another hour on that boulder scouting the set, but it would not have changed our rocky fate.

"What if we start with a backferry?" Ann suggested. Backferrying is a technique where both parties paddle backward to move slowly through the rapids, giving the paddlers more time to respond to obstacles and to maneuver from one side of the river to the other. The tricky part is that the bow and stern paddlers switch roles: the person in the bow takes on the responsibility of directing the canoe and the person in the stern becomes the powerhouse, focusing on backpaddling until the bow paddler requests their assistance with a pry or a draw to help turn the boat. It was a conservative play to enter the set backferrying, but the sharp tips of the large river waves spooked us into making what we thought was the safest decision for our first big rapid set of the trip.

We untied our boat and loaded our most precious cargo, Myhan, into the middle of the canoe behind the bear barrel. Ann told her to be on her best behavior, like a mother would say to their kids before taking them out in public. "Don't mess this up for us, Myhan!" I followed. We were new to parenting, but I enjoyed working as a team with Ann to care for our fluffy, mischievous child. Myhan, struggling to translate the words directed at her, was looking forward to her upcoming rollercoaster ride.

"Bow is stern, stern is bow. Angle the back of the boat to the right side of the river. The bow is stern . . ." I internally repeated our plan in my head, worried that once we caught the current my memory would quickly float downstream with it. We started backpaddling. The stern of the boat swayed from right to left as we adjusted until it settled in at a slight angle, pointing toward the opposite shore. But we were moving too slowly. We started drifting too far to the right as we entered the set. The first wave crashed around our canoe. I saw the bow dip below the surface as water rushed over the spray skirt like rain over pavement. The submerged rock to our right got closer and closer. Why was it moving toward us so quickly? I briefly considered that the rocks were really trolls bent over, strategically changing the course of the rapids to interrupt our foolproof plan. *SPLASH!* Another wave crashed over the spray skirt and brought me back to reality. I needed to focus. Our canoe just missed a large pillow as the current continued to pull us much farther to the right than we had anticipated. Our well-thought-out plan was hopeless. "Screw backferrying! Paddle forward!" Ann yelled from the stern. "Amen, sister," I thought. It was every woman for herself. If either of us saw a rock or obstacle, we would make a split-second decision and hope we were executing a similar strategy.

Myhan felt the chaos and decided it was a good time to stand on top of the bear barrel for a better view and perhaps a more exhilarating ride down the rapids. I glanced back briefly to see her towering high above the gunwales. I was initially impressed that she managed to fit all four of her fluffy feet within the small circular top of the barrel. But then I felt how tippy our canoe was as it swayed from side to side, with Myhan swaying along with it. It hit me that we were probably going to swamp. The whole canoe—our gear, dog, everything—bobbing down a class III rapid set like amateurs on inner tubes. What happened to our whitewater skills? Had we been off the rapids for too long? For a brief moment we went broadside (perpendicular) with the current, highly unrecommended. We straightened out just in time to hit the large waves at the end of the set. Water engulfed the bow and crashed around us as I blindly paddled forward. I was glad I couldn't see Myhan. I could only imagine what life looked like through Ann's eyes at that moment. Then everything went still.

It took me a moment to realize that our boat was still floating upright and that all expeditioners, dog included, were accounted for. I looked back to see a wet Myhan still standing on top of the bear barrel with a crazed look of adrenaline on her face. She was like a child who just went on her first fair ride and immediately wanted to go again. Ann's expression was similar, but had sprinkles of luck and fear mixed in. I appreciated their strange resemblance. "Hey! We made it!" I said, trying to sound proud. But we both knew we had messed up. Even though we made it through unscathed, I felt as if thousands of people had just watched us struggle through those rapids and weren't quite sure how to respond, as if our attempt had been broadcast across the nation under the headline "Female Canoers Less Capable Than Anticipated." Or worse, Milton was right: "They'll never make it to the Bay!" I could see him clutching his Bud Light Lime and shaking his finger at the camera.

The river continued through a narrow rocky canyon with small swifts and ripples that gently guided us through the corridor. The steep granite walls hugged us on all sides as if to comfort us after our bad show on the rapids. We spent a great deal of time analyzing where we went wrong and how to improve for next time. Whether or not it was productive, it passed the time and made us both feel better. It would not happen again, we agreed.

I kept one eye on the map to make sure the next set, "Hell's Gate" (not a comforting name), didn't take us by surprise. I asked Ann, "Have you thought about your plans after the trip? I mean, what you wanna do before school starts up?" I was nervous to ask this question because it hinted at the end of our journey. And I knew we weren't ready to talk about that yet.

"I'll probably head out to Alaska for a few weeks. Hitchhike out there and visit some friends," she responded. "You?"

"I dunno. Probably hang out at your parents' cabin as long as possible!" I laughed, half-jokingly. Unlike Ann, who was heading to graduate school in Colorado that fall, I had no plans whatsoever.

I carried the weight of a woman who desperately wanted to do great things but didn't know what they were or how or where to do them. I didn't want the type of job they had us "test" for in high school. I didn't want to be a nurse or a policewoman or a lawyer or a doctor. I wanted to make a mark on the world that was unique and impactful, to do something untraditional and totally out of the box. After a long silence I said, "Let's be honest, I'll probably just move back in with my parents and work at Starbucks, if they'll have me."

"If Starbucks will have you? Or your parents?" Ann jabbed.

"Both," I responded in a surprisingly serious tone.

Ann must have noticed I had left the present world to live in a scary unknown future because she started pointing out the different species of trees, mostly black spruce and tamarack. Around the next bend we saw a moose and her calf wading by the bank of the river. They stared at us, just as surprised by our sudden appearance as we were by theirs. Myhan looked like she wanted to bark but didn't know how. The current pushed us around the bend, and the moose disappeared in the canyon behind us. We were definitely not on the Minnesota River anymore.

SPRING BREAK AT HELL'S GATE

T HE LOW HUM OF RUSHING WATER grew louder as we approached its source—Hell's Gate. We were more than a little concerned by the name. The Hap Maps suggested that we could run the set on river right, around a rock island, and then ride out the V to the end. We pulled over on river left and listened for the rapid, which sounded more like a large waterfall than a run-of-the-mill set. Finally, we emerged from the spruce to find a ledge running across the width of the river that we were definitely *not* going to run. Instead, we portaged through the thick trees and put in at the middle of the set to ride the waves out to the end.

During one of multiple trips carrying our gear downstream of the ledge, I realized that we didn't often venture into the woods without a path to guide the way. Here everything felt untouched. The air was moist, and a rainbow of green mosses carpeted the forest floor, covering hidden boulders from long ago that were slowly sinking into the wet earth. Though I knew it wasn't true, it felt like we were the first people to make a mark in the soft ground beneath us. There were no signs of other footprints, human or animal, along our path down to the river. Once back in the canoe, we expertly maneuvered the second half of the set. Even Myhan redeemed herself, staying low in the canoe and only slightly lifting her head above the gunwales to enjoy the ride. This time I hoped Milton was watching from his inn at Gull Harbour. We continued on the winding river until it widened into a large lake, where we looked for a place to camp.

We sang loudly as the moon began to rise over the still waters of Lake Opiminegoka. The sun had just set, though we couldn't see it beyond the dark sky looming on the horizon. It looked like rain was on the way. In his journal from his Hudson Bay expedition in 2005, Scott mentioned that he met a couple who owned an island cabin on Lake Opiminegoka. Our killer instincts from the Minnesota and Red Rivers kicked in. We hoped that if we sang loud enough, that same couple would magically appear to offer us a room in their cabin for the night. But the world seemed quieter the louder we sang.

In the waning light we saw a small structure on an island in the middle of the lake. We pulled up to the dock and turned on our headlamps to explore. Briefly, images from every horror movie I'd ever seen flashed in my mind (ax murderers!). Those thoughts quickly dissipated as Myhan ran along the perimeter of the island like a trained night guard. Trash littered the ground everywhere from the dock to the cabin. Perhaps a bear had scavenged the island before our arrival, or maybe we had just missed a big rager in the wilderness. We stopped at the thin plywood door and looked at each other, waiting for the other person to push it open. Pandora's box? Zombie jail? Who knew what we would unleash into the night. Ann bravely opened the door and stepped inside as I followed. Her headlamp flooded the empty room with light to reveal a kitchen area and two wooden structures that looked like cots.

"Well, should we move in?" I said, hoping that Ann and I were on the same wavelength. She shrugged and nodded. So began what we affectionately called "Hudson Bay Bound Spring Break: Good Decisions 2011."

Our last spring break in college had checked all the boxes for what a college spring break should be, including an attempt to entice a goat into a canoe with carrots, but that's another story. College is a weird time. For me, it was filled with escapism so I could briefly forget my impending undefined future. HBB Spring Break was no different. Maybe it was the upcoming whitewater sets or the week we would soon spend in polar bear country.

Whatever the reason, we came to the conclusion that now was a great time to sit back and relax. Until, of course, the guilt of inactivity surfaced and pushed us forward again, as it always did.

For two nights we lived comfortably on our very own island. We decided that clothes were not necessary. We played music and took naps in hammocks. We fished and swam and wrote poems that no one will ever read. Myhan barked for the first time at a fish flopping on a granite slope before we killed it, filleted it, and fried it for dinner. On the second day we wanted to make sure we knew how to load and shoot the gun in case we needed to use it. Unlike when we first shot the 12-gauge in Ann's neighborhood near Minneapolis, the cops were too far away to hear the loud boom. I pressed the stock into my shoulder and aimed for the endless forest across the lake. BANG! My body jolted back. Two bald eagles frantically flew out of the trees where I had arbitrarily aimed my bullet. That shot, on a remote island on Lake Opiminegoka in northern Manitoba, was the last time I fired a gun.

We used our satellite phone for the first time to call a reporter in Minneapolis, who agreed to be our blog ghostwriter for the more remote sections of our trip. After we recounted our travels since Norway House, the reporter told us that there had been fifty-seven polar bear sightings in Churchill just last week. York Factory was a mere 194 kilometers south of Churchill. If it was an active polar bear year in Churchill, it would probably be busy at the mouth of the Hayes River, too. The news reminded us that we had somewhere to be. Even if a parade of polar bears was waiting for us at the finish line. It was time to go.

The next morning we pored over the Hap Maps before waving goodbye to our island vacation spot. There was a short stretch of river to paddle before Windy Lake, followed by four rapid sets that would dump us into Oxford Lake. Oxford House, home to the Bunibonibee Cree Nation (formerly known as Oxford House First Nation), is located on the eastern shore of Oxford Lake. The Muswagons had called ahead to let the council know we were coming, and Chief Irvin Sinclair offered to host us at his house when we arrived.

A slight wind from the northeast moved gently across the lake, rallying the water to march southwest for the day—a headwind for us. Ever since Lake Winnipeg, whenever I saw the wind blow across the water in the morning, I would instinctively think, "We've gotta go. And fast." Too often we let the hours pass in the calm early morning only to be windbound in the afternoon, when the high sun pulls the air across the landscape. But what would Windy Lake be if not windy? After Marsh Lake, Hairy Lake, and Hell's Gate, how disappointing would it have been to not experience the namesake of Windy Lake, too?

The waves picked up as the river widened into the lake, getting larger and larger as we paddled out of the protected channel. I was reminded of our upwind battle on Mud Lake before arriving at White Rock Dam, the beginning of the Bois de Sioux River. Back then, the waves seemed enormous and difficult to handle. After paddling Lake Winnipeg, those same waves, now on Windy Lake, appeared calmer and more manageable. Everything is relative on an expedition. I may never paddle again in conditions like those we faced on Lake Winnipeg. Admittedly, there were times when we should not have been out paddling at all. But now the moderate headwind felt safe and easy. Windy Lake was just another day on the job, another experience soon to be backlogged in our minds to help determine how concerned or comforted we should feel when taking on a similar challenge in the future.

As we paddled I thought about how this perspective might apply to my life after the trip. Surely being able to paddle large waves was not a gold star on my resume. Once we reached Hudson Bay, what then? Ann had to be in Colorado by late September to start a master's program in statistical ecology. She mentioned visiting a friend in Alaska beforehand. Either way, she had a solid date and a location. I didn't have anything. After more than fifteen years of school I had no point of reference for what it was like to be out on my own. For the first time in my life there was nothing backlogged to assure me it was going to be okay.

I thought back to my very first Menogyn trip, when our group of six high school girls and one guide got stuck in a bad storm in the Boundary Waters. It was the first time in my life that I could not simply go inside to wait out the bad weather. I had no previous experience telling me that I would be okay as the wind picked up and the lightning flashed freely in the sky around us. But everyone was in it together. And because of that I felt safe and supported in the chaos. I could only hope for a similar community as I ventured into adult life after our expedition.

～～～～～

The rapid sets after Windy Lake were fast and fun. We strategically cruised around boulders and weaved in and out of small islands in the river. It felt like we had an outdoor carnival all to ourselves. We rode the thrilling current through amazing scenery, with something new and entertaining to see around each bend. We portaged over the last rapid set for the day and set up camp on the shores of Oxford Lake, where we would stay much longer than anticipated. The next morning we enjoyed a relaxing breakfast.

"Ready? Who am I?" Ann set her bowl of granola on the mossy ground and looked up while dramatically pointing into the sky. I rolled around laughing at her theatrical impression of what was clearly our friends who joined us for a paddle on the Red River, awestruck by every bird we saw.

"Okay, okay, who am I?" I switched roles between freaking out and pretending to be a slithering snake. To the best of my ability, I pretended to sword fight an invisible monster just as Ann had fended off the snakes on the desolate shores of Lake Winnipeg. I think she knew what I was reenacting before she said it to encourage my continued tomfoolery. There is nothing quite like making a complete a fool of oneself in the thick of the forest.

"The great snake encounter of 2011, of course!" Ann laughed and looked out at the lake through the trees. "We gotta go, Nat. Look at the wind starting up on the lake." She was right. We packed up and only briefly glanced at the maps before launching on the large lake.

Oxford Lake is not the place to briefly glance at a map and think you've got it covered. It stretches over 240 square kilometers and is littered with islands, peninsulas, and bays that team up to confuse canoeists on their way east to rejoin the Hayes River. I could almost hear our compass, now sitting at the bottom of Lake Winnipeg, chuckling as we ventured off into the watery maze with only our wits and paper maps to guide the way.

The waves picked up throughout the day until they became so large that water began to trickle into our canoe every time we cut through a crest. Perhaps it would have been wise to put on the spray skirt. Now, in the middle of the windy lake, was not the time to think about what we should have done. I thought that after Lake Winnipeg every wave would seem harmless, but fear was starting to creep back into my bones as I dug my paddle into the fierce water. Navigating maps took a back seat to staying safe and keeping the boat perpendicular with the waves.

Ann was in the stern. She was in control. I noticed that she was cutting the waves too far to the east.

"Ann! I think we need to go left of this island!" I yelled from the bow without looking back.

"What?" she yelled in return.

"Left! I think we need to go more left!" I tried again. The ten feet between us might as well have been ten kilometers. The sounds of the howling wind and crashing waves engulfed us entirely—it was impossible to communicate. I let it go, but my heart told me we were headed the wrong way. We realized our mistake when we found ourselves in a bay about fifteen kilometers off course. After a quiet and tense lunch on the beach we rerouted and battled the unforgiving headwind to Oxford House.

The sun slowly sank lower in the sky as we continued east around a large peninsula. The wind eventually settled into a whisper as the sky began its nightly display of pink and yellow fireworks. The silhouette of a small island without trees came into view. In the distance, a motorboat sped east from the island to what must be Oxford House—our destination. After twelve hours of continuous paddling, we were almost there.

The fresh and familiar smell of the north woods changed. I inhaled deeply. Could I smell the town from kilometers away? The scent worsened as we approached the treeless island. I noticed its unnatural silhouette in the waning light. It was entirely covered with trash: the local landfill.

There are no roads or trains to Oxford House. The only way to get there is by boat or by plane. In that sense, it was very different from Norway House, which was a ten-hour drive north from Winnipeg. We had traveled 960 kilometers (as the crow flies) northeast of Winnipeg to one of the most remote areas of the world. I was initially saddened by the presence of garbage in the middle of such a pristine lake. To be sure, it is a strange sight to see after living in the wilderness for so long. But it made sense. Where else would the Oxford House community dispose of their trash? It's not like a garbage company was going to show up to haul it away and out of sight. An island seemed like a good location to deter unwanted wildlife from getting cozy near town, too.

Home to the Bunibonibee Cree First Nation, Oxford House is a community of around twenty-five hundred residents located at the eastern end of Oxford Lake at the mouth of the Hayes River. It was established in 1798 by the Hudson's Bay Company as a fur-trading post in between York Factory and Norway House. Many Swampy Cree Natives, a band of the Cree Nation occupying lands in northern Manitoba, were forced to settle at Oxford House. Cree First Nations, including Norway House and Berens River, first signed Treaty 5 in 1875 and 1876. Oxford House did not sign on to the treaty until 1909, agreeing to a permanent relationship with the Canadian government. Through Treaty 5, the Bunibonibee Cree First Nation hoped to receive annuities and access to resources and reserves in return for their land. Similar to Norway House, each resident of Oxford House receives an annual payment of $5, the band leader receives $15, and the chief receives $150.

Treaty 5 provided smaller reserve areas and fewer resources than previous numbered treaties. Because the First Nations negotiated terms orally and in their own language, which were not accurately translated onto paper in English, the circumstances surrounding the signing of Treaty 5 have received warranted scrutiny. Many people speculate that if the signatories of the treaty really knew what they were agreeing to—surrendering their land and livelihood to the government—then they would never have signed it.

We landed on the beach in the dark, hopeful that Chief Sinclair was still awake and awaiting our call. There was cell phone reception, but Ann's phone had been dead for almost two weeks. We went to a nearby gas station and waited while it charged, struggling to keep our eyes open after the long day. The countertop by the soda machine looked comfy enough for a night's rest. My eyes were involuntarily flickering closed and flinging open again when I realized that I was falling asleep standing up. The lights in the gas station seemed much brighter than I remembered unnatural light being. It had been a full week since we had seen anyone or anything besides the shapes and colors of the wilderness. If this small town seemed overwhelming, I wondered what it would feel like to get off the train in Winnipeg or to return to city life in Minneapolis or, better yet, Miami.

I could hear the faint ringtone through Ann's phone, pressed awkwardly against her ear. Her face saddened as each ring went by. Had we arrived too late?

"Hello? Ladies? Are you here?" a voice answered excitedly. Within minutes a crew of people showed up in a pickup truck. The chief and his entourage emptied our loaded canoe and threw everything into the truck, expertly tying the canoe to the top.

"Well, what are you waiting for? Let's get going!" Sinclair smiled and signaled for us to hop in the bed of the truck with our gear.

We swerved through the dark woods, bouncing up and down on the bumpy dirt road. The night sky peeked in and out of the treetops. I caught glimpses of the stars, just starting to shine for the night. The cold wind blew the tiredness right out of my body and replaced it with the sensation that I was here and nowhere else. Fragments of my thoughts incessantly occupied with histories, futures, and relationships briefly sprang together into one place. Instead of worrying about becoming someone, I was aware of being someone. Here, bouncing around in the back of a pickup truck with my best friend, our dog, and a group of complete strangers, I felt alive and whole.

We pulled up to Irvin Sinclair's house and unloaded our gear by moonlight. After briefly meeting his daughters we were shown to our room. We fell asleep in our own twin beds with Myhan resting on the carpet between us. It was her first night sleeping with us instead of wandering through the woods.

The next morning, we went into the kitchen to make breakfast. Irvin's two daughters, seventeen and eighteen years old, didn't seem interested in hanging out with us. They avoided us for most of the day. Craving a relaxing afternoon, we watched several movies in a row, repeating one because we liked it so much. We were slowly becoming part of the couch like high schoolers on summer vacation.

"Ladies? Are you there? It's Irvin!" My weak legs wobbled through the kitchen to answer the door. My upper body was becoming increasingly large and muscular as my lower body was quickly shrinking to all but skin and bone. It was a miracle I didn't topple right over.

"Would you like a tour of the town? We can visit the conservation house, and you can attend a council meeting, if you want."

"Sure!" We were still standing at the door. I thought it curious that he didn't just come right in, since this was his house after all.

The conservation house was an old log building with a small office and gift shop. The conservation officer greeted us and almost immediately began to pray loudly over us while we stood there awkwardly. We were sick of getting prayed over. It felt less like a peaceful blessing and more like a concern for our safety, like a socially acceptable way for people to publicly express doubts about our trip. I was surprised to find that most people in the town identified as Christian. We learned that the United Church played a major role in the development of the community. Ministers and their wives were the first nurses and teachers. When the officer was done with his prayer, he gave us a survey to fill out.

Question 1. Do you like trees? Answer yes or no.
Question 2. Why do you like trees?
Question 3. Do you like rocks? Why or why not?

The survey went on like this. I wondered what data they were looking to collect. We received two Hayes River mugs to add to our collection of unnecessary items.

Irvin gave us a tour of the town and brought us to the council meeting. There was something different about our interactions with the community members here compared to our experience at Norway House, but I couldn't quite put my finger on it. From Mike's stories I knew of the injustices and struggles of the First Nation communities. But everyone we met here seemed to be saying, "Everything is peachy at Oxford House! Tell your friends in the States how great it is here!" Unlike the open conversations we had with the Muswagons, it seemed as if everyone we met at Oxford House painted only a positive picture of their home without any reference to poverty, food access, education, or any of the other issues we had recently learned about from Mike.

We stayed at Oxford House for three nights. The rain came down for days, and temperatures dropped into the forties in mid-August. On the evening of the second day, we returned back to the house to find that everyone else had "moved out." We had been welcomed into the Sinclairs' home, but they decided to stay elsewhere during the rest of our visit. Had we watched too many movies? Did we do something to insult them? I had a feeling that they wanted us to have the best experience possible and did so by isolating us from the town and its issues. From then on, we were left all alone in their house, waiting for the rain to let up so we could depart with dry gear for the journey ahead. The leaves were starting to turn yellow, signaling that we should not linger much longer.

I looked over at Ann sitting on the couch. She had a daze about her, her eyes glazed over, as we settled into our seventh movie in three days. Could we be depressed? I, too, had little motivation to do anything or go anywhere. My eyes shifted from Ann to a shelf stacked with CDs next to an old boom box. I remembered that today was Ann's trail birthday. She hadn't said anything about it, and I wondered if she thought I had forgotten. Then I spotted the answer to our funk: *Crunk Hits Volume 4*. Nothing cheers up Ann like a little Lil Wayne. I put it on full blast and started singing and dancing around the couch where she sat. Whenever I'm feeling low I like to blast some old-school jams and dance my heart out. We danced the night away and took advantage of the oven to make a cake for Ann's fake birthday (she decided to turn nineteen, again).

KNIFE RAPIDS

~~~~~✕~~~~~

THE NEXT MORNING, AUGUST 18, we portaged our gear from the house to the water and took off toward the rocky rapids and polar bear country ahead. There was nothing but wilderness between Oxford House and York Factory. No more sleeping indoors or waiting out bad weather. No more procrastinating the inevitable end of our journey, of our life together in a canoe. Or so we thought.

As we paddled away from Oxford House toward the mouth of the Hayes River, the current sucked our boat into the channel like a vacuum. There are forty-five sets of rapids and falls on the Hayes, most of which were still ahead, spread across the 380 kilometers between us and the shores of Hudson Bay. Our maps suggested it would take fourteen to eighteen days to paddle the rest of the river, which would put us at York Factory at the beginning of September. But the maps had also suggested it would take eight to ten days to paddle from Norway House to Oxford House, which we did quite lazily in seven, including our HBB Spring Break. With nowhere else to stop along the way, I had a feeling we would make it there faster than we thought.

The day ahead was filled with treacherous whitewater sets that were much longer and rockier than previous ones. There were few easy places to pull off the river to scout, but it didn't always matter since some of the sets went on back-to-back for kilometers, making it impossible to plan a route through the rushing water. We had to navigate as we went and hope that a quick decision would not lead to a rocky fate farther downstream.

"Rock! Go right!" I yelled from the bow. I felt Ann respond.

The rock brushed by on the left. This went on for hours. Right! Left! Left! The water calmed down briefly. I stood up in the canoe, eyeing Myhan to stay low, as if to say, "Just because I do this doesn't mean you can do it, too." We felt comfortable in *Kawena Kinomaeta*, our home, and knew how to stand in moving water without upsetting her. Just like our paddles, she had become an extension of our bodies. She was our feet on the water. We stopped trying to scout the water ahead. Our brains processed the terrain and hydrology as rocks and riffles appeared in front of us. Both our arms and the canoe responded almost effortlessly. We continued in this way through class I and II rapids, weaving in and out of islands and shallow waters. We clicked as a team, as if we could read each other's minds.

"I don't see a good way through this one." The trance was broken. Ann was right. There was no clear path ahead, just a small ledge across the width of the river. We were always taught to look for the horizon line. If we could not see the continuation of the river, if everything seemed calm but there was space unaccounted for in between the water and the trees on the shore, that meant trouble. "Let's pull over and scout," I said. The days of my unwillingness to take charge of our safety were forever windbound on the sandy shores of Lake Winnipeg. Luckily my disagreements with Ann had faded before running whitewater, a skill that requires teamwork and clear communication. There was no room for resentment in our efforts to safely navigate the risky waters ahead.

Myhan jumped out of the canoe while we were still feet away from shore. She just barely landed on the dry rocks, glancing at the water with disdain. She had yet to go swimming or show any interest in getting her paws wet. Was she old or young? Had she decided on what she liked and disliked yet? Her age was a mystery; so was her breed. Could she really be part wolf? She bolted into the woods for some much-needed exercise after three nights of sleeping indoors.

Ann glanced from where Myhan had disappeared into the forest back to the rocky ledge across the river. "She'll come back. Let's line this one?"

"Yep. Good call." We untied the painter lines from the bow and stern. I was excited to line the upcoming set. When done well, lining a canoe through whitewater is like playing puppet master—a quick pull of the string could make the boat dance through the rapids or twirl into an eddy. Essentially the canoe rides the rapids without us while we control its movements from shore. The painter lines were twenty-five feet long, so we could get some good distance in between us and the boat. We waded through the shallow water near shore, carefully guiding the canoe over the ledge before pushing it off into the rapids alone. I wrapped the rope around my wrist multiple times. I didn't realize it was so tight around my skin until I started losing circulation to my hand. "Pull!" "Loosen up!" "Let's go right!" We shared command after command until we made it to a spot farther downstream that looked paddleable again. But where was Myhan? It had been a solid forty-five minutes since we saw her dart into the woods, without any sign of her since.

"Myhan!" "Myhhaaaannnnnn!" We screamed in unison, holding on to the gunwales of our canoe while we waited. Minutes passed. Trees rustled in the distance much farther downstream. Then we heard a "bark!" but it seemed distant. Rustling and barking, rustling and barking. Was she stuck? Did she need our help? Polar bears had been seen as far inland as Oxford House. As we worried about her safety, I realized that she was not live bait after all. She had given us confidence when we feared the future, but we had no intention of letting a polar bear eat her. She was our protector, and we were hers.

"Look! On the rock!" Ann pointed downstream. Myhan leaped onto a large boulder on the river and stared in our direction, puzzled by how to get back to us. "Let's go get her," I responded.

We ran the rest of the rapid set and skirted past the rock where

Myhan stood. She leaped into action and ran alongside us on the shore until it was safe to pull over. "Well, I think she likes us!" Ann smiled as Myhan jumped back into the canoe and settled in on top of her favorite pack. The jubilee of officially feeling like a pack only lasted a short while, as our next challenge was around the bend: Knife Rapids.

Knife Rapids, too, lived up to its namesake. Rocks like shark teeth stuck out of the river, sharp as knives, slick black, and almost impossible to spot. Kevlar canoes can be easily punctured, and ours was certainly not ideal for these conditions. But as we always said, "A free boat is the best boat." Until it wasn't. We had heard stories of people getting stranded on Knife Rapids with holes the size of basketballs in their canoes. One couple was stuck here for seven days before they were rescued. We pulled over and scouted to the best of our ability, but the rushing river snaked around the corner beyond sight. It didn't look like anything to write home about. The waves were no larger or more intimidating than our very first rapid set on the Hayes. But the rumors of Knife Rapids echoed in our minds. We agreed to go slow and keep a sharp eye out for rocks below the surface.

The plan was clear. Backferry left, backferry right, backferry middle. Zigzag around obstacles left to right, right to left, as slowly and as carefully as possible. "What if we puncture the boat?" I asked Ann. She shrugged, hinting it was an unhelpful question. I already knew our options. We would patch it. But the weather didn't look promising. It was the type of gray overcast day that makes you forget the sun ever shone or think it will never shine again. Could you patch Kevlar and fiberglass with epoxy in the rain? I hoped we wouldn't have to find out. We pushed off from shore and into the chaos.

So began our five-star performance: two women and their furry companion jumping through hoops, dodging shark teeth, virtually high-fiving while chortling downstream on the speedy waterway. Or at least that is how I thought it must have looked from shore before we hit rock bottom. It was a sneaky demise. We aimed for large-volume waves in the middle of the V near the end of the rapids. The bow lifted with the first large wave, and the lip of our skid plate, a protective layer on the bow and stern, caught on the tip of a sharp rock. The upward movement of the bow pushed the stern down. CRACK! A small line appeared in the boat beneath Ann, like in a cartoon when someone with super strength punches the earth and it begins to crack open, one splinter at a time.

"Keep paddling! It's okay! It's going to be okay!" I heard Ann yell from the stern. I kept paddling as if I had not just felt our canoe slam into a brick wall. We were still floating, after all. We eased out of the set and pulled over at Trout Falls to portage our gear to the other side of the waterfall. There was water in the canoe, but not much. The crack looked more like a long ridged line than an open gash. We felt like failures for not completing the rapids without any scars. There was nothing to say, no comforting words that were not already understood. Not even muttering "It'll be fine" could change how we felt at that moment. We ate lunch in silence while looking out over a rushing waterfall.

After Trout Falls, the current slowed as the river entered Knee Lake. I noticed for the first time that I was wet from head to toe and quite cold. I dipped my fingers into the lake. It felt warm. Perhaps a swim would feel nice. My body told me the water was warm, but I knew that couldn't be right. We were on an Arctic river that was frozen more than eight months out of the year. I was a long way from Miami Beach.

Thunder rumbled behind us, and the gray sky threatened rain as we pulled over to camp in Painkiller Bay. "Is that a good namesake or a bad one, you think?" I asked.

"Could be a natural painkiller, like you don't need them because it has natural healing powers. Or it could be so treacherous that we'll need to take lots of painkillers. Let's go find out," Ann responded jokingly.

On another day, a warm sunny day, it would have been the former. A large granite rock sloped like a sand beach from the trees to the water's edge. The lake was calm until raindrops disturbed its mirrorlike reflection. My hands shook violently as I cooked dinner. Ann set up the tent in the rain. We ate standing up, interchanging bites with jumping jacks to keep warm before running into the tent for the night. I curled into a ball in my sleeping bag and was awake all night trying to get warm until, hours later, dim light shone on the blue tent flap—the beginning of a new day. I watched the raindrops fall, collect, and trickle off the sides of the tent until Ann woke up.

~~~~~~

"IT DOESN'T LOOK GOOD," Ann said as she looked up from the canoe after examining the damage from Knife Rapids. "We need to patch it."

I rummaged around in our packs and pulled out the Kevlar repair kit, which consisted of sheets of fiberglass and epoxy glue. "It says we need to patch it in a cool dry place. And that it needs to dry for at least twenty-four hours."

"Where are we going to live? What are we going to eat?!" Ann began to laugh. I looked at her, crouched down by our cracked canoe in the cold rain, and began to laugh, too. We decided to continue with business as usual. If water entered our canoe we would bail it out, and we would be extra careful on future whitewater sets. Pam Raiho would not be pleased to hear we had broken our boat and that we were paddling it anyway in the rain. Whenever anything happened, big or small, her famous one-liner was, "What are you going to do? Where are you going to live? What are you going to eat?"

We paddled out of Painkiller Bay with wet gear, a wet dog, and an inch of water in the bottom of our canoe. Paddling brought warmth back to my body. I never wanted to stop, afraid of another cold and sleepless night.

"Do you see that, too?" I needed confirmation from Ann that I was not hallucinating when a beautiful lodge came into view. We didn't expect to see anything like this until the historic buildings at York Factory.

"Yeah, weird," she responded. The unmistakable sound of an ATV hit our ears. "I think someone spotted us!"

A man got off the ATV and ran onto a dock, signaling for us to pull over. A sad display of old damaged canoes came into view as we neared the shore. Some of them were completely trashed; one even had plywood nailed over a large hole in the stern.

"It's the canoe graveyard," the man explained. "This is where people usually end their trip after Knife Rapids. I see you've made it through!" He smiled and waited for us to get out of the canoe. "I'm Mark. It's nice to meet you. I haven't seen people in six months, except for the pilot who drops off my food, of course!" he explained, perhaps to justify his enthusiasm. "Any chance you'd like a hot shower and a room for the night?"

I shrugged and looked at Ann to say, "Why not?" It was not in our plan to dillydally after our stint at Oxford House, but between my lack of sleep, the dreary weather, and the enticing idea that we could patch our boat indoors, it seemed like a good idea.

Mark looked like we could trust him. There was no hint that he was a creepy serial killer living in the woods waiting to murder young canoeists. Ann and I had found the world to be much more gentle and welcoming than what was typically portrayed in the news. We learned over several cups of hot chocolate that he was a musician before he went into the Air Force. After a kid and a failed marriage he ended up here as a caretaker, living all alone on Knee Lake at a five-star lodge in the middle of nowhere. The lodge was closed for the season while Mark made improvements. This meant we could take over the luxurious lounge to patch our canoe, which we took full advantage of. It was a seemingly out-of-place thing to do next to a pool table.

Usually fishers would be flying in to enjoy the abundant lakes and rivers paired with modern comforts—a chef, large spacious lounges with fireplaces, and big fluffy beds in private cabins. But this year, it was just him and the wolves. They howled all night, beckoning Myhan to join their pack and live the wild life she was born to lead. Luckily, our slowly diminishing bag of dog food kept her around, for now. We cozied into what was usually the maid's room. Once again, we found ourselves sinking into soft blankets and pillows.

"Maybe that skeptical outdoor rep was right. This trip is a vacation!" I joked as we giggled about the fortuitous day. But my hands still felt the cold sting of the rain that morning. The possibilities of polar bears and dangerous waters ahead weighed heavily on me as I fell asleep in a bed for the last time before reaching the Bay.

Our Kevlar patch successfully dried overnight. In the morning, Mark fed us breakfast and brought us a bottle of wine. "Open this when you get to the finish line," he said proudly. Unlike so many other people we encountered along our trip, Mark never expressed any concern or doubt in our ability to finish. We added the wine to our pack of mementos. Tricky portages lay ahead, but it gave us something concrete to look forward to, something to mark the true end of our expedition in what would otherwise be a blurry whirlwind of bears, planes, and trains.

OUR PREVIOUS TRIPS through the Boundary Waters, Quetico, Wabakimi Provincial Park, and Nunavut, Canada, were littered with difficult portages. We felt like we had seen it all: downed trees, swampy land, steep slopes, and unclear paths extending for kilometers. But this next portage was incomprehensible. The type of feat you think about and say, "That can't be right" before realizing there is no other option.

There had been a fire. New vegetation was slowly pushing up around the burn area. Burned and fallen trees created a maze of small fences across kilometers of shoreline. Like a barbed wire fence, sharp wooden spikes protruded from the sides of tree trunks where branches used to live. The river was too rough and shallow to paddle. We had to portage. I was reminded of the scene in *Sleeping Beauty* where the prince plows through tangled thorns to get to the castle to save the princess. Except he had a sword (instead of more than fifty pounds of gear). Our day had already been filled with lining and running whitewater sets after we left Knee Lake. It must have been late afternoon, but it was hard to tell. We looked over the endless expanse of fallen death traps ahead of us.

"Well, should we set up camp and tackle this in the morning?" Ann asked.

I exhaled loudly and watched my breath float away. For a second it looked as if I was blowing smoke. The air was icy cold and getting colder. "Let's camp," I said after some thought. Getting warm was a priority.

The next morning it took us several hours to cross the burn field. It was each woman for herself. I tried taking the path of least resistance to find that it only led me in circles, farther and farther from the river. The only way across was above or below the fallen trees. The sting of sharpened branches cut my legs. For a while, I walked only on top of the trees, portaging on a rickety balance beam, until I fell again and again into the thorny underbrush. It was tempting to just sit and think about how unbearable it was. But we inched forward. Eventually it was over, but not without battle scars.

The river rewarded us with a tailwind across Swampy Lake followed by a fun section of class I and II rapids braided in and out of some small islands. On the maps, the river looked like interwoven strings, some leaving the main channel for several kilometers before returning. We were moving so quickly through the fast current that it was hard to find where we were on the maps. Beware the horizon line . . .

"Ledge! Backpaddle!" I heard Ann yell after hours of smooth sailing.

I saw it too late. We frantically backpaddled, but the current was too strong. We were only feet away from being launched over a class V ledge.

"Well, here we go!" Ann shouted. Her voice suggested there was nothing more we could do to avoid the waterfall.

Reserved energy stored in my muscles exploded through my arms, hands, and paddle. We had been training for this moment, building our strength every day since our departure on the Minnesota River. Our backferrying skills were honed on previous rapid sets. If there was any time to bust out our strength and skills, it was now.

The canoe slowed and began to shift to the right. Somewhere in geologic history a large boulder had fallen into the river, where it sat for centuries. But it created an eddy to our right that miraculously saved us from a wet and rocky fate. The stern hit the eddy. Ann expertly thrust her paddle into the river from the bow, spinning the boat 180 degrees. This threw us fully into the eddy, where we were protected from the strong current. We forward ferried closer to shore where one of the braids in the river branched off to the right. With no discussion, and without even looking at the maps, we headed for the narrow side channel, spurring away from the river, assuming we could connect back farther downstream.

I previously thought that paddling upstream was the slowest form of transportation. But wading waist-deep in water while guiding a canoe down a series of small waterfalls, mixed with crashing portages through the woods—*that* is the slowest form of transportation. We traveled five kilometers in seven hours with no sign of rejoining the main channel. Soaked from head to toe after walking our boat, gear, and dog through the last cascading falls, we finally found respite.

"Wow. Natalie, look," Ann said in awe. I glanced up. Five waterfalls flowed into a small lake with an island in the middle, just big enough for a tent and a cooking area. We were lost, but we had found paradise. After that day, anytime I was asked to envision a heavenly place, a place where I felt most myself and at peace, I would relive that moment again and again. That evening we sat in silence on our small island while looking out at the waterfalls. Living in the wilderness for so long had blurred the lines between river and canoe and woman. The river was my home. It ran through my veins. Not just this river, but all rivers everywhere. Each day my connection with nature deepened. My understanding of water as home, as life, continued to grow.

The next morning we packed up camp and prepared to leave the island in search of the main channel. I was loading the canoe when I saw half of a granola bar on a rock by the water. Ann noticed me looking at it and explained, "It's an offering for the Sasquatch."

We rejoined the river and found our bearings on the map. The current flowed quickly but smoothly through the valley as the land around us grew in elevation from swampy lowlands to rolling hills. Brassy Hill, the highest elevation on our route (almost five hundred feet), appeared in the distance. The land ebbed and flowed with the river. Light faded in the sky until the blue water darkened and we could no longer spot obstacles. It was time to camp. But where? There was nothing but brush and thick forest all around us. If we kept going, we would encounter two class III sets that would not be fun to run at night. As it would turn out, they were not very fun to run the next morning, either.

We moved a fallen tree to make room for our tent. Our home looked sad scrunched between trees and slanted on the uneven ground. But it would do.

"What's for dinner?" Ann asked as she emerged from setting up the tent.

"Welcome to the kitchen!" I said in a British accent. "Tonight's specialty is . . . pancakes, again!" The kitchen was a small patch of dirt behind a fallen tree. Our nonstick pan had become quite sticky, so I made pancakes in a soup pot. This was our fourth meal of pancakes this week. The thought of real food made me salivate.

POLAR BEAR PARADISE

WE WOKE UP AT 6:00 A.M. to pack up camp. Ann bustled around while I lay motionless in my sleeping bag, my body refusing to enter into the cold morning air. I gave myself a silent pep talk: "Get up and get moving, sister! We've got a big day ahead!" I finally crawled out of the tent and stood by the vestibule watching Ann move in double speed to get packed up and on the water in a timely fashion. My teeth chattered and hands cramped in the icy air. I was convinced that if I stood there long enough I would become an ice cube. How was Ann functioning? She looked at me with a smirk and said, "Got that Miami blood, huh?"

Our first rapid set was a class III but not as technical as our previous sets. It looked innocent, so we decided to go without the spray skirt. Each wave crashed into our boat from the bow, filling our canoe with water until we were paddling a small swimming pool down the river. I slowly turned back to assess the damage. Myhan was drenched and in shock. Her thick fur was matted down over her small frame, making her look like a helpless fawn. Ann hadn't noticed the degree to which our boat had flooded because she was preparing for the next set around the bend.

"Ann," I said calmly. "Don't freak out. Move slowly and bail as fast as you can." Our boat was close to becoming a submarine. When there is a lot of water in your canoe the smallest movement can make it tip. It didn't help that Myhan was freaking out in the middle of the boat. I could tell Ann was concerned, but she kept cool as we quickly bailed the water out with old milk cartons, keeping our hips steady while slowly floating toward the next rapid set. The urgency of staying afloat distracted me from noticing that I was shivering from head to toe. There was no room for error where we were now. Hit one rock, go over one ledge . . . if anything happened, we would have to call for help on the satellite phone or, worse, use our emergency device, which would send out an SOS with our GPS coordinates, and wait for air rescue. We waded down a small ledge, hopped back in the boat, and ran the waves from there on. It was affirming to run a set so flawlessly after our previous mishap.

We ran the rapids until we reached Whitemud Falls, our last set, last portage, last *anything* before a solid two hundred kilometers of free-flowing water out to Hudson Bay. I knew that after this portage there was nothing that could stop us from making it to York Factory (except perhaps a bear encounter). The last few days had been overcast, cold, and wet. All of our gear was soaked. Even our toothbrushes were beginning to mold. After almost three months on trail, we were finally ready to end our trip and return to modern comforts, at least for a little while. I felt a lack of nutrition had worn on my health, and I couldn't wait to eat fruits and vegetables again. While the hope of York Factory and relaxation was at our fingertips, we still had kilometers to go on the river, and the rumors of polar bear country echoed in our minds.

We paddled hard. Stamina and endurance are our strengths. Our plan was to make the four-day trip from Whitemud Falls to York Factory in a mere two days. Ann and I paddled for fifteen hours before the sun made us retire to the shore. The moon failed to show as I built a fire to fight the cold. We hoped to stay up all night, afraid of letting our guard down in polar bear country. But after an hour, we felt the weight of our exhaustion and gave in to the comfort of our tent and sleeping bags. Despite our concerns about bears, Ann quickly fell into a deep sleep. I slept, too, aware of the shotgun resting, fully loaded, inches away from my sleeping bag. I was in and out of consciousness, unable to separate dream from reality. I dreamed of creatures surrounding the tent and felt a deep sorrow that we would never actually make it to the end.

We left camp that morning without breakfast and continued on the Hayes. People had warned us of the thick fog and dark clouds typical for this section of the river. The trip journal we had from 2005 read, "It was so foggy that if a polar bear were to come, it would eat us before we even saw it." Luckily, we had a clear morning. We approached the turn where the Gods River flows into the Hayes and saw our first woodland caribou swimming across the water. I was reminded of the great distance we had traveled since leaving Minnesota, where these endangered creatures once traversed. The current quickened at the junction, and we ate a floating lunch of cold quinoa and chili powder from the night before. With ten hours of paddling ahead, we felt as far away from York Factory as we ever had. Our wrists ached, our clenched hands throbbed, and our minds struggled to accept our inner conflict of desperately wanting to arrive somewhere while not wanting our time together to end. The scenery was beautiful— high white-mud cliffs towered to our right, low-lying spruces lined the left, decorating the shoreline, always reminding us of our desolation. Our strokes slowed and stomachs turned. We became desperate for the hours to pass.

BOOOM! A huge clap of thunder came from behind, spooking us both. While we contemplated the threat of oncoming weather, a pack of wolves, five total, one black, came out to the riverbank from behind the spruce. The air was still. There was a suspicious calm. The wolves stopped in their tracks when they felt our presence. We stared. They stared. Myhan barked. A bird sounded a loud cry. The sound brought goosebumps to our skin. We glanced at the dark cloud floating behind us, and we were off with the motivation reminiscent of our efforts on the Red River.

We reached "The Rock," a big rock on the riverbank signaling our remaining distance of fifty . . . forty . . . thirty kilometers. Two more hours. We sang every song we knew, including some Christmas medleys. We saw seals, caribou, and black bears. Every rock looked as if it were swimming our way, and I joked that someone should spray-paint them all black to soothe the nerves of canoe-ists paddling through polar bear country. We were ten hungry, tired, desperate kilometers away. It felt like something could still go wrong. Could we really arrive unscathed at York Factory after eighty-five days of ups and downs? We reached the point where the tide effect would slow us down, but we were still moving steadily toward the Bay. We turned left. A huge expanse of water appeared before our eyes: Hudson Bay.

Delusional and overwhelmed with hunger, Ann and I didn't joyously celebrate the sight of the Bay. We just solemnly pad-dled toward it. I thought about what to say to Ann, but nothing sounded good enough. The last few days had been some of the most trying of my life, and I knew I could relax now, but I felt an emptiness as well. Part of me wanted to break down and sob on the shore for every fear we had overcome and every moment we had shared. The other part of me felt numb, like an old tired woman at the end of her life who just wanted to eat some vege-tables and go to sleep.

There was no party or trophy waiting for us at York Factory. Just a crooked set of stairs leading up to a building that once man-ufactured York boats. As we walked up the steps, I wondered how this had become a major destination for canoeists. Eric Se-vareid and Walter Port made paddling to the Bay a rite of passage for modern paddlers, but it is just a vast shoreline with a few his-toric buildings. We emerged above the steep riverbank at a sign that read "York Factory. National Historic Site of Canada." The site looked abandoned. Across the tundra we saw a large anchor in front of a white building with a green sign that read "Hudson's Bay Company." When Eric and Walter arrived at York Factory in 1930, it was still a community of about three hundred people. Es-tablished in 1684, it was a Hudson's Bay Company fur-trading post for over 270 years. They built York boats, similar to the large boats we saw at Norway House, and branded them with the fa-mous YF logo on the side. Many of the buildings are gone now, and the only people living here today are seasonal employees hired by the Canadian government to take care of the land and remaining structures.

Myhan stretched her legs around the grounds while we walked on the boardwalk looking for any sign of human life. We turned the corner around a building and took two of the caretakers completely by surprise. After explaining who we were, they said, "It's a good thing you made it today. The season is ending early and we are all leaving tomorrow!"

We couldn't believe it. The suggested paddling time from Oxford House to York Factory is fourteen to eighteen days. We had paddled it in seven. If we had arrived one day later we would have been greeted with silence. It wouldn't have been the end of the world, of course. We would have camped and used our satellite phone to call the float plane. But it was safer to stay inside. Camping along the shores of Hudson Bay was not recommended because of high polar bear activity. The caretakers graciously offered us a small cabin with a bunk bed for the night.

I saw them talking to us but could not process what they were saying. My stomach painfully twisted and turned. We hadn't eaten in hours. It was all I could think about. We had been so cognizant about every paddle stroke bringing us closer to Hudson Bay that we didn't want to waste time eating.

". . . and then we can show you all of the historic items that just pop out of the shoreline! The bank recedes an average of eight meters a year here due to the melting permafrost. We have actually had to move that big white building three times! It's the oldest and largest structure built on permafrost in Canada, you know. It used to be smack-dab in the middle of the river channel. The river has changed so much . . ."

"I'm sorry. We really need to eat," Ann interrupted, trying not to sound rude. She looked like a ravenous wild creature. Her hunger was reflected in her body, eyes, and facial expression. She was the closest thing I had to a mirror these days.

We set up the stove and cooked a glorious meal of hash browns, black beans, and dehydrated eggs. I could feel every bite travel through my body, slowly satiating my hunger. A man on an ATV rode over to say hello. His name was Lenny. We had now officially met the whole village.

"You ladies should really go inside, you know. Lots of polar bears around lately." Lenny expressed his concern while towering over us with a shotgun around his shoulder.

"Sorry, we are really hungry. We'll be done soon, and then we can go inside!" I replied, returning quickly to my hash browns.

"Suit yourselves. I'll stand watch," he responded. He stood there watching us eat for several minutes. This seemed a little much, but neither of us had the energy to tell him we didn't need protection.

Just then, a polar bear came into sight around the peninsula, lumbering slowly in our direction. Our minds sprang to Myhan: where was she? Would she know to stay away from the bear? We called and she came bolting toward us from under the boardwalk. It seemed ironic that we had agreed to take her along for protection from polar bears and she was our main concern when one actually came around.

I looked up at Lenny. "Okay, we're ready to go inside now."

~~~~~

"Natalie, wake up! You gotta see this!" Ann whispered into the dark. I reluctantly fumbled down the bunk bed ladder and walked over to the open heavy metal door, where Ann stood gazing out into the sunrise. I appreciated her enthusiasm, but hadn't we seen enough sunrises? Couldn't we sleep in for once?

The sun had just begun to peek above the horizon, providing a serene backdrop to the strange scene in front of us: a polar bear was running across the boardwalk. A large German Shepherd, the caretaker's dog, was chasing the bear. Lenny was riding an ATV chasing the dog, holding a gun. From a distance, they all seemed to be moving at the same speed, gliding across the tundra through the morning fog. I looked at Ann and said, "I think it's time to go home."

That afternoon we branded our paddles with the same YF logo the Hudson's Bay Company once used on their York boats. Paddlers who make it to York Factory get to do this as a ceremonial closing to their expedition. I pushed the hot metal deep into my wooden paddle and felt a fleeting wave of accomplishment for what we had just done. But our travels were not over yet. After branding our paddles, we began our long journey back to Minnesota. Our float plane landed at the delta where the Hayes River flows into Hudson Bay. We loaded our gear, boat, and dog and took off into the skies.

The river we had paddled day after day looked like a piece of string in the large landscape below. Our three months of traversing the land and water from Minneapolis to Hudson Bay suddenly seemed distant: our upstream battle on the Minnesota River, long days on the fast and winding Red River, the hopelessness we felt on Lake Winnipeg, and the remote wilderness of the powerful Hayes River. Every painful moment of bone-chilling cold and sweltering heat. Every close call and lucky escape. It was all behind us. But the experiences we had were forever ingrained in our hearts and would shape the women we would become.

The end of our expedition was too much to take in. So much so that I promptly vomited into the brown paper bag in front of my chair. Ann laughed as I tucked the vomit underneath my seat and apologized to the pilot, who assured me it happens all the time. It provided some comic relief to an otherwise sobering moment of departure, reflection, and new beginnings. I knew it wasn't just the rocking of the plane that made my body respond that way. It was the resurfacing of fear I had felt in the last week and the realization I was finished with the life I had lived in a canoe with my best friend. High in the sky, our adventure slowly transitioned from present to past.

We flew in silence for a little less than an hour before landing on the Nelson River in Gillam, a town that is home to three of Manitoba's largest hydropower dams. As we unloaded our gear from the plane Ann looked at me with a knowing grin and said, "We oughta crack that bottle of wine, dontcha think?" I smiled. She always knew exactly what to say. That night, after sneaking Myhan into our hotel, we opened the bottle we had been carrying since Knee Lake. We clicked little plastic cups together and toasted our success before stretching out for a well-deserved night of rest.

The next morning was filled with strange to-dos, like searching the small hydro town for a dog crate so we could take Myhan on the thirty-five-hour train ride back to Winnipeg departing that afternoon. We creatively constructed a rope collar and leash for her before portaging over to the train station. After several games of cribbage I remembered something I had been longing to do when we ended our trip.

"Ann! Do you still have the number for that inn on Gull Harbour? I think it's time we gave old Marvin a call to let him know we made it to the Bay. He owes us a keg of beer!"

Ann's eyes lit up. Not everyone gets the chance to tell their skeptics they were wrong, that we could do it, that we *did* do it, and to top it off they owed us beer. We clumsily operated the pay phone at the train station.

"Yes, hi, Milton! Sorry, I mean Marvin. This is Natalie and Ann. We just wanted to let you know that we made it to Hudson Bay!" I waited for his congratulations.

"Who is this?" he responded.

How quickly he had forgotten us. Yet his words had played in our minds over and over again throughout the most challenging parts of our trip: "I bet you a keg of Bud Light Lime that you won't make it there 'til October!"

When we reminded him of our deal he said, "Oh. Uh, I don't think you can ship beer. Sorry," and hung up. It was less satisfying than we had imagined, but the call helped pass the time until the train finally rolled in from Churchill. We loaded our canoe and gear into the baggage car and a reluctantly caged Myhan into her new kennel before finding our seats. She cried almost the entire way home, unused to her new domestic life. The following thirty-five hours felt like summer camp. Ann and I played the ukulele and travel guitar, singing songs for everyone and sharing tales from our journey. At every stop we would quickly walk Myhan and run back to our seats as the conductor yelled, "All aboard!" Many of the passengers were traveling home from polar bear and whale watching along the shores of Hudson Bay. We were all adventurous vagabonds stuck together on a train, tumbling through the tundra for an ungodly amount of time, until we finally reached Winnipeg.

It was prime rush hour when we arrived downtown. The sun blinded us as we crawled out of the dark train cabin onto the busy streets. Car horns echoed loudly through the cityscape. People in suits with briefcases were busily bustling about, talking loudly on their phones and urgently whistling for cabs. Everything seemed to be moving in fast-forward. The sounds and colors of the city, especially the neon lights, shocked our systems after months of river waves and bird calls, of brown, green, and blue. We spotted our ride, a large white van with a canoe trailer on the back, and began our very last portage through a flowing river of pedestrians.

"Congratulations, ladies!" our friends Megan and Austin yelled through the crowd. Seeing familiar faces warmed our hearts. It had been weeks since we had seen anyone we knew. Frantically loading the van, I paused to look up at Ann. Her wild tangled blond hair in a messy bun, muddy shorts, tan hairy legs, and Muck Boots. She was standing outside the train station during rush hour pumping our 12-gauge gun to empty its shells before we crossed the border. People just kept streaming by her as if nothing unusual was happening. I watched in amusement as she successfully emptied the loaded gun and wondered if we had completely lost our ability to operate under social norms.

People told us that crossing the border into the United States was going to be more intense than our crossing into Canada had been. It was hard to imagine anything more tense than the six border patrol agents who had personally "pulled us over" on the Red River. But we were concerned that our newly acquired furry companion might complicate things, so we swung into a vet to get shots for Myhan. Finally, we pulled into a long line of cars and waited for our turn to talk to a border agent. Megan collected our passports and rolled down her window. Everyone was silent. I ran through possible questions and answers in my mind: *Did we pick up a stray dog from a Cree community? Yes. Did we fire our gun while in Canada? Yes. Did we know buckshot was illegal in Canada? No, sorry.*

A fierce-looking woman approached the van and took the passports from Megan.

"What were you doing in Canada?" she asked sternly.

"Well, these two women just paddled all the way to Hudson Bay!" Megan exclaimed.

"No shit! That's awesome!" said the agent. "Go on ahead."

"We picked up a stray dog and we have a gun!" I blurted from the back seat. Ann gave me a loving but exasperated look that said, "You can't just stay quiet for once, can you?"

"Sounds like you had a great trip. Come back soon." The woman waved us on.

~~~~~

TEN HOURS LATER we arrived at Ann's family cabin at the end of the Gunflint Trail in northern Minnesota. We should have been exhausted. We should have rolled into bed and slept for days. But we stayed up for hours, drinking champagne and sharing stories with friends and family, singing and laughing late into the night.

The next morning, I woke up to find Ann sitting on the porch, sipping coffee and looking out at the lake, Myhan by her side. For the first time in nearly three months there was no map to tell us where to go next, no goal we needed to reach that day. I poured myself a cup of coffee and sat down in the large wooden chair next to her. I glanced at her and attempted a smile. But no expression or words could say anything that she did not already know. We had acted as one person for three months. Every decision we made was made as a team. My memories and feelings were hers, too. We had learned to compromise, challenge each other, surprise each other, and take care of each other. In the process, even through our trials and frustrations, we had learned to love one another more deeply than any friendship.

"The lakes here seem smaller now, don't they?" she said quietly, keeping her gaze on the opposite shore. I nodded. We clinked our coffee mugs together and sat there for several hours without speaking, staring at the water, our once and forever home.

AFTERWORD

Natalie Warren and Ann Raiho

It's BEEN TEN YEARS since Ann and I made our historic journey to Hudson Bay. We paddled two thousand miles over eighty-five days, battled unbelievable weather, picked up a dog, ate a hell of a lot of granola bars, and burned more calories than we can count. Though we're as close as ever, I don't see as much of Ann as I used to; she went on to earn a PhD in biology at Notre Dame and is now in Colorado doing postdoc research. This trip impacted our lives more than we could ever have possibly imagined, and writing this book gave me an opportunity to reflect on what it all meant. Ann and I recently had the chance to reconnect and talk about the Hudson Bay Bound experience and why expeditions like this are so vital to environmental change.

Ann
We didn't really realize that this trip would be so important. Sometimes I struggle with the "first women" thing because, really, we were only the fourth documented trip. It confuses me a little that when you add "first women" to that sentence it changes the trip so much in people's minds. It's like they don't even have to know where you went to be impressed. Maybe that's a good thing, but it's also interesting to me that not a lot of people really know where Hudson Bay is. A lot of times I'll say, "I went on a canoe trip with my best friend after college," and people are like, "Yeah yeah yeah, I've been in a canoe before." But when I say the trip was two thousand miles and we were the first women to do it, it blows people's minds. To be honest, I get embarrassed to say all those details and usually try to avoid it because I'm worried that people will think I'm like a show-off or something. But at the same time, it's like, when can I do it again? Be the first to do something. I like

the idea of the unknown. That I can't really be doing it wrong because no one else has done it before.

Natalie

We were often asked why it was important to be the first two women to re-create this historic route. My first thought, and Ann's too, was that we were surprised no two women had done it before. We did not possess superpowers beyond other paddlers. In fact, many of the women we knew from Menogyn were far more badass and talented in a canoe than we were. Ann had simply struck gold finding a beloved canoe route and story to "re-create" that women had not attempted yet, and I was smart enough to say yes. Hundreds of people dream about doing this route. But I think the most impressive thing was not that we were two women roughing it in a canoe but that we took action and *chose* to be two women roughing it in a canoe. Honestly, I didn't understand how sexist our society can be when I was twenty-two. The more I learn about it as an adult, the more impressed I am with what we did. I was nervous to do the trip in the first place because of the looming story that if we make one wrong step in life then we might mess up everything. That somehow we need to constantly orient ourselves toward the things that we think we want or else we may never get them. In my case, I worried that if I didn't enter the workforce right away after college, I would somehow fall behind and ruin my chances at building momentum in my career. Looking back, I see how ridiculous this sentiment was and how pervasive it still is in society (especially among college students). Two women going canoeing for three months tells an alternative narrative to life, one that is not heard enough. I'm so proud of us for doing this trip. I hope it made a statement and an impact on others. It sure changed our lives.

Ann

I've always wanted a sister, and I feel like Natalie became my sister on that trip. Unconditional friendship in the end. I feel really lucky to have gotten to spend that time with Natalie, and I don't think we would have stayed as close without our trip.

Natalie and I have a pretty special dynamic that most people are never fortunate enough to find in a friend. Seriously, though? My best friend wrote a book about our friendship. Who is that lucky? We pretty much can hear what the other is thinking a lot of the time, even though now we don't get to spend that much time together. I think we had to sort of make a choice to get to know each other that well on this trip. We could have easily just kept to ourselves more, but we wouldn't have gotten as close on the trip. There were times when we could have thought like, "Forget it, she's annoying," or whatever, but we never made that choice. I'm really fortunate that Natalie made the choice to want to be my friend. I honestly feel like she could do just about anything and I would still want to be her best friend.

Natalie

I always thought Ann was too cool for me. I think she initially thought I was cool because I'm from Miami. We used to joke about how she assumed I had a Jeep and a tan boyfriend and just hung out at the beach all the time (which couldn't be further from my real upbringing). Ann is a total badass of a woman who can and does do anything she sets her mind to. I admire her so much and strive to be like her in so many ways.

We never left each other's sight on our expedition. It was comforting to have someone I knew and loved around when tromping onto new land and meeting new people. I honestly don't think I could have done this trip with anyone else. We literally trusted each other with our lives. I often joke that Ann is the only reason we made it to the Bay. I tend to make riskier decisions. But she always grounded me. I like to think I pushed her on occasion, too. We made the perfect team.

Ann

I remember looking down at Myhan and thinking, "This dog will be with me until I'm thirty!" Now I *am* thirty, and it doesn't feel like I'm that old or that I've even had her that long. Looking back on adding her to the canoe makes me feel like we must have had some incredible balancing skills. Our canoe was so full of stuff and she was this little puppy perched on top. It's amazing that we never really tipped!

When people ask about Myhan I'm always like, "She's Canadian!" and no one laughs. But then I tell the whole story about finding her in the parking lot under the northern lights and feeding her hot dogs and putting her under the seat in the canoe. People probably think I'm lying sometimes. Myhan has been a blessing. She's moved with me to Colorado, Indiana, Boston, Berkeley, back to Indiana, and back to Colorado. This dog has swum in three oceans! She's been mountain biking with me in ten states and three provinces! She's amazing and I'm so grateful I get to feed her every day.

Natalie

I think Myhan represents something significant about our friendship and our expedition. I've been on expeditions with other people when someone would suggest something out of the ordinary and other people would shut it down. Deciding to get a dog represents what I love most about traveling with Ann. It was a really big decision. We could have easily talked ourselves out of it with a million excuses. But we knew it would be okay because of the trust we had in each other. There was little we could predict about our day-to-day on the river anyway, so adding another expedition member fit perfectly into our already wild lives.

Myhan has showed up for Ann in big ways, as an adventure buddy and as emotional support during challenging times. I can't help but smile when I think of them together.

Ann

One of the biggest things that I took from that trip was learning to be kind to myself. I think that I hadn't really gotten to know my inner voice as a teenager, and spending so much time with yourself makes you really listen to what's going on in your head. I would say that it even amplifies what's going on in your head because there aren't really any distractions. It took me a long time even after the trip to realize that at times I'm pretty hard on myself for almost no reason.

It's important to have things in your life that you can lean on and think, "You know? I can do it. I've done a lot harder things before." It's probably why a lot of people are drawn to running marathons. These experiences really ground you and prove to yourself that you are capable.

I didn't realize it at the time, but this trip really solidified for me that I want to use whatever skills I have and wherever my career takes me for the benefit of the planet and the wilderness. I feel like it's my calling to work with, protect, and understand nature, and I got to hear it because of the time spent that summer paddling to Hudson Bay.

Natalie

This trip became my life and my career. It allowed me to see that self-organized expeditions are possible, which led me down the Mississippi River in 2013 and the Yukon River three years later. It also prepared me with the planning and outreach skills to organize support around a cause. I started a nonprofit organization when I was twenty-three that took youth on canoe trips to learn about water quality on the Minnesota River. We stayed with farmers and advocates of the river, many of whom we had met paddling to the Bay. We led expeditions down entire rivers. I felt like, if I had learned so much about the land and water through paddling it, maybe others could, too, at even younger ages. My love of rivers eventually led me to jobs in public speaking, outdoor journalism, environmental policy, and even back to school to study environmental communication. Everything I have done since our expedition has been directly related to rivers—consulting, policy making, writing, advocating. I can't imagine a better focus for my life or a better way to kick off my career in rivers than an eighty-five-day canoe expedition.

Ann

We were often told back then that we should seize this opportunity because we wouldn't have time when we got older to get away for so long. At the time, I thought that was sort of a presumptuous thing for people to say because I really saw expeditions as a big part of my future. But ten years later it's not just that I have more responsibilities, but also that I want to be home more than I did then. Taking that time when we were younger was so important because it taught us important lessons about taking risks, communicating, and being with ourselves. I think that even more than ten years ago teenagers today are faced with this incredible amount of pressure to succeed, and having time without all those distractions is really important.

Obviously there is a balance between loving yourself and being self-centered. And the wilderness allowed me to find the time to come up with the balance for myself. In our society, commercialization and social media can have a big impact on how you feel about yourself. Taking time in the wilderness allows you to get a little bit away from that to see what is going on behind the scenes of your internal self-image. Cultivating that loving-kindness toward myself and Natalie during that trip pushed me to become a better person.

Another thing I always think is a very useful life skill from living outdoors is that you learn very quickly how to deal with whatever comes your way and make do with the things in front of you. Since this trip, when little things happen to me, like I get a flat tire or I forget something, etc., I can always come up with a solution.

Nothing is ever too much to overcome, and I think that is from having to solve problems for myself in the wilderness as a young adult. And my parents trusting me to do things. I think Natalie would say the same. I've never seen Natalie give up.

I feel strongly that I would do anything to protect the wilderness. Just for the sake of the wilderness. I think that feeling is because of all my time spent on trips as a young adult and the value I put on getting to know myself better through the wilderness. To me it seems like an invaluable and even underutilized tool for humanity. People really need that time with nature, and I think a lot of loneliness stems from this self-hatred that people never realize they have inside themselves because they don't have time in wilderness to really hear it. Although I am also extremely fortunate to have an amazing support system that I always have with me in my internal voice, too. So I guess I don't know how it would go if you don't have that. I'm certainly not advocating for people to go out there unprepared. We were lucky that during our teenage years we got to build up this self-confidence and self-reliance through our trips at Menogyn, surrounded by friends and family. I'm also lucky my parents always supported our trips. They were there to help all of the time, and I think that still makes me feel like I can do anything.

Natalie

At the end of our expedition, we calculated that we had spent more than one hundred days together, by each other's side. Spending that much time with another person helped me look inward to my strengths and flaws. I felt like I was always working on my character and striving to improve myself on the expedition.

My day-to-day in the city consists of perpetual busyness. I feel anxiety from an increasing disconnect between myself and stillness, myself and nature. I strive to find the therapeutic benefits of stillness that used to be unavoidable when living in a canoe. I try my hardest (and often fail) to carve out time in my day to sit, even just for five minutes, without doing or worrying about something. I'm so thankful that I took the time after college to give myself space to think. That's mostly what expeditions are: time. Lots of time spent in your head, talking, thinking, creating, re-creating, understanding, exploring. Time that we do not often allow ourselves otherwise. Time to get to know ourselves, to step off the treadmill of life and question what it is we really feel and who we are when we are stripped from our props, roles, and societal goals. Without that foundation, I wonder if I would still be searching for my core self.

Expeditions can also reframe our environment. The rivers we traversed were and still are our homes. They are like mothers to us. We spent time getting to know them, in their best and worst moods (and ours). I would not poison my mother or harm her in any way, just like I would not pollute or damage a river. But we do. It is still legal to pollute rivers, even though we know how valuable they are to maintaining a healthy ecosystem and sustaining the human population. Even though we see the scars we have made on the eroded banks, the algae when the flow slows, and the dangerous contaminants that seep into our drinking water. The unsustainable systems that support our farms and industries turn a blind eye to the damages they cause to the landscape. Rivers are out of sight, out of mind. They are for human use, capital gain, and extraction. Until you get to know them. Until you paddle their waters and see the damage for yourself. To spend time on the land and water is to build a relationship with it, to learn to love it, and to fight for its protection. For me, expeditions have blurred the line between human and environment to understand everything as connected, dependent, and in need of great care.

Ann

People sometimes don't think about Canada as a place impacted by climate or land use change because it's so far north and cold a lot of the year. I now study changing ecosystems, and it often comes up that entire biomes are shifting northward. Natalie and I passed through three to four biomes on our trip, and to think of them slowly shifting away—it changes everything for the people and animals living there. It's just not the same place that Eric and Walter paddled or even the place that Natalie and I paddled anymore. People really need to think about that when they place so much value on "historic," "pristine" ecosystems because really they are changing very quickly, but it's not always due to a fire or something that you notice the very next day. Plants especially change very slowly if they aren't disturbed and can persevere through changing climate, but if you really look back to see what it was like in *Canoeing with the Cree* you will see that the ecosystems are all very different. They didn't see the first deer of their lives until they got to Canada! The water was really clean in the Minnesota River. But also people lived where they don't live now, like on the east side of Lake Winnipeg and at York Factory. So some places are sort of "rewilding," too. (I also like to bring up that you can see the algal bloom in Lake Winnipeg from space.)

Natalie
Paddling through our nation's Corn Belt was so eye-opening for me. I couldn't believe that the corn and soybeans that litter the landscape don't directly feed people. Yet somehow this has become the norm. We unnecessarily squeeze them into syrups and processed foods and subsidize their production into ethanol or feedlots that pump cows with corn that they have trouble digesting. What if we actually grew food to feed people in nearby cities and communities with those hundreds of thousands of acres currently used to grow commodity crops? Not to mention, the GMO crops require the use of certain toxic pesticides that flow into our groundwater, lakes, and river systems, causing serious damage to wildlife and presenting risks to public health. Ultimately, I do not believe it is up to individual farmers to change their practices. The entire system is based on political decisions made at pivotal

moments in history. I feel like our agricultural system has forgotten its main goal: to feed people safe and healthy food to support life on this planet. Instead, it has become a corporate operation with capitalist interests that disregard sustainability and public health. We have to find a way to feed people without polluting our water resources through significant top-down changes.

Ann and I traveled through stolen land for much of our expedition, and we saw firsthand the effects of silenced communities forced onto reservations. It is important to remember the traumatic history of the route we took. To not only remember but to begin our own journey of decolonization. What if we actually acknowledged the treaties made with First Nations? What would it look like to think about land and water as reparations? Native communities are still fighting for their rights. And their stories are still being silenced by those in power who are trying to maintain and justify what we took. On our expedition, Ann and I had only begun to understand the fight for justice, for rightful land and a healthy environment, still going on in places like Norway House and Oxford House.

To echo Ann, the world is changing quickly. The route we paddled nearly a decade ago would be very different today. Every expedition team will encounter different social and environmental scars on this route. It is easy to ignore the changes from our homes in the city, but it's life-changing to see them unfold in person, to understand the urgency of a changing climate in our own backyards.

Natalie Warren is one of the first two women to have paddled 2,000 miles from Minneapolis to Hudson Bay, recreating Eric Sevareid's route from *Canoeing with the Cree*. She was nominated for *Canoe & Kayak*'s 2012 Expedition of the Year and has since paddled the length of the Mississippi River and won first place in the women's voyageur category in the 2016 Yukon River Quest, paddling 450 miles in fifty-three hours. Along with writing for outdoor publications and being an avid public speaker, she has worked with organizations on land protection, outdoor recreation, and environmental education, and she advises communities on how to increase paddle sports tourism. She is pursuing her PhD in communication studies at the University of Minnesota and lives in Minneapolis with her husband, daughter, and dog.

Ann Bancroft is one of the world's preeminent polar explorers and the first woman to have achieved both the North and South Poles. An internationally recognized educator, speaker, and philanthropist, she founded the Ann Bancroft Foundation in 1991. With Liv Arnesen, she is the author of *No Horizon Is So Far: Two Women and Their Historic Journey across Antarctica* (Minnesota, 2019).